To: Sarah With thanks!

I hope this book Unravel your hidden gems!

UNRAVEL YOUR HIDDEN GEMS

A COLLECTION OF INSPIRATIONAL AND MOTIVATIONAL ESSAYS

BY:

TOLU' A. AKINYEMI

28/07/2021.

First published in Great Britain as a softback original in 2018

Typeset in Bembo

Editing, design and typesetting by UK Book Publishing

www.ukbookpublishing.com

Published by T & B Global Concepts Limited

ISBN: 978-1-9998159-9-8

Email:

tolu@toluakinyemi.com
author@deadlionsdontroar.com
author@www.tolutoludo.com

Website:

www.toluakinyemi.com
www.deadlionsdontroar.com
www.tolutoludo.com

ALSO, BY TOLU' A. AKINYEMI

"Dead Lions Don't Roar" (A collection of Poetic Wisdom for the Discerning)

COMING SOON

Dead Dogs Don't Bark (A collection of Poetic Wisdom for the Discerning Series 2)

Tolutoludo's Fables (A Collection of Short Stories for Children)

DEDICATION

Unravel your Hidden Gems is dedicated to God Almighty for helping me to Unravel, to my ever-supportive wife Olabisi, to my Parents, for teaching and influencing me positively into the Man I am today and to the people of Newcastle, United Kingdom – the CITY of my rising STAR.

CONTENTS

PREFACE

Unravel your Hidden Gems follows closely after my first published book, Dead Lions Don't Roar, an astonishing poetry collection that has been well received and widely acknowledged as a wonderful book by book lovers, critics and enthusiasts the world over. Unravel your Hidden Gems is a collection of Inspirational and Motivational essays and is a culmination of my life's journey until now. Unravel your Hidden Gems is a Life Manual that everyone will find useful irrespective of age, race, career level, leadership position or spiritual beliefs as it covers topics that include Personal Development, Motivation and Leadership, Relationships, Career Development and many others. Always remember that we all have something of value that we can offer to the world.

I wrote these essays to Inspire people who would hitherto sleep-walk their way through life or settle for the norm that they can be more, do more and achieve more with their lives if they choose to Unravel that Hidden Gem within. Note my emphasis on the word "choose"; always remember that our life's outcome is a culmination of our daily choices. I would have been a local champion, an unknown entity until I made a choice to Unravel my Hidden Gems and my life's story has not been the same ever since.

There is a lot to learn from this collection of essays to bring out the best in you, the aim of this book is to raise a new generation of leaders on every front. We can have healthier and fulfilling relationships, enjoy an illustrious career and have a better life by reading through the principles in this book. Always remember that you are not a victim but a victor. Stop the pity-party; you deserve to be celebrated by all and sundry if we Unravel that Hidden Gem. Do not let anyone talk you out of your life's vision, mission and purpose. You are much more than the ordinary, there is always an extra that we can bring to the table – if we refuse to settle for the norm then truly we can be EXTRA-ordinary.

Tell yourself and young ones that they can be much more, tell them to dream big, tell them that they have so much talent within, the World awaits your Roar. There is so much that we can do; a lot of people come to the world to add to the numbers and statistics. However, we can put our gifts and talents to use when we Unravel that Hidden Gem. Whatsoever your hands find to do, do It with all your power and might. So, if your talent is writing, don't stop writing; if it's singing, painting, dancing, blogging, sports, and other magnificent skill-sets you possess, please keep working at being the best version of you. Always remember that we can only Unravel our Hidden Gems when we are alive; the cemetery is filled with a lot of unpublished books, unreleased albums, and a vast number of talents that would have added colour to our world if only they had Unlocked their hidden potentials.

Unravel your Hidden Gems I can assure will inspire everyone who reads it; there is something to learn from this book that will help fuel the fire of your dreams. The lessons shared in this book deserve to be read in the entire world. If you are truly blessed by the life-lessons I have shared in this book, kindly buy a copy and gift it to someone who needs to Unravel their Hidden Gems. There is a whole lot of difference between going through the motions in life and living an excellent life. There is no person in the universe without a gift or talent, but most times we cover it up and do nothing with it.

As you go on to read through the pages of this book, which I have written especially because of you, I do hope that you will find it a truly rewarding and life-changing experience.

ACKNOWLEDGEMENTS

Writing this book gives me immense joy and immeasurable satisfaction as I believe it will truly inspire my generation and generations after me to "Unravel their Hidden Gems", put their gifts and talents to use and leave their imprints on the sands of time. When the curtains are drawn on my life, my soul will radiate so much joy knowing that my name will live on because I chose to Unravel my Hidden Gems. Writing a book of over 85,000 words takes a lot of time and effort – hence, I would like to thank some special people in my life who supported me through this Journey.

Special thanks to my jewel of inestimable value and darling wife, Olabisi, for your understanding and support, through the extremely busy periods when my attention was really divided. I will always love you till the very end.

A big thank you to my wonderful children, Isaac and Abigail. You light up my world and inspire me to live my dreams. I would also like you to know that the world is your oyster, go forth and conquer it. Dad will always be there to support you throughout life's journey.

Special thanks to my dad and mum. What a great privilege to learn at your feet, thanks for teaching me great wisdom; I appreciate your sacrifices, investments and selflessness and for being there at every step of the journey. Dad, let me also say thanks for the massive effort on Dead Lions Don't Roar, I am proud to let the whole world know that I have an amazing dad. If you did not train me and Invest so much in me, this book would never have been a reality. I am a product of your school of mentoring, and thanks for living a life worthy of emulation.

Special appreciation goes to my siblings, Shola, Seyi and Ireti. Always know that I love you come what may. And to my in-laws, The Osiyoyes, I appreciate you for accepting me as one of your own. To Segun and Ireti Akerele, thanks for all the outstanding effort on Dead Lions Don't Roar in the past year. To my nephew David Akerele, Uncle Tolutoludo loves you so much.

Thank you won't be enough to Antonia Brindle, my creative and brand manager, for the outstanding effort to grow the Tolu Akinyemi brand in the past months – we are making great inroads and I am very optimistic for the great promise the future holds.

I would also like to thank my friends and brothers, Nzubechukwu Alutu, Daniel Dada, Seye Morakinyo, Gbenga Obakin, Emmanuel Alawode, Biodun Coker, Aaron Lee, Oluwaseun Alele, Oke Ayoade, Ayotunde Ogunleye, Ayo Zubair, Dapo Arofin and my young apprentice Kenneth Robson (a.k.a. Kenny Toludo). I appreciate your constant support throughout the past year.

Sincere appreciation to Pastor Akinkunmi Thomas, Pastor Nath Ogundipe, Pastor Sekumade and Pastor Eghosa Best Agho; thanks for the tremendous support and encouragement always.

Special thanks to my editor, Ruth Lunn, and the team at UK Book Publishing. Appreciation also goes to the book designer, Jason Thompson, I am indeed proud of your work and honestly, I can't wait for the design of Dead Dogs Don't Bark; It keeps getting better and better.

Special shout out to Omas Anyanwu and Evelyn Aneni (Bookworm), your advice and feedback throughout the process is greatly appreciated. A word of thanks to Sarah Garton, Alexandra Yeatman, Jonathan Weetman, Moses Erim, Abi Oguntubi, Sandra Bamfo and Hakeem Olagunju – thanks so much for believing in my talent.

Sincere thanks to Rabiu Wasiu, Abodunde Ojikutu, Gbenga Adelakun and "Funmi Ogunleye"; from the bottom of my heart, thank you for believing so much in me.

It will be very hard to bypass these other great leaders without whom the story would not be complete: Chris Mulrooney, Nick Morrison and Karl Richardson, you will forever hold a special place in my heart.

I would also like to acknowledge the support of Moyosore Faith Agboola (Founder African Writers), the great support in those early days is greatly appreciated. Also, my friend from Red Clover Ghana's Golden Boy, Kwadwo Kusi-Frimpong, you are such a great guy with a very bright future. Thanks to my wonderful friends Oluwaseun Arewa and Amaka Offia, your support is very much appreciated. Thank you to my fellow creative Oluwole Amoye, you need to write those books as the world needs to hear your story; and Tayo Adebiyi, my talented friend, I have so much love for you and I will not let you rest until you publish your books.

Lastly, to the numerous friends, colleagues and acquaintances who have gone to great lengths to support the Tolu' Akinyemi brand, even though I am constrained by space to mention everyone. Thanks a lot for all the support; I have nothing but love for you all.

PART 1

ARE YOU PREPARED?

Preparation is the first order condition for success in Life – show me a successful person and I will show you a person who was well prepared. Nothing happens by chance or accident in our world; there is no prize without a price.

In your quest to be the best in your chosen field of endeavour, adequate preparation is the best price you can give to yourself. There is a lot of training and preparation that great athletes like Usain Bolt, Tiger Woods, Roger Federer and Rafael Nadal go through before their houses can be filled with many trophies. There is a place of intense training, self-denial, strict fitness regimen and work outs they had to follow before they had the enviable trophy cabinet.

I remember I used to wonder if it was possible to disregard the normal cliché of sleeping for eight hours without dire consequences, but it is abnormal for me to be in bed for more than five hours in recent times. Anytime I wake up and I see people on the streets either going to work, praying or doing some fitness work, it reminds me of the Ten virgins who were waiting for the arrival of the bridegroom; five had enough oil that could last them for the coming of the bridegroom while the other five did not have. This same scenario also applies to our present-day environment: students now believe that the best way to achieve success in exams is either by cheating or bribing lecturers to pass their courses. Most people in the present-day world are looking for short cuts to success instead of paying the price by towing the path of adequate preparation.

I discovered that the pastors who are dangerous to the devil are those who have studied the word to show themselves approved; the consultants who are managing the best projects in town are those who have prepared well; and the big law firms who handle the major cases are those who have gone through various preparation stages.

Do not discount the effect of adequate preparation before you start that project, course, career and other things that might interest you. A builder counts his costs first before the commencement of a project, before artistes churn out award winning songs they have gone through various stages of training – adequate preparation is the seed for every great result.

Are you well prepared to pursue your goals, dreams and aspirations? Are you willing to go the extra mile to see your dreams become reality? Are you ready to step out from being a victim and wear the toga of a victor? What are the things that are limiting you from getting prepared to get the best from life?

Good harvest is the result of a great seed; don't be afraid to pursue your dreams, water your seed before the sun comes out and watch your seed yield bountiful harvests.

Repeat these words of affirmation:

I will give my best in this race, I refuse to short circuit the process to get the result, I will prepare as if there won't be another opportunity, I refuse to waste my time, I choose to reduce activities and increase my level of productivity. I will prepare for my success; I will put in my best to be the best.

BEAUTIFUL BUT IMPERFECT WORLD

It's a beautiful but imperfect world, a world where strange things happen and given that we are humans the flesh will always fall short of being perfect.

I choose not to live in the shadow of any human, not necessarily because I don't have great mentors but because everyone has their unique gifts. I see people who have stayed outside the ring for too long and have lived the greater proportion of their lives chasing the wind.

When you go to the Car Dealer and order a wonder on wheels, your dream car, but you later discover it has some manufacturer's error, it is not because the manufacturer fell short of meeting the standard of production or some cost cutting measures; instead it shows it's a beautiful but imperfect world.

Most times we go after the crumbs, the tasters and forget the main course because we are in awe of the ephemeral, we lose track of our own lives' agenda because of a rare appointment or meeting with a supposed perfect being. The problem is not your failure but what you do after that seeming challenge. Many people live their lives on the make-believe, they are a replica of the best-selling authors, they have discovered twenty-one ways of doing it right, forty-eight ways of being a perfect husband or wife, fifty secrets of highly successful people and they are having issues replicating those success stories in their lives. Don't chase shadows; we all have our special characteristics in this beautiful but imperfect world.

Carve your own niche; every human has their own unique selling point; discover yours. Help others to get along in life but remember to pursue your life's goals. There are a lot of people who live their lives for other people. Always remember that your major assets in life are your mind and time – if you don't maximize this vital resource other people will help you use it.

Time as a resource waits for no man; maximize it. That is the only resource that is available to every human in equal proportion. Shun time wasting activities; there is no opportunity to turn back the hands of time. When you waste your time, you waste your life.

Always remember that the grace comes with a proportion of pain; pay the price to get the prize.

If you are experiencing failing ambitions, an abusive relationship, a failing marriage, unemployment or any other issues in Life, don't weep for too long; don't give up on yourself, tough times don't last as we all know.

No matter how clear a photocopy is, it can never be like an original copy. The human mind is a well spring of ideas; discover your originality, that which makes you different and unique, shun the crowd mentality and live a purposeful life.

CELEBRATE PEOPLE

Some people believe success in their pursuit comes with long and fiery prayer points, so you see people in this school of thought perpetually in the sanctuary seeking God's face in their lives, hoping to get the result they want.

Some others believe they have been diligent in their ways, served God with all their heart and never seem to progress in Life – why am I stuck here, why is my life moving in slow motion and not the turbo fast movement I expect? Why is God being partial to others and never seems to have me on his radar? A lot of times people in this school of thought get depressed and begin to question God.

My question for you today is do you celebrate the success of others? Are you envious of the success of your friends, neighbours and colleagues? Do you as a fact think the success and accomplishment of a friend is not deserved? My number one tip I would like to share with you is that you should rejoice with them that rejoice, celebrate the success of people around you.

A woman who is barren and is looking for the fruit of the womb must not be envious of other people's children or beat the children of her neighbours but show children around her love with the understanding that her own fruits will come. A Yoruba proverb says, "the sky is large enough for all birds to fly through without colliding with one another".

You need a car, celebrate those who have cars; you are a tenant who aspires to be a landlord, don't despise landlords and use their properties as if you have been destined to be a tenant. If you are in the position of being able to help people move up in life, do not withhold good to whom it is due if it is in the power of your hands to do it.

The fact that the heart of man is desperately wicked and full of evil intentions does not mean you cannot be a shining light and bright spot in this murky world. Some people just hate other people for no just cause; you will hear phrases like "Is he the only one?" "Why is my own like this?" Your own is like that because of the envy in your heart. The moment you start celebrating with others, you will experience internal peace and your own blessings.

So many people are poor not because they deserve to be poor, but because they have not learnt the attitude of the wealthy. Being rich is a state of mind, it comes from the within before it becomes obvious in the without. The time you spend discussing other people can be spent in productive ventures, the time spent ridiculing the success of your friends can be spent in the pursuit of your own personal dreams and aspirations.

God is still in the business of blessing his children; the fact that he blessed your colleague will not stop him from blessing you. Remember life has its times and season. I see a lot of people who have become increasingly frustrated with a system that does not guarantee the future, a life of struggles, unhappiness and depression.

Be thankful for that which you have and are, many people also strive to have the opportunities you feel is nothing to you, so develop an attitude of praise and thanksgiving. Thank God in advance for the beautiful future, the high paying job, the thriving business, wonderful children and all that you desire. The past might have brought its pain and difficulties, but everyone can have a fresh start.

Celebrate others then you will also be celebrated.

RELATIONSHIPS: THE CURRENT THAT CONTROLS YOUR LIFE

Every relationship in your life is a current, moving you towards your dreams or away from them.
– Unknown

Show me your friend and I will succinctly tell the kind of person you are, show me your mentors and I will tell the direction your life is moving. "Iron sharpens Iron" – your network determines your net worth. True wealth can be calculated in the value of friends we keep and relationships we grow.

As you are reading through this essay, run a checklist of the seven most important people in your life, write down their life's vision, what they live for and what values they would die protecting, what do they stand for?

The quotation above can inspire us to chart a course for our lives. A good person with a bright future who resides with fraudsters is also a fraudster, and an innocent man who lives with criminals will also be termed the same.

Where is the current moving you to? Are you moving faster towards your dream or away from your dream? Are your relationships helping to build you or reduce you? Are your friends' assets or liabilities to you? Take a plain sheet of paper and write out seven achievements of your seven closest friends in the last two years. Are they progressing in life, seem stuck or regressing? How much influence does your close circle have on your decision-making ability? Do you have your free will and ability to swim against the tide or are you currently being tossed about by the current?

There is always a period when we need to do a reality check on our relationships and see if it is a host-host relationship, or a host-parasitic relationship. If that friendship is meant to ruin you or destroy your future, it is time you show him or her the exit door and stop tolerating the fellow when you can see the danger signs in CAPITAL LETTERS.

Good Friends are the most valuable assets anyone can have, so be careful of your association, don't follow the crowd, and have your own silent moments where you can develop strategies to move your life forward. Success has many friends, but failures and derelicts are scorned by the society. I have heard about young people, who lost their lives when they went on a night out with friends, some others went to the beach and never returned.

Who you hang out with determines your financial success, who you listen to determines your outlook on life; birds of the same feather flock together.

I have seen a lot of people, footballers and celebrities move from a state of opulence to poverty because of the people they chose to hang out with, the people they chose as their life partner, the people they chose as their role models and chose to emulate.

Be in control of your relationships for it is the current that controls your Life.

RELATIONSHIPS: THE CURRENT THAT CONTROLS YOUR LIFE 2

Every relationship in your life is a current, moving you towards your dreams or away from them
– Unknown

To get the best out of our lives, we must as a necessity evaluate our relationships. Are they moving us closer to our dreams or away from them? Our association this year will determine whether we will be able to achieve most of our set goals for the year. Birds of the same feather they say flock together; you cannot grow beyond the capacity of the people who inhabit your close circle.

If you aspire to get to the top this year, let your life revolve around people who are on a mission; if you desire excellence you must despise co-habiting with mediocre people. Our relationships can have a positive or negative effect on our life's outcomes. A lot of people became miserable and depressed due to being in the wrong relationships; some others paid the supreme sacrifice with their lives because of their association with the wrong people.

Evil communication they say corrupts good manners, so no matter how good you think you are, you must carefully select those I will call the influencer group in your life. Many men and women have been deprived of lifelong happiness based on their choice of life partners. Differences in values, ideology, and outlook on life are some of the minor issues that might eventually crystallise into a frustrating end from a beautiful beginning. There is no point being tolerated when you can be celebrated elsewhere.

Our choice of Mentors, place of worship, business circle and those we call friends will go a long way in determining our outcomes for the Year. There are some relationships that are parasitic and emotion draining, some others are time wasting in nature; it is time we evaluate all our relationships, who are the parasites, time wasters, mediocre people that we carried over into the New Year? Don't be afraid to delete into the recycle bin of history anybody who is not adding value to your life.

You must carefully select who you listen to, you must develop your own personal growth strategies, and you must have your own life's vision, mission and be desirous of making a success out of life. Do not let the disappointments of the past negatively affect your relationship with people. No man is an island; hence we need others to grow.

The electric current is strong enough to determine the longevity of gadgets, when the current is stable or destroy electrical gadgets within a household when the generated output is above the expected, so also our relationships have the capacity to build us up or destroy us when we are in the wrong association. As much as possible, avoid gossips, time wasters, rumour mongers and any parasitic relationship that drains us in all aspect of life.

Choose the right relationships for this is the current that controls our life.

NO ONE IS INDISPENSABLE

Don't think of yourself as indispensable or infallible. As Charles de Gaulle said, the cemeteries of the world are full of indispensable men.
– Donald Rumsfeld

I have seen various circumstances where humans get to a level where they feel there can be no other person except them in the completion of a given task or assignment; they feel indispensable and begin to see themselves as irreplaceable. They believe there can be no other person as good as they are on their project team, no one else who can implement strategies in their company. A certain president said there was no one capable of steering the affairs of a nation he was presiding over at that time, but after his exit from government three people have occupied the seat of the President and the country is still intact and experiencing peace.

There are ministries with very large congregations who the senior pastors believe exist basically because of their polished preaching style and charisma, but the truth is there is nobody that is indispensable in this world. With the shake-up in the Nigerian banking industry so many years ago, I was concerned about the survival of the banks after the era of their founding CEOs, but I learnt from this experience that continuity is a basic requirement in Life.

Orphans have learnt to cope without their parents; parents who lose their offspring have swallowed the bitter pill and have moved on with their lives. The greatest lie anyone can tell you is without your presence their lives will be incomplete. We as humans get tempted when we attain an iconic status, and we begin to feel as though life will not continue without our presence. But the truth is "YOU ARE NOT INDISPENSABLE"; every living being has an expiry date and with or without us lives will go on and generations will come and go.

Always live with the consciousness of being privileged to be in a position of authority; that you are the leader does not make your followers incapable or does not change the fact that there are hundreds of thousands who could have done it better.

I remember different love lines that has the "without you" phrase – without you my life is incomplete and other love lines – but I discovered that all those lines were thrown into the recycle bin of history the day the relationship hit the rocks.

Beware of sycophants and praise singers who derive their Joy from making you feel indispensable. I feel bad when I see the way Presidents and Governors have been turned into mini-deities simply because everyone in their close circle feel they are indispensable.

Live your life with the mindset that you are only here for a set time, and if you don't make yourself available for a project there are hundreds and thousands of people who will do it better.

You are NOT INDISPENSABLE, No Man is; Only God is.

THE LAW OF CONTINUOUS MOTION

Nothing moves until you move
– Unknown

"Don't Ask God to Guide Your Footsteps if you are not willing to Move Your Feet"
– Unknown

I discovered that Life is a moving enclave; everybody seems to be in motion either going somewhere or coming from somewhere. We are all engaged in continuous motion either in our business, workplace, school, place of worship and every other place we find ourselves in Life.

Whether we use our Time or not, the hands of the clock appear to be in motion all the time. Every morning that I wake up for my exercise regimen, I discovered that I cover more miles and burn more body fat because I am in continuous motion; it's not a start stop exercise, but I am propelled by the fact that I need to make my day count, hence I need to start the day firing on all cylinders.

With the configuration of humans, we have been destined to be in continuous motion.

Man will always be in continuous motion when he discovers there is a prize attached to his endeavours.........Tolu' A. Akinyemi

Usain Bolt is always in continuous motion to remain relevant on the tracks; to remain relevant in your sphere of influence you need to be in continuous motion, so find ways to improve yourself and aspire to be the best.

Show me a prosperous man and I will show you a man who is always in motion; even when the road seems blocked and things seems not to be working: keep moving. When Life seems to be at a crossroad and you feel like giving it up, Keep Moving.

You have a vision, give motion to it. A car without fuel will never move, a generator without diesel is unlikely to work, so the same formula applies to our lives – before we can experience growth in life we must always fuel our lives with positive energy. There is no great innovation without significant effort. Before you see that edifice with all the architectural aesthetics, men and women toiled day and night to make it happen. The aircraft will only get to its destination if it is in continuous motion, the moment it stops mid-air there is a problem.

To succeed in life, always be in motion. Don't stop learning; don't stop reading. The few who are on the top rung of the ladder either in the economic, entertainment, entrepreneurial, social, political and other strata of society are those who have learnt to always be in motion.

Winners don't quit, they are always in motion, looking for new techniques to improve old ways of thinking and turning supposed impossibilities to possibilities.

As you choose to be in motion, the reward can be mind boggling and I wish you all the best as you make a conscious effort to move from where you are to where you want to be.

THE SEQUEL TO THE LAW OF CONTINUOUS MOTION

Nothing moves until you move
– Unknown

Don't ask God to order your steps, if you are not willing to move your feet
– Unknown

Generations come and go, as deaths are recorded daily so do we experience the birth of new-born babies every day. The configuration of our lives entails motion, being active. On motorways, speed of vehicles and trucks are very essential – it could be dangerous for a car to be moving at a slow pace on a high-speed lane, so life entails us to keep moving on its motorway. Stagnation is a crime; we become ingrates to the one who has given us our life if we become motionless. A tree that does not bear fruits is not useful to itself and becomes a liability to the ground that it uses as an abode.

If our lives are investments, will it be profitable for people to invest in, will our lives yield dividends and bonus for investors or will it just be an unprofitable venture? To be in motion in life, we must continually make ourselves relevant wherever we find ourselves. As much as possible, we must not despise personal development, we must crave education, continuous learning, seeking out new-information and enlarging our reference base. A classic example of how profitable it is to be in continuous motion is highlighted below.

A young Nigerian while working as a casual staff in a complex organisation was studying for his degree. On completion of his degree, he applied for a team lead role and was subsequently employed. He became a higher-ranking staff to his supposed former senior colleagues, and contemporaries. There is a lot to gain from gaining speed in life; there is no knowledge that can be lost in life.

Man will always be in continuous motion when he discovers there is a prize attached to his endeavour……...Tolu' A. Akinyemi

Whether I am self-employed or work for an organisation in the future, my knowledge and expertise will always belong to me and will always make a way for me. The world will only pay you for your knowledge and expertise; there is no prize for being mediocre. You have a vision, give motion to it. To experience success in life, we need to move from the realm of dreamers to actors.

Ask the world's top organisations, they will tell you that a whole lot of funds go into research and development; they know and understand the benefits of being in continuous motion with their product range and service offering. So, there is a need to remain relevant with the times and the season – you don't expect consumers to buy a 1990 Jaguar, for example, when there is a more fashionable 2018 model. In the Nigerian banking sector in the early 80s, bankers were employed with their secondary school certificate; those who had the foresight studied for their bachelor's degree and when the mass retrenchment of the 90s surged through the sector like a whirlwind, those who remained motionless without any form of development were displaced from their work roles.

Inasmuch you are alive, keep moving, don't stop gaining speed and give motion to your vision.

HAPPY PEOPLE

I dedicate this essay to all men and women worldwide who have risen above their situation and circumstance and have embraced HAPPINESS AS A WAY OF LIFE.

Happiness is an emotion that is characterized by a feeling of absolute contentment. It is the feeling of being where you should be, getting what you want and needing little else.

According to the free online dictionary, happiness can be defined as

1. Characterized by good luck; fortunate.
2. Enjoying, showing, or marked by pleasure, satisfaction, or joy.
3. Being especially well-adapted; felicitous: *a happy turn of phrase.*
4. Cheerful; willing: *happy to help.*

Below are quotes from great people I would like to share with you:

Happiness is when what you think, what you say, and what you do are in harmony.
Mahatma Gandhi

Happiness is that state of consciousness which proceeds from the achievement of one's values.
Ayn Rand

Happiness is something that you are, and it comes from the way you think.
Wayne Dyer

Happiness is essentially a state of going somewhere, wholeheartedly, one-directionally, without regret or reservation.
William H. Sheldon

Happiness is not a reward – it is a consequence.
Robert Ingersoll

Happiness is different from pleasure. Happiness has something to do with struggling and enduring and accomplishing.
George Sheehan

Happiness is the meaning and the purpose of life, the whole aim and end of human existence.
Aristotle

Happiness is not something you experience, it's something you remember.
Oscar Levant

Happiness is not a station you arrive at, but a manner of travelling.
Margaret Lee Runbeck

Happiness is the spiritual experience of living every minute with love, grace and gratitude.
Denis Waitley

Happiness is the antidote to loneliness, the true essence of our life and living.
Tolu' A. Akinyemi

Being happy is a choice. Some find pleasure in getting into depressing moods and they do not experience a state of happiness; happiness is a journey, not a destination. There are two ways to show happiness: you can either be the light that shares it or the mirror that reflects it.

I have made a conscious effort to embrace happiness, to stop getting worried over things I cannot change. Some people complain about depression and mood swings, but I have made a choice to be master over my emotions. To be happy, you need to be contented always, you need to rejoice with those who succeed in your environment, do not despise anyone and stop the hating. Show love to everyone that comes across your path; stop the strife, envy, malice and bitterness. Life is too short to hold grudges against anyone. Sickness like hypertension is prevalent with people who worry; happy people live healthy lives and are free from diseases. Happiness also enhances longevity of life; happy people live longer than those who worry.

Happy people give thanks all the time, they are always grateful for the present times, knowing that the future holds much Joy.

THE MAGIC WAND

It's a season when people want to see the God of plenty magic in action, the God who can turn stones to bread, the God who can turn paper into money, the God who can change a man's location from the slum to a castle without lifting a finger; many people are interested in the very sharp God or the extra smart God.

The God of the magic biro, that can write plenty of notes in the exam halls. The God who can make your cheat sheets invincible to the examiner. The God who gives the product without the process, the God who produces the gold without the pruning, the God in the fast lane, the God of fast cars, the God of fast money (some will not mind if the money is blood), the God who throws manna at all his children, the God who does not even consider us to be tempted, the God of the overcrowded ministries, but wait, have you not heard that God is Love, even though you have been lost in the desires of the flesh and you are wont to satisfy its lust thereof, remember that God's time is the best.

My God is not a magician, he blesses those who know how to diligently obey his commands, and he does not bypass the process and churn out the product. Many times, people ask God why their life seems stagnated and they seem stuck in a spot in life, in business or other areas, but we need to understand the concept of God's time and our time. God will not give you a car if he knows that car will be the cause of your death, so while you are busy rebuking the devil for your lack of funds to buy a car, God is telling you that, my son, I am still the Alpha and Omega. He is the God who knows the beginning and the end of our lives.

The problem humans tend to experience most times is that we tend to resolve the issues of our life based on human intellect and calculations; we relegate the God of all creation to the background and when we get stuck we run back to him.

Truth be told, there is no magic wand from heaven that will restore lost hope, lost business, lost opportunities, lost careers and other things that have been lost to the world if you don't study the word, act the word and let the word work wonders in your life.

The solution is not in the white handkerchief or the anointing oil, for my God is not a magician. To get the best from God, do not despise the process; it might seem tough, the road might be bumpy and the whole terrain might look difficult, but keep trusting in the Lord.

Always come before the Lord with praise and thanksgiving on your lips and watch him turn your life around for the better.

THE MAGIC WAND 2

People go to the presence of God these days expecting to hit a divine jackpot. When you hear prayer points of some believers you will be scared a Spiritual hurricane is about to hit their office account, the state treasury and whatever department they oversee.

I want you to know that my God does not cut corners, he is not a God of Awilo Sharp Sharp, there is no abracadabra in his kingdom; let's stop this mockery of God all in the name of the craze for riches and wealth. People run from one church to another all in the name of a quest for miracles or magic; people have forgotten that there is reward for dignity in labour.

Instead of seeking information that will enrich their lives, instead of attending seminars that will improve their destinies, they can be seen in the four corners of a church evoking the death penalty on their enemies even on a Monday morning when all their contemporaries are off to pay the price in the quest to gain the prize.

In the quest to be prosperous, the people on the top rung of the ladder only use some timeless principles which turn all their efforts into excellent results; they have money working for them and were not in pursuit of magic in their quest to get to the top.

Have you heard stories that moved you to tears, testimonies that made you weep like a baby? Have you seen such poverty that even the poor called them poor? Those are the stories of the people who went through much pruning before they became the role models and super stars we all adore today.

Don't be deceived that the magic can last forever; either it is internet fraud or yahoo plus or whatever form the magic is coming from. Always remember that there is nothing as pleasing as enduring wealth. Buy tapes and CDs of the successful, attend seminars and download materials that will help improve your reference base. Seek the face of the Lord and patiently wait for his reward.

The patient dog eats the biggest bone with plenty of biscuits on it as add-on, eat the word, study the word, bathe in the word, let what the word says be your reality and not what the world says.

There is great folly in magic and death for the one who trades their soul for the allure of short term results.

CORE VALUES

You can succinctly tell the direction an organization is moving towards through its application of its core values, the same way you can accurately predict where you will be in the nearest future by checking out the values that you can live by, die for, and stand for even when no one is watching.

The business dictionary defines core values as Operating philosophies or principles that guide an organization's internal conduct as well as its relationship with the external world. Core values are usually summarized in the mission statement or in the statement of core value.

What is your core value? Which philosophy are you operating your life upon, what is your relationship to the external world, what are your fundamental principles in life?

Your core value is a summary of your life's mission, and your "mission" is your purpose in Life.

Have you discovered purpose or are you still using a trial version operating system as a guide to destiny? Many people claim to have a beautifully scripted life mission's statement but are you living in the radar of your mission? Is your core value mere rhetoric and meant for personal aggrandizement or are you truly living the dream?

A lot of people can afford to live the quiet life, probably because they have their mentors and guardians watching their every step and guiding them on the right path. Are you ready to stay true to your life's vision and mission even when you are alone without any advice from guardians or is that an opportunity to misbehave and lose focus?

We need to develop a good values system and hold on to it tightly, we need to have strong principles that defines our existence. Are you ready to stay committed to this cause even when no one is watching, when no one is there to mentor and motivate you, when there are no tapes, pastors, blogs, motivational speakers to inspire and motivate you, will you be willing to follow those values that define who you are?

A man who does not drink alcohol can only justify that when he is confronted with free beer and wine and does not compromise; a pastor who preaches about fornication and adultery can only justify that if he is faithful in his marriage or relationship when he is confronted with temptations and stands strong.

To succeed in life, we must have a set of defined principles that will push us closer to our dreams. Check out the people who have succeeded in life and I will show you individuals who cannot be lost in the crazy frenzy of this world, they have been sold out to their dreams, aspirations, philosophies, principles and they are not ready to fall for anything.

How far can you go without compromising on your set standards?

For those who do not have set standards or principles they live by, do you know that if you don't stand for anything, you will fall for anything?

You can start by writing in a notebook, principles, standards and sets of core-values that will be your guide to that desirable future of yours. Nothing happens by chance; to get the PRIZE you must be willing to pay the price, let go and give up some habits and you will be amazed at the transformation you will experience.

DISCOVER YOUR PLACE

When a man discovers his place in life, he ceases from struggles and trying to run from place to place thinking God's blessing is a function of location. My dear friend, God is not interested in your house address or the class of neighbours who live in the same area with you; he is not concerned whether you reside in the city capital or the remote part of the village.

When you discover your place in life, you will begin to know your speed limits and will not be in a haste to fulfil destiny or trying to bite off more than you can chew. I have seen lots of people who went in search of the golden fleece and greener pastures and still do not have any worthwhile achievement to show for it.

I have also seen people who came to cities empty-handed, conquered those cities and dominated territories; I have seen individuals who were tagged as "nobody" yet rose to become people the world cannot do without. When you come to an understanding of your life's purpose, everything else begins to fall into their right dimensions and you will experience joy and happiness in all you do.

This essay is dedicated to people who think their blessing is a function of location and have been doing every possible thing to leave their present domain. It is the Lord who decides whom he will have mercy upon, it is not of him who wills, plots and strategizes, neither of him who runs, but it is a function of God who shares the blessings.

My prayer for everybody reading this today is that you will discover your resting place in life, you will discover your own Greenland, and you will not miss your own blessings in Jesus' name.

Stop trying to be like somebody else, we are different and unique in our own special ways, discover your original calling. Your human wisdom is too small to help you achieve anything in life, leave the knotty issues of your life to God for him to help you resolve. He is the potter and we are the clay, we are vessels in the hands of the father.

The race is not always won by the fastest runner; the strongest people do not always win the battles in life. When you discover your place in your career, everything else begins to fall on fertile ground for you. People who are fulfilled in their career find it easy to advance in other areas of their life.

Those who discover their place with their choice of life partners will always have rest all the days of their life; when you miss it in that area it is very difficult to get it right in other areas.

Always remember that God did not bring you this far to leave you alone, he will not forsake you or let you down. Know for a fact that even twin babies have different destinies; don't use someone else's timing to determine your own.

ENLARGE YOUR SPHERE OF INFLUENCE

We always think our father has the biggest farm until we go to someone else's father's farm and we discover what we pride as the biggest in our eyes is infinitesimal to what other people have.

This essay is meant to challenge business leaders, entrepreneurs, lawyers, bankers, economists, researchers, youth development advocates, human and business consultants and those whose occupations have not been listed above. I hope this will spur you to see a need for a paradigm shift.

The fact that you have been a local player in your field of endeavour for a long time is enough reason to let you know that there is a need for a shift in focus. You must always look for ways to enlarge your sphere of influence. The key thing we should always remember is: all things might not remain equal in the years ahead; the economic, business and other factors which are a boost for your business in this season may not always be constant.

You must make your life a school of continuous learning. Don't be satisfied with the status quo, and constantly look for ways to do things differently. Stuck on old ideas? Look for ways to make those ideas relevant in this present time. Check out the businesses that cascaded our landscape in the early nineties – how many are still functioning in this present day?

When you change your paradigm, you change your life. Enlarge your sphere of influence, break new ground, and chart new territories. Don't be too comfortable in your present zone, get an education, read books, get a mentor. The quality of information available is the difference between the rich and the poor, so source the right information.

Always remember that the future belongs to those who see the possibilities before it becomes obvious, imagine the possibilities, and don't short-change yourself in life.

Think Global, dare to be different. The fact that you tried several times and the challenges seem insurmountable is not an excuse or reason to quit. Think of how you can add value to the economy; be a solution provider. Turn your frustration into positive anger, thrash the victim mentality, and break yourself free from the trap of self-doubt.

Don't just be an addition to the numbers in the world; make your life count, be an agent of positive change in your immediate environment. Imprint your footprints on the sands of time.

FOCUS IS KEY

Whenever we set our gaze on a key accomplishment, we must do it without a shift in focus. I discovered many people in life miss the main course and are lured by the add-ons, the starter and other freebies before the main menu is served. Sometimes the extras may look so alluring that we tend to forget the reason why we really want the main course.

Individuals who achieved accomplishments of note are those who kept their eyes on the prize while they paid the price without looking back. I have seen a lot of people lose the essence and value of their lives because of the side attractions; they forgot completely about the main course.

To everything there is a season and a time for every accomplishment under the sun; we have separate times and seasons in our lives: there is a time to be born, a time to attend nursery school, primary school, secondary school, university, work, marriage, and other events as people's individual choices differ. A school student who is supposed to be laying the right foundation for their life but shifts their gaze from the essential; whatever outcome derived from a consequence of decisions taken should not be blamed on other people or on society.

For people who want to maintain an elevated level of focus in their projects, marital life, business, work and education, questions like "Why am I here?" should always come up from time to time. It is also essential that we do a periodic evaluation of our lives, make a deep reflection of the past and the present which will tell you if you are on the right track for the future.

The mistakes that people make is they tend to live for the moment, the present; many do not even want to remember the past; many people have become lost in the present and prayerfully hope the future will sort itself out.

The people who pride themselves as the key achievers in our generation were able to achieve those enviable heights because even in the face of daunting challenges, trials, sleepless nights, business failures, pitfalls and other obstacles which came their way, they never changed their focus, they were undaunted by the seemingly temporary failures, they kept their focus on their set goals – which is the main reason they are celebrated in our generation.

Do you desire success in every area of your life? Are you keen to achieve a faster turnaround time in your projects? Then, the secret lies in your ability to concentrate the bulk of your time doing the things that are essential, which will give you a more productive outcome.

No matter the side attractions that might be on offer, always remember there is a main course which should be our main target. Make your life count; don't forget that Focus is vital to all that we ever want to do in Life.

DEVIL YOUR CHIEF RESPONSIBILITY OFFICER OR NOT

The devil has really had a tough time with the people of my generation, people who are capable of making the right choices but refuse to, and have made the devil the Chief Responsibility Officer for their lives. I find it quite amusing the way people blame all of their woes on the devil – the armed robber who goes out killing innocent people and robbing them of their belongings will tell you it is the work of the devil the day he meets his Waterloo; all the time he has been shooting and maiming innocent people, the devil was his right hand man but the day the long arm of the law catches up with him the devil becomes the victim, he gets all the blame.

The paedophile who rapes innocent and underage girls will start pleading for forgiveness when he is caught and blames it all on the devil. If the devil removed his trousers, did the Holy Spirit not minister to him not to involve himself in such acts? But he hardens his heart, removes his shorts and after defiling young girls blames it all on the devil.

I still find it difficult to understand why people have given so much false importance to the devil, a Christian who has a headache begins to cast and bind the devil – stop giving importance to the devil; he does not deserve any of the attention he is getting.

I was watching a crime fighters programme on television many years ago. A young man who stabbed a mad woman to death was being interviewed and he blamed all his woes on the devil; he had smoked Indian Hemp and was no longer in control of his senses. The mad woman stepped on him and he ran inside his house, brought out a knife and stabbed her to death on the neck. He was apprehended and found himself in the police net. If only he had made the right choice by not smoking that night, maybe the devil would not have been blamed for the act.

I want us to know that we all have the chance to make a choice, we all have the chance to do it right, we all have the chance to be in control of our lives by evaluating every decision critically and allowing the Holy Spirit to minister to us before pleasing the desires of our mortal bodies.

It's a sign of weakness and irresponsibility to transfer the dominant role of the Chief Responsibility Officer of your life to the devil. Try out the Holy Spirit – he will always be there to minister to you and help you make the right choices in Life. The most significant element you need in Life is the God factor and the second one is the power of your choices; do not dismiss that small, still voice that tells you not to involve yourself in evil acts.

As you start anew in your decision-making process, you must learn to take charge of your life and exercise self-restraint, your decisions must seek to glorify God and I pray that we will not lose the control of our lives to the devil.

THE BOY DIED, WE MOURNED

I find it disheartening when we lose young people to the cold hands of death. Our heritage from the kings of kings is long life so we must come to an understanding that premature death is not our portion. We must understand this notion and free ourselves from the fear of death.

The same way millions of babies are born daily, so also many young ones and old people die day-to-day. To everything there is a season and a time to every purpose under the heaven. A time to be born and a time to die. The promise of God to his children is that none shall cast thy young in the land and he promised to fulfil the number of our days in the land; in some other versions he promised us a full life span. Anytime I see people who are cut off in their prime, I am always saddened that potentials and resources are lost whenever we record a death.

The boy died, we all wrote wonderful eulogies, cried our hearts out, mourned and talked about his charitable deeds while on Earth and we prayed that such evil occurrence should not happen in our midst again. Have you forgotten that it is better to go to a house of mourning than to go to a house of feasting, for death is the destiny of every man; the living should take this to heart. So anytime a young person dies, we should always remember that we are on planet Earth for a time and season; no human has permanent residency on Earth, we are here for just a short while.

Do not store up for yourselves treasures on Earth, where moth and rust destroy, and where thieves break in and steal, but store up for yourselves treasures in heaven, where moth and rust do not destroy, and where thieves do not break in and steal. For where your treasure is, there your heart will be also. "Therefore, I tell you, do not worry about your life, what you will eat or drink; or about your body, what you will wear. Is not life more important than food, and the body more important than clothes? Look at the birds of the air; they do not sow or reap or store away in barns, and yet your heavenly Father feeds them. Are you not much more valuable than they. Who of you by worrying can add a single hour to his life? But seek first his kingdom and his righteousness, and all these things will be given to you as well. (Matthew 6:19-21, 31-33)

Don't lose sight of your assignment on Earth, even as we are daily confronted with life's daily challenges, looking for ways to make ends meet, in our quest for survival, in our quest to make the best out of life; always remember that we came to the world with nothing and we will return to our creator the same way we came.

CREATE YOUR BUZZ, CELEBRATE YOUR SUCCESS

The moment we learn to create that special buzz around our own lives, the more we learn to appreciate the power of God and be thankful for what he has done. Every human has enormous potential, the can-do spirit, but most people tend to undervalue their own gifts and abilities and celebrate the success of others. The human mind has been discovered over time to be the breeding ground of ideas and the engine room of powerful inventions. While you are moaning about your personal situation and giving excuses for your failures, look at the positives, celebrate your success. You never know what you can do unless you put in that extra nudge; the sense of fulfilment that comes from knowing that you also are a treasure who has been designed for success cannot be measured.

Spend the next thirty days celebrating your personal success, reminisce on the past, be thankful for today and tomorrow will surely be a best-seller. From my experience, I also discovered that those who envy the success of their colleagues, friends, and family never achieve anything meaningful from life.

Stop living your life as a sycophant; no one is permitted to make you a slave if you don't permit them. The difference between a success and failure is positive action; without acting on your goals, dreams and aspiration all you will be doing is wishful thinking.

No man has ever succeeded on wishes – have an action plan for your life, make the vision plain upon tables so that you may also understand it.

Be thankful for every breath, make every moment count, and don't stop believing in yourself. Everyone has opportunities in life no matter how infinitesimal; the difference is how we maximize our potential on a personal level. Some had opportunities to succeed in life which they misused; it has nothing to do with your background, a silver spoon or muddy spoon.

Every time I think of the failures in my past, I am always thankful for the success in my present. Don't stop believing in your abilities; add works to your faith. Create an aura of success around your life; always remember that you are in control.

MEASURING GROWTH

There are diverse ways we can measure our advancement in life. The growth process is quite important, and I can succinctly say it is an unavoidable development. As we are wont to admit, the only constant event in life is change and with humans it comes as a core requirement. Either we choose to embrace it in terms of maturity in our daily living or the enforced growth that comes with changes in the human cycle and development.

Our configuration has humans detest stagnation, hence the human mind tends to flourish in a dynamic environment where change is of the essence and daily growth of high value.

The free dictionary defines growth as development from a lower or simpler to a higher or more complex form; evolution. **Growth is also** an increase, as in size, number, value, or strength; extension or expansion: population growth.

When you stop changing, you stop leading. To function as an enigma in your sphere of influence, you must be open to changes which are a vital ingredient in the growth process. Growth entails embracing new ways and patterns of doing things and discarding old ones. Some individuals always find it difficult to try out innovative ideas because they do not want to alter a winning team, are comfortable with the old pattern and find it difficult to think outside the box.

Permit me to say: when we stop growing, we stop living. Only dead people experience stagnation; hence they are alienated from growth.

How can you measure your growth?

As with humans which has a visible growth process that can be ascribed to the evolution of man and the development phase from childhood to adulthood, we can measure our growth using visible and invisible parameters as the case may permit. A student who advances from bachelor's degree to the master's degree level and doctorate degree can aptly say he has experienced growth in his academic pursuit based on the progression from one stage to the other.

Using another scenario of a political office holder who starts as a councillor, moves on to the role of a local government chairperson, then later becomes a Member of Parliament, the politician can be said to have experienced growth in their political pursuit.

To truly measure growth, we need to do a critical evaluation of the major changes that have occurred in our lives. We also need to do an in-depth analysis of the events and people in our lives – either it has helped in our advancement, making us forward-looking or has relegated us to the trenches and consigned us to the count in the data pages of those whose growth has become stunted.

We can all grow up as a matter of necessity when we make a conscious effort to embrace positive change. Growth is a prerequisite to our daily living and existence.

THE BALANCED SCORE CARD

The most difficult part of our existence as humans is trying to achieve perfection in every area of our life; you might say "What a daunting task". How do we align our life's mission, with our vision statement and streamlining with our purpose to achieve an optimum result? How do we make a head-way in our finances, education, marital life, work, time management, social activities and spiritual walk with God without an area of our life being in reverse gear? Who can you point to as a model that has been able to achieve this highly tasking yet achievable score card?

A student who checks his result might prefer to see credit grades in all subject areas than to get distinction in some areas and fail in other subjects. Truly we can live a balanced life; our score card can be very impressive as to warrant emulation by the upcoming generation.

The first step to achieving a balance in every one of our endeavours is to plan our life effectively – he who fails to plan, plans to fail. We must learn to prioritize and rank every one of our activities to ensure life's success. Enough of whatever will be will be, we must consciously thrash the tomorrow will take care of itself attitude. Planning ensures cohesion in our decision-making and gives us a sense of direction.

The right balance is truly possible; truly it is achievable. Every worker should know a vacation is not a luxury but a necessity to guard against the breakdown of the immune system to illness and disease. Another factor which will work in our favour to ensure optimum balance of our life is discipline. Effective planning without discipline will throw our plans into disarray; hence it is important to be disciplined in life. An individual who is interested in watching his or her weight will need to be disciplined to eat the right balance of food.

Those who have been able to maintain a balance in their life do not have addictions. What is that idol or time-wasting device that is affecting your ability to maintain adequate balance in your life? I remember a time I was so much in love with my Sony PlayStation 3 that I barely had time to do any other worthwhile thing. There is no way we can achieve any meaningful success in life when we have addictions. The truth is when we waste our time, we waste our life.

To achieve a balanced life is not impossible; it entails consistency and conscientious efforts to realize it. Activating the right balance will help us to achieve our life's objectives faster and will help us save time that might be lost pursuing other things.

Always remember that the right balance is within reach if we desire and work towards it. We can do it right when we do everything we desire within limits and in the right proportion.

THE PASTURE IS NOT ALWAYS GREENER ON THE OTHER SIDE

Eyesight Advisory: This essay may not be pleasing to everyone who reads it. Viewers' Discretion is advised.

Whoever told you there is a greener pasture anywhere should have his head examined. This essay is envisioned for Nigerians who have sought refuge in different countries looking for the golden fleece and greener pastures. The truth be told there is no green pastures anywhere, the only green pasture I see lies in the resilience and power of the Nigerian man and woman on the street striving daily to make ends meet, from Lagos, Abuja, Port Harcourt, Ibadan, Warri, Benin, Ado-Ekiti, Ilorin and Jos. I see the never say die spirit of the true heroes of my fatherland.

Whenever I see my fellow countryman on the streets working as cleaners, security guards, train station attendants, and in departmental stores in different countries of the world, I see people who have short-changed themselves of the opportunity to lead successful lives back home and deny the country of vital human resources. No place like Nigeria, our heritage, a land flowing with milk and honey, blessed with the lightweight crude oil even the United States of America is glad to be our trade partners, a country with excellent weather conditions, blessed with rich human resources (engine room of development), free from natural disasters and other plagues experienced by countries of the world.

In the search for the greener pasture, a lot of people have left their heritage for various countries just because they believed the jackpot is within their grasp in their new abode, but many come back disappointed or unable to match their expectations because those lofty dreams of picking free dollars on the streets of America become a mirage.

My clarion call to all Nigerians who have enslaved themselves all in the name of travelling abroad, my candid opinion today is that it is very easy to succeed in Nigeria if you are diligent, hardworking and if you have acumen for spotting opportunities. If your excuse is unemployment, there are a lot of problems that can be converted into Job creating ventures. The government or lack of development should not be your excuse; don't look at what Nigeria can do for you but how you can bring change in your own little way.

I remember a young man who told me how he walked through the desert to Sudan because he felt his good luck was not in Nigeria, he said many people died on that journey because of lack of water; most times bones and decomposing human bodies were evident in the desert.

I applaud those Nigerian professionals who are contributing to the development of various countries in the world through their in-depth knowledge and expertise, the medical doctors, bankers, Financial Crime Analysts, World Bank Executives, nurses, mathematicians, professors, pharmacists, engineers, IT gurus, fashion designers and all those who are contributing through their pool of knowledge to the development of the world – I feel your pain that most times your ingenuity is not rewarded in your own country hence your decision to pursue a new life outside.

I remember reading a soft sell magazine that reported the story of a young man and his sister who married each other, because of the desperation to travel abroad. Many people have lost thousands of naira to fake visa agents, who use the desperation for greener pastures to swindle unsuspecting victims.

This essay is meant for the hustlers, those who work long shifts and have no rest, those who have traded their destinies for a plate of porridge in a foreign land, and those who lament daily about the lack of development in our fatherland but are in no way making a positive contribution to see my heritage move forward. The pull Nigeria down syndrome, those journalists who sit in their posh offices in Atlanta, Georgia and paint a gory picture of Nigeria, it is not as bad as you think or is being projected; Nigeria is the land with the pastures green.

Nigeria will fulfil its potential one day and very soon. Nigeria is crying today; if you can't contribute to my development please don't pull me down.

NO CONDITION IS PERMANENT

I dedicate this essay to every living soul who metamorphosed from a state of knowing the nicknames of poverty to a state of opulence through diligent work and perseverance. To those who were despised and disgraced on various occasions because of their lack of money, who are now blessed beyond measure, this essay is also dedicated to you.

I dedicate this essay to the young man and woman who are disenchanted and have lost hope in life and keep on asking the creator when they will be blessed.

From summer to winter, through sunshine and rainfall, and from the morning dew to night fall, no condition is permanent.

Life and its configuration favours growth – that is the main reason we can say no condition is permanent; a little child yesterday in a few years becomes a teenager then a youth, an adult and the circle revolve the same way till old age when our eyesight becomes dim.

Since I was born and now that I am old, through all my existence as a living being I have been privileged to know that there is no condition in life that is permanent.

The fact that you have failed in some aspects of life or you are not living up to your potential does not mean life will remain this way forever. I have seen tenants become landlords, jobless people employed and servants ride on horses. There is nothing that is impossible for my God to do; he is the only one who can give us joy and add no sorrow to it. He is the God who lifts the head of man in life without any condition.

Dear Friends, do not despair no matter what situation or circumstances life might throw at your doorstep. Life's success is not a function of family background, location or good looks; there is a time and season for everything that happens to us. Always remember that there is light at the end of every dark tunnel and after the night comes the morning.

If you weary not in well doing, in due season you will reap if you faint not. Trust in the Lord God with all your heart and lean not on your own understanding. In all your ways acknowledge him and he will direct your paths. Let's shun desperation; in the quest to get rich, your father owns the title deed of all properties in the entire world, never give up on God. God's ways are not our ways neither are his thoughts our thoughts, no matter how the last year might have been for you, this year is going to be your best year yet.

I have a father who makes the barren fruitful; he is the God, the lifter up of our head. No matter your condition, put a smile on your face for this too shall pass.

QUIT HATING

The world will be such a better place when we quit hating and show love to our friends, neighbours and contemporaries. We must learn to celebrate with those who succeed and not the pull him down syndrome that is a common occurrence in this part of this world. There is a blessing attached to those who show unequivocal love even to their enemies. The heart of man is desperately wicked and full of evil, it is hard to understand – have you seen smiles filled with indignation and derision?

The Bible talks about showing love to our neighbours as we love ourselves, but how many people can lay claim to being in love with their neighbours? Instead of showing love, we live all our days in envy and hate; it's very simple and logical – the sky is large enough for all birds to fly therein without any collision or accident of any nature. The barren that is expectant of the fruit of the womb must be caring towards children around her and not despise them. The tenant who intends to be a landlord someday must use his rented apartment as if it were his, not damaging any of the fittings therein.

Life is an individual affair; even twins born on the same day have different destinies and life's purpose. What if your class mates, age mates, colleagues are even younger than you are? Is that a parameter for life's success? It's time to wake up, God's blessings are not shared based on age or family background.

It's the same rain that falls on the yam, which falls on the maize; when there is life, there is hope for a better tomorrow. I learnt one secret of success from my dad: he taught me to celebrate with those who succeed in life. No matter the situation that life might throw at me, I spend my life celebrating people around me and to not bring anyone down. Take a clue from that; bitterness against fellow humans robs us of our blessing from God.

Be happy always and put your trust in God almighty, no matter what may come our way in life. God can bless us and lift us up.

We must spend our time productively, for how we spend our time invariably determines the outcome of our lives. Shun spreading rumours, negative news, and gossip about your friends but our lives must epitomize the love of Christ. We must be a harbinger of good news and not a channel of discord among our friends.

The power of life and death lies in the tongue, so use your tongue wisely; we must learn to evaluate the consequences of our actions before taking them. No man has the capacity to turn back the hands of time. Make your life count, let Love be your hallmark, don't just be the hearer of these words of wisdom but let LOVE be on the template of your heart.

QUESTIONS WITHOUT ANSWERS

The rich also cry; everything is vanity, so it seems. Life could be called a mystery – why do terrible things happen to good people and good things to bad people? When do we attain the level of optimum satisfaction? The rich are getting richer and the poor are getting poorer. So many questions that need answers but clueless we are. Can money truly buy happiness? If yes, then why are the rich not contented but always seek to get more even when they have surplus? If No what is the actual cost of happiness?

I find it hard to comprehend why young people die and the aged want to live on forever. So many questions that need answers in this world, but we have a God who knows it all. No matter the seeming level of perfection that can be seen in a man's life, never make any human your standard in Life. Behind the seeming perfect pictures, there is that human perspective, the areas where we are weak and can do nothing on our own accord.

Remember that with the grace comes an element of pain, the weakness, the part that defines our humanity. Most times we worry ourselves with the ephemeral, what we will eat, drink, clothes to adorn, what people think about us, our life partner, our future family, cars, houses and all other things of the world, and we begin to solve all these issues with our imagination.

What has been revealed unto me, most times we think it's about how much effort we put in, how much we struggle, how much we want to attain, in terms of salvation, money, power, status, respect and claim to knowledge. But the truth is, it is not of him who wills, neither is it of him who runs but of the Lord who shows mercy. If only we can understand that God's ways are not our ways, and his thoughts are entirely different from ours. Our definition, criteria and assessment will reflect a new pattern when we come to this knowledge.

No matter the issue in life that has made you grow weary and the situation that has thrown up numerous questions in our hearts. Always remember that there is a time and season for every occurrence in life. In all situations give thanks. The reason why David enjoyed so much grace from the throne of mercy was because he understood that God revels in our praises and thanksgiving, so despite his human frailties and weakness he enjoyed tremendous grace from the throne of mercy.

Even as we have numerous questions without answers readily available, always remember that there is a God who controls the affairs of humans. Make him the kingmaker in your life and experience life in a new way and higher dimension.

EGO: A TIME BOMB

Ego has been discovered as a time bomb that has the potential to destroy the carrier; ego has destroyed many relationships, made many jobless, closed many doors that could previously have been opened. Ego has turned kings into forgotten men and princes to servants. It has the capacity to make the wise foolish and the intelligent stupid.

I have heard different clichés during wedding ceremonies that a man loves his ego and the woman should do all within her power to massage that ego and not bruise it, but it is still that same ego which has destroyed many men, an inability to admit their mistakes and pronounce the five letter word "SORRY"; the same ego brings out the animal in man, showing some men as if they originated and live in the pre-medieval era. I have seen people who because of false ego ascribe some importance to themselves when truly they are nothing.

What about people whom acts of service are rendered towards and refuse to say thank you – how can I thank him, is he not my mate, or questions that can make the fall of man inevitable come up.

Ego has a lot of children; it leads to malice, hatred, strife and an unforgiving nature. People who are egotistic attach some false importance to themselves and they believe they can do no wrong, they are the Lord, the opinion of others does not matter to them and they are swift in making decisions without thinking about it.

To tame your ego, try humility. A few years ago, I was driving opposite the African shrine in Lagos, Nigeria and my car scratched the car of a senior assistant to the Governor. He almost lynched me and used his powers to get the Traffic Management Authority to levy fines against me. He ranted, do you know who I am and, in his bid to manhandle me, he locked his car keys and could not open the car and was stuck there for a few hours.

Talk about self-aggrandisement, that's another name for the people who love their ego. Many people have missed the goldmine that came in the form of animal manure because they cannot imagine themselves doing that kind of job. Look around you today, fake people, fake lives, all in the name of show off, because I am a celebrity or motivational speaker, people should not see me pushing a car. A lady who cannot afford a taxi wants to show the guys that she is hot, it's all for the ego.

People who love their ego live above their means, possibly borrow to maintain previous lifestyles, imagine a whole me (Chief Titus) who used to take my whole family on vacation to the States, so they continue to live in the make-believe world until they assist themselves to finish their glowing future.

Any ego that cannot be tamed ought to be bruised and that is always the lot of the egotistic person.

PART 2

LIFE – AN INDIVIDUAL AFFAIR

More often than not, we tend to ascribe our failure in life to other people, a rich brother who never taught us how to fish, an uncle who did not sponsor our education, the reason we were born into a muddy spoon family, the government, and a thousand and one reasons space will not allow me to mention. My dad had an adage he always emphasized to my hearing in my formative years which kept me on my toes. “Life,” he said, “was an individual affair”, and he told us a story of my mom, how she had to carve out her future by herself rather than relying on her brother’s wealth. Dad always capped the story by admonishing us to put our trust in God and not in any human. Anytime a member of the family was ill, Dad would say no matter the love we show for the sick member, it is the person who is ill that feels the pain. The same is applicable to our future: if we have a beautiful life we get to enjoy the benefits that come with living successful lives. The story touched my heart for many reasons; it taught me that I had to strive to be the best in all that I lay my hands upon and not depend on any man for survival. Do you know how much joy you will feel, when every child in the family is excelling in their chosen career path without a local champion dictating the pace, or how much indignation you will feel when there is a family head that the cap no longer fits?

We must know that the shape of our lives and invariably the future path lies in our daily routine. Check out what you do with your time, the people we believe cannot succeed without our input. We can live good lives despite the failings of the government and the society we live in.

LIFE SERIES: THE TOP IS WHERE YOU BELONG

We need to fight our way to the top in all our endeavours; the basement is always crowded in every sphere of life. Check out our universities; only a fraction of the total students graduate with a first-class degree. There is always stiff competition for those who desire the best, losers are always timid and are not in a hurry to achieve results.

Theodore Roosevelt said, and I quote: "It is not the critic who counts, not the man who points out how the strong man stumbled or where the doer of the deeds could have done them better. The credit belongs to the man who is actually in the arena, whose face is marred by dust and sweat and blood, who strives valiantly, who errs and comes short again and again, who knows the great enthusiasms, the great devotions and spends himself in a worthy cause, who at best knows in the end the triumph of high achievement and who at the worst, if he fails, at least fails while daring greatly, so that his place shall never be with those cold and timid souls who know neither victory nor defeat."

I know I can be what I want to be if I work hard at it, I will be where I want to be. Like I always emphasize, without the test there can be no testimony. I put myself under consistent pressure, so I can achieve my set goals and plans for my life. Many people live life at their own pace; you hear phrases like I cannot kill myself. I knew early enough in life that the zenith is where I belong, and I have not been deterred ever since to get to the top. There have been days of disappointments, the silent tears, the frustrations in business; there have been days when I had to cry and ask God some questions; there have been days of breakthrough in business. The joy I felt when I made my first million in my early twenties; the joy I felt when I bought my first car; the business success as an undergraduate and the grace to succeed in the business world even after my university days. I remember vividly the days I was a phone dealer and I toiled day and night till I was able to make it big, I remember all those times with mixed feelings. I remember all my hustling in life; I remember the prophetic nights with a passion; I remember my dreams, my aspirations to be a better man.

I remember this new season of my life, how I have been able to impact upon lives; the wisdom has been phenomenal, and it can only be God. I pick up my laptop and write down whatever comes to my mind without a script or book as a guide. I owe everything to God; the feedback and response has been phenomenal. I am not perfect, and I have my flaws as a human being and I am just a vessel in the hands of God.

Give motion to your vision; don't stay at the background – the spotlight is where you belong. No matter the problems you encounter in life, always remember without the process there can be no results. You might have tried and failed so many times; don't give up. If you weary not in well doing, in due season you will reap if you do not faint. Life is too short not to engrave your footprints on the sands of time.

What you need in life is the strength of character, character to stand up for the truth, the strength to pursue your dreams after your failures. Being crowned a champion is not a one-day effort – it takes consistent preparation over a period. Draw up a road map and a work plan for your life, develop a vision and mission statement and do a review from time to time to see if you have achieved your objectives periodically.

Those who have a relationship with me understand the fact that I am always motivated and happy always, no matter the challenge and turbulence life throws at my feet. That is one of the secrets to my writing ability; don't despise the days of your little beginnings; Life is not a bed of roses – for some people the bad patch they have experienced is more significant than any rose life can give them.

Pursue your dreams, be passionate and you will succeed. Always remember that every great person in life has a story, your story will be heard all over the world.

LIFE SERIES: TAKE RISKS

The reason why people tend to let go of their dreams, goals and life aspirations is because of the fear of failure. Everything in life is a risk and comes with a price. Every invention that has gained prominence also has its attendant risk; the aeroplane has shortened travel time and is very convenient, but plane crashes always leave few or no survivors at all. The fact that plane crashes do occur has not stopped people from travelling by air. Road accidents have been the bane of motor vehicles, trucks and motorcycles, yet people still buy cars and travel on the road every day. A lesson from the above illustration is the fact that the downside has not prevented people from enjoying the benefits that come with various inventions.

Failure should not be an excuse to quit; remember quitters never win, and winners do not quit. No matter the challenges confronting you in your daily life, keep forging on. A lot of the successful people out there had their difficult moments as well, but after the dark cloud comes the morning.

Do not be afraid to follow your dreams and convert your ideas into reality. Nothing is impossible to those who believe, that you tried and failed does not determine who you are. The fact that cultism is rampant in some higher institutions of learning has not stopped people from going to school; football players get career threatening injuries on the field of play, yet still many people look forward to a great footballing career. Be ready to throw your hat into the ring; do not be afraid to take risks. You never know which of your seeds will bring forth bountiful harvests.

To get the prize, you must be willing to pay the price.

LIFE SERIES: IT'S AN INDIVIDUAL AFFAIR

I believe that everyone is the architect of his own fortune and misfortune, success and failure; we have the capacity as human beings to determine what we make of our lives. We all came to the world as a distinct and wonderful creation designed by God to fulfil a purpose on Earth. So, if you are out there wondering what you can really make out of life, or you are not yet in your desired comfort zone, there is hope for you, because everything God created was good. You will truly succeed when you begin to develop the mentality that you are responsible for your success and failure.

The sum of our daily activities will give us a picture of the future we desire, so if there are some events in your daily routine that will not ultimately take you to your promised land, please press the delete button or you can throw it into the recycle bin system of your life. When I have malaria, I feel the pain alone. My loved ones will always ensure I get the best medical treatment, but I feel the pain in my body. The same analogy also applies to life; it is the person who the shoe pinches who knows where it hurts. I have seen people who complain about a rich uncle, brother, father and sister who has not been fulfilling their responsibilities, but I beg to differ – they are not under any compulsion to give you what they have. They made better use of the opportunities at their disposal.

God has given to every person talents and gifts for use on the face of the earth; how you use it is entirely dependent on your decisions in life. Everyone has the chance to make a choice; our choices will either make or mar our future. So, the next time you are looking for a pawn to blame for your woes, try and recall the major decisions that shaped your life. Your love or apathy towards education and technical skills will determine how far you can go career-wise; your creative ability and gifts will determine how much impact you can make; your choice of a life partner will determine your marital happiness or regrets. The tiny details in our day to day lives do count; our choices today have an overbearing influence on our future.

Many of the people in the intensive care unit of hospitals who are suffering from ailments because of addictions in their early years always wish they can turn back the hands of time. If only they knew that their decision in their early years would leave an imprint on their lives forever. Remember, it's an individual affair.

My prayer for families most of the time is that every child should be successful, so there is no liability and castaway who feels intimidated by the success of other siblings.

Spend your life well; it is your currency to lifelong fulfilment.

LIFE SERIES: ACT YOUR SCRIPT

We are all actors with distinct roles in the blockbuster movie called life, the movie script has been given to us all by the Movie director (God Almighty) and we are to play our part, as actors, boss or crowd. The kind of effort we put into acting our assigned role is dependent on our commitment to churn out a good movie for the viewing public. Some people's scripts or assigned roles are best-sellers but they can also conspire to re-write their script or history as we might call it, when the movie director finished his work of creation and he saw that everything he created was good, so all the bad and sharp practices that have become common in the world is as a result of people deviating from the original plan of the movie director.

When you realize that the life you live is not your own, then we need to exercise more caution in the way we handle our life issues. The same way a movie director can remove any erring actor from set, is the same way our Movie director can dismiss us from location without our permission. We had no clue when we were born, we did not have any idea of the kind of family we will be born into and we had no power over our gender so that tells us that before he created us, he knew us and even knows all the issues pertaining to our life. Whatever role that has been assigned to you from the director, please act your script well. If you are a pastor or a religious leader, please lead the sheep in the right direction as the Shepherd of the flock; if you are a politician please give the people good political leadership; the same also applies to other areas of assignment that space will not allow me to mention.

Life is a teacher, no matter the lessons you have learnt since birth, keep striving to be the best. Play your part well; make an impact in your world. Always do things for the benefit of mankind. Some people died many years ago and the world still talks about them to this date even when they died many decades ago. Ask yourself this question, if I die tomorrow what will I be remembered for? Will I truly be missed or are people going to hiss that he is better dead than alive. Many people are on Earth to add to the crowd and make up the numbers; don't just add to the numbers, live your life every day with the belief that you can imprint your footprints on the sands of time.

Always walk in the consciousness that you are a special creation and the Director who knows the times and season of our lives will perfect all our weakness and give us strength in return.

Remember that your life is a book; today is the page you are reading.

LIFE SERIES: DISCOVER YOUR APTITUDE

I am a king, I am divinely inspired, I am a sent man to my generation. Every individual has a royal trait within; until you discover your royal status you are subject to abuse. Everyone within my nuclear family know and accept the fact that I am a king, I have been a king for a long time but until I began confessing my kingship through words it began to enter the consciousness of my family members that they have a royal priest within the household. To add value to my status, I also have a royal name as my middle name. A plasma television without its manual cannot work to its full potential, so if a poor person wakes up every day for the next five years and begins to confess I am divinely connected with my helpers of destiny. I believe somewhere along the line, their confessions will speak and make a way for them. Do you know that you are a royal priesthood, a chosen generation and a peculiar people?

Many people are living with innate abilities and potential that are under-utilized; your gifts are meant to be made evident and not hidden. I had a visitor many years ago who got me thinking with his confession; he has a mindset that his success is a function of how well his boss likes his face. I made him realize that God decides who he chooses to have mercy upon; the sky is large enough to accommodate all birds. God is still in the business of transforming lives, no one was born a failure, and our attitude to life will eventually determine our altitude (how far we can go in life).

Life challenges are not supposed to act as negatives in the quest to get to our desired future. I told my guest his situation is not the worst and if he listens to other people's stories he will begin to give thanks to God. God needs children who have discovered their rights in the kingdom; we need to change our prayer points from asking for manna to getting the real substance. A lot of people have traded their birthright for a plate of porridge and lost the right to their originality due to lack of understanding. My people perish for lack of knowledge; God created you an original not a photocopy of anyone. Until you begin to walk in the consciousness of who you really are, you will not be able to achieve your dreams and aspirations.

LIFE SERIES: DROP THE MILK AND START CRACKING BONES

God needs children and not babies; he needs sons and daughters and not outcasts in the kingdom. God needs children who are not swayed by the machinations of the enemy; it is one thing to be a son and another level entirely to understand your rights as a son in the house. Babies always lean on their mothers for help, they need milk to stay alive and they depend on others for survival while children always use their initiative to sort out the difficult puzzles of life.

The prodigal son had to come back home when he realized he had to drop milk (slavery); even if he was a servant in his father's house he would enjoy the benefits of being a son. Many Christians do not realize they have enormous power at their disposal and they fret at every wind that blows in their direction. The devil lost the battle over your life two thousand years ago, when Christ died for the sins of all mankind. Don't magnify the devil because you are Christ-like; the spirit of God lives on our inside and we can do all things through Christ who strengthens us.

There is no enchantment or divination that can stand against you or your destiny for the Lord is on your side; a trap that the devil always uses as a weapon against Christians is sin. Remember, for all have sinned and fall short of the glory of God, and are justified by his grace as a gift, through the redemption that is in Christ Jesus. (Romans3:23-24)

The grace of the Lord is sufficient for you. I remember I had an altercation with a woman many years ago who promised to kill me, and she went to her sect to report and promised to attack me. I told her if she can kill Jesus then she has every right to kill me. I knew my rights in the kingdom of God and I was not afraid to confront the enemy. Then came the spiritual attack in the dream but the God of Abraham, Isaac and Jacob stood for me. If God be for us; who can be against us? I have tasted Jesus and there is no one like my God; the devil will give you one leg and collect two bones in return. But my God makes me rich and adds no sorrow to it.

I was in an aeroplane some years back and at the slightest shudder, everyone started screaming the blood of Jesus. I was calm because I know the God that I serve.

This essay is a challenge to someone out there, who is trying to resolve every issue of their lives through their own wisdom and ability, lack of money (fraud/internet scam), marital problems (divorce/infidelity), unemployment (streetwise) and other problems too numerous to mention. Put your trust in the Lord; children understand the fact that God knows all about us. He is the potter and we are the clay; he decides of what use to put every vessel.

Use your ticket as a son or my God will raise stones to have his kingdom established here on Earth.

LIVE YOUR LIFE

Our uniqueness as humans lies in our individuality. No matter how much of the same features twin children possess, there are still habits, virtues and principles that set them apart. This essay is meant to challenge us to shun crowd mentality and live our own lives so that when our epitaph is written, statements to depict that we truly lived will be made about us. A lot of people are just here to add to the numbers, make the world a bigger place and leave without imprinting their footprints on the sands of time.

I have been fortunate to be a mentor to many young people and when I ask them why they have picked up the habit of smoking at such a tender age or other delinquencies, they have no real reason but all the answers I get always flow in the same direction: I am smoking because my friends are doing it, or I chose this negative habit because everyone is doing it. I begin to tell them that your life is yours to live, nobody should influence you negatively as life is an individual affair.

We all came to the world independently; if you have a headache, you suffer the consequence of the pain alone. No matter how much love your family can show you, all they can wish you is a quick recovery, but no one is going to help you carry the burden of your pain.

In living your life, always remember that life is in phases and we all have our times and season. Don't let any burden or pressure make you live a false life; a lot of people live their life based on illusions depicting what they are not. Greatness is hidden in small packages, so if you want to be big, starting small is the way to go. A lot of people are in the world to follow the crowd, and they get what's on offer in equal measure; a lot of habits and negative vices are common in our world today, so whatever path we choose there are lots of things on offer like different meals on a food menu.

I have many mentors who I admire but I don't want to be like them; they are great individuals, famous, have been blessings to generations, but I choose to live my life and not be like anyone else; I love who I am. In trying to live our lives, we must carve a niche for ourselves and be distinct from everyone else; we must not just count the days but as a matter of urgency make the days count.

Steve Jobs said, and I quote; "Your time is limited, so don't waste it living someone else's life. Don't be trapped by dogma which is living with the results of other people's thinking. Don't let the noise of others' opinions drown out your inner voice. And most importantly, have the courage to follow your Heart and Intuition. They somehow already know what you truly want to become, everything else is secondary."

LIFE IS ABOUT PERSPECTIVE

An optimist is a person who sees a green light everywhere; while a pessimist sees only the red stoplight... the truly wise person is colour-blind.
– Albert Schweitzer

Always borrow money from a pessimist; he doesn't expect to be paid back.
– Author Unknown

The kind of future you get revolves around the predominant thoughts in your mind and your perspective on issues. While some people like to view life on the positive side, some others are full of negativity and already know a million and one reasons why things will not work.

Do you always feel angry when sycophants sing the praises of corrupt politicians? Those supporters most times have embedded in them fixated mindsets that choose to suffocate the negative public image of their Icons and only project the perceived positives to the populace.

Some people out there believe there are contracts they cannot get because they don't have any connections in the corridors of power, while some others believe they have built capacity to access any government contract notwithstanding their lack of connections.

Most graduates in this region will tell you they cannot get jobs with their qualifications because they don't know anyone; because of their mindset it is always hard for this set of people to get jobs, while some others get jobs because they believe their qualification will get them the kind of jobs they want.

What is your perspective on life? Do you have a positive or negative outlook on life? Remember that the future belongs to those who see the possibilities before they become obvious, so you have to see it, think it, plan it, believe it, work at it and watch it become reality.

You will hear phrases like this: rich people are wicked people; someone who plans to be rich someday will stop hating the rich because he knows someday he will be among the rich. I have a very close friend who achieved an ambition; most people would have perished the idea and rebuked the devil if the thought came to their mind, but today he is living the dream.

You need to develop a CAN-DO attitude on issues; there is no impossibility to those who believe. What do you believe in? You must also be mindful of your confessions; your words are the seeds that propel the engine of your life.

You must also have the mindset of a solution provider; I have heard people say that they were able to break through in life because of the perceived problems in their industry or a sector of the economy. While some people moan and groan about the problems in the country today, some others are amassing a fortune because they have developed the right perspective to issues.

A pessimist sees only the dark side of the clouds, and mopes; a philosopher sees both sides, and shrugs; an optimist doesn't see the clouds at all – he's walking on them. ~Leonard Louis Levinson

LIFE: AN OPPORTUNITY COST

Investopedia defines opportunity cost as the cost of an alternative that must be forgone in order to pursue a certain action. Put another way, the benefits you could have received by taking an alternative action. The life we live is an opportunity cost in all its facets; never take it for granted. The fact that your mother did not abort your pregnancy is the main reason why you are here.

There are two sides to a coin in life: the cost of your decisions and the cost of not taking the alternative course of action.

The opportunity cost of my writing this essay will either be my sleeping time or my leisure time which is being given up.

The fact that you chose that career path and you seem to be successful does not mean you would not have been more successful if you had chosen an alternative path in life.

When we evaluate the opportunity cost of our decisions before taking them, it will help us become better individuals, and hence enhance the quality of our decision-making process in life.

When you are sitting an exam that is theoretical in nature, it tends to be very difficult but the moment you are sitting an examination that is objective in nature, even if you are not sure, you can guess your way through to the correct answer. That is part of the benefits of having different options and evaluating them appropriately before you arrive at your decision.

I am always fascinated whenever I watch the millionaire game show and participants on the hot seat use the 50-50 lifeline – the cost of their choices could be winning or losing the prize money at stake.

Life is all about the power of choices; we are obligated every day of our lives to make choices. The quality of our choices will determine the quality of our lives. Evaluate both the decision and the opportunity cost of your decision, make effective use of your chance and choices, and don't do tomorrow what you can do today.

Procrastination is the thief of time; use your time wisely. Don't be swayed away by the present gains and discard your future happiness – for every seed you sow today, sow an extra in your future.

Dare to be different; you can do all things as far as you can imagine. You might have experienced failure because of your past decisions, but don't let it dampen your spirit; you can have a brand-new start and rise again. The failure is not the problem; your decision not to take the chance to have another attempt might be the major problem.

How are you making use of your talents? Our choices are the talents that act as the propeller to our future destination. Don't live life regretting and dwelling on your past; the future is all yours to conquer if only you make it a duty to evaluate the cost and opportunity cost of every action.

MENTORS WATER

I dedicate this essay to every person worldwide who by their exemplary lives have shown great compassion to the poor, through their initiatives have liberated the sick and the oppressed, through their kind hearted nature have helped to lift up the poor and destitute, to the exemplary individuals who have liberated countries, delivered free education, fought for the emancipation of their countries and lost their lives pursuing that cause; I also dedicate this essay to all mentors worldwide, those who live their lives helping others to rise and also acting as a catalyst for change; this essay is dedicated to the people who are sold out for the cause they believe in.

Death is an inevitable price we all must pay at some point; Martin Luther King Jnr, I deeply appreciate that which you have done for the black race – without the struggle a Barack Obama presidency would have been a mirage. Dr Obafemi Awolowo, the seed of free education you sowed in the western region of Nigeria has made people from that region educationally savvy. Warren Buffet who gave a large chunk of his wealth to the Bill and Melinda Gates Foundation; the super-rich are always looking for ways to increase their wealth and not to give it out, but that singular act of yours is set to spark a paradigm shift in the way the world's rich people view wealth. Bill and Melinda Gates, for your conscientious efforts at providing support for those with health problems, the poor and helping to meet the education and information needs of under-developed countries. Nelson Mandela, your life is a true reflection of that which you fought for, "Freedom". Sam

Adeyemi, for breaking the barriers of poverty and acting as a role model to thousands of youths. Fela Durotoye, for living your life as a role model to thousands of youths in Nigeria. Gabriel Akinyemi, a true mentor and role model to lots of young people, thanks for birthing in me the seed of greatness. Kudos to Deng Xiaoping, who sparked up the industrial revolution in China, I say big props up to you.

The generous man will be prosperous, and he who waters will himself be watered (Provs 11:25). The truly great heroes are those who live life with an understanding that we are in this world but for a moment, so whatever position you find yourself "your predominant thoughts should be what will my legacy be, if I am opportune to read my obituary tomorrow, what will it read, what will people say about me".

Don't forget to open your taps and let people come and drink of it; there is much blessing to him who scatters and much pain to the man that withholds. Don't be afraid to be a blessing, help the poor and the oppressed, be a change agent and a catalyst for change and development in your country, spread positive information. Build your life around developmental initiatives, share your knowledge, and don't be selfish; those who eat alone die alone (literal terms). There is no success without a successor, pass your wealth of knowledge to a protégé, groom others, invest in people and pass the baton, grow your business beyond borders; the truly great are those who build businesses that outlive them.

Be a shining light; let your life illuminate and give hope to the weary. To all those who by their lives have inspired hope among this generation, I say thanks for showing up in my time.

LIFE AND TIMES OF MAN

As I sat in the bus on my way to the Redeemed Christian Church of God for the Festival of Life Holy Ghost Service in the Excel Centre many years ago, I was inspired to write on the life and times of man. Everything is so short, the difference between life and death is the same difference between embarking on a trip to the next town, the same difference between sleeping and waking up, and traveling from Nigeria to the United States or Ghana as the case may be. We are here but for a moment. If today was my last day on earth, the question should be: will I die knowing I lived a life worthy of emulation, would my life have been an exemplary one?

There is a time for every activity under the sun, a time to be born and a time to die. Do not spend your life in misery or frustration because you lack the basics; always remember that no condition is permanent; weeping may endure for the night, but joy comes in the morning. Is there anyone who has been trusting God for one miracle or another? There is great gain in waiting on the Lord; there is nothing too hard for my God to do.

He makes the wretched person wealthy and distorts the thinking and comprehension of humans. Stop trying to resolve the issues of your life based on your human thinking; your brain is too small to imagine and know God's purpose for your life. Who are you, oh man, that calls to question the purpose of God? We will someday account for this life which heaven has entrusted into our hands, and everyone is on borrowed time. Our life is like a script from a movie; we all must act our part and leave this world someday.

A man who is tagged "nobody" today is entitled to be somebody whom the world cannot do without tomorrow; it is not a function of human permutations, but the Lord decides to have mercy on us all at his own specific time. Don't be in a rush to hit the jackpot, don't be too hasty to see all your dreams become reality – the race is not always won by the best of runners, the patient dog will not be killed by hunger as people are inclined to say.

Don't sell your birthright for a plate of porridge; do not mismanage your destiny and make the devil your whipping tool. Everyone has the chance to do it right and make it happen. Understand the times and season; the reason why things are not working is not because you have been doomed to fail, it is to let you appreciate the better days which are ahead of you.

There is a reason for every season in your life, always give thanks in all seasons and watch your life become that which everyone covets.

THE ROLE OF A FATHER

This essay is for all fathers, aspiring fathers and everyone who is curious to know more about the role of a father. Fathers have been the butt of jokes on various occasions, especially those who fail in their responsibility on the home front. For guys who feel they can't control their sexual urge and they are considering marriage, it is not for the feeble hearted and it's not all about sex. A wise man once said Marriage is like watching DSTV and staying glued to CNN for the rest of your life; you are not permitted to change channels even for a second. Fatherhood entails Leadership; a father must be able to lead and coordinate effectively every member of his family. Check out children who have their father as a mentor, and you will discover the father has lived an exemplary life worthy of emulation. A father must be sacrificial, he must learn to give up or lose that which is precious to him for the benefit of his family. I experienced a situation when I was involved in a life-threatening situation and my father showed up and he sacrificed a whole lot, much more than I could ever have imagined. Jesus also died for us when we were yet sinners; he died that we may live, so as fathers there is no price that is too much to pay for the seeds God has given to us. A father must be visionary; a blind man cannot lead anyone on a journey; remember, where there is no vision the people perish. He must learn to plan his life and set specific goals; the Bible says teach us to number our days that we may apply our hearts to wisdom. I remember my father used to set specific goals when we were kids; all the goals of yesteryears are now today's reality. He did not just set the goals and idle away; he made a conscious effort to turn his dreams into reality. A father has been licensed to be the spiritual head of the home, he must be able to stand in the gap effectively for the family in spiritual and physical matters; he must learn how to effectively communicate with the whole family and above all he must be teachable – a father must learn how to accept his mistakes and be subject to corrections in areas where he is weak.

In truth, most men out there have ego problems and they want their egos massaged and not bruised; a father must learn to be accountable to the family. If he is going out, he should reveal his destination to the family, and a father must not be a perpetual liar. He must not say he is in London when indeed he is in Chicago; he must have the spirit of accountability in all his decisions and leverage on the synergy that marriage has afforded him.

PRICE FOR PRIZE

In any endeavour we lay our hands upon in the journey of destiny, there is always a price to pay to earn the prize. Being a success in our career, family and the country at large comes with a price. For the successful business moguls making the greatest impact within our generation today, they paid the price before securing the prize. They don't sleep until very late in the night, rarely socialize and are basically strategic thinkers.

What we pay for in life is our ignorance; I mean services rendered to us due to our lack of knowledge – mechanical engineers fix our cars and carpenters our furniture etc. It is what you have that you can sell to the world; knowledge is power. I pray every day that there might be problems in Nigeria because every problem needs a solution.

The late Isaac Durojaiye (Otunba Ghadafi) of DMT TOILETS was a solution to the problem of having to use the toilet at public places and events in Nigeria. We can be the solution to the myriad problems Nigeria is currently facing. Don't look at what Nigeria can do for you, rather what you can do for Nigeria.

Also, do not despise your days of little beginnings as you start out the journey in life. As they say, life is an individual affair; we should not downplay the process for us to achieve the result. Life is not a bed of roses and success comes with a price.

In conclusion, we have the power to rule our world. What is your life's vision statement? We cannot go farther than what we see in life. To have a secured future, we must be willing to pay the price in order to earn the prize.

CHARACTER

Character is doing what is right when nobody is looking. According to Abraham Lincoln, character is like a tree and reputation like its shadow; the shadow is what we think of it, the tree is the real thing. The character of every act depends upon the circumstances in which it's done. People seem not to see it that their opinion of the world is also a confession of their character.

I have steadfastly advocated the idea that how a person conducts himself/herself in their private life reveals their character, and character is of paramount importance when it comes to choosing a leader. This essay presents me with an opportunity to highlight the difference between a person with a good character and those with a faulty character. Much of life's fruit or result comes from good character and character comes from spiritual growth in the ways that God has ordained. To make life work, focus on character growth first not just results. Most people set out to succeed in life in two primary areas, relationships and work; what they do is launch into those arenas on autopilot. No matter how hard we try to make life work, no matter how much effort we put into it, we will always hit the ceiling that our character make-up dictates. We can be brilliant, for example, but if we lack perseverance and courage then we will never build a business or a career. We can be talented, but if we are not trustworthy, people will not invest with us, promote us or want to be married to us, at least for long.

We all need to build up Godly character, because we are all a reflection of our character. You will succeed.

THE BIG PICTURE

What do you see constantly daily? What pictures play out in your mind consistently over a period? Most times people fail not because they lack ideas, connections and positive thoughts, but the ability to see yourself in the big picture.

A quote says you cannot feature in a future you cannot picture.

Whatever dreams and aspirations that you hold dear to your heart, begin to imagine vivid pictures where you feature prominently, begin to imagine about that big project, the beautiful marriage and cheerful home, begin to think about your future happiness and banish every negative thought that pervades the society.

There is a lot of sad news everywhere, negativity and people who are ready to run down your vision; they know lots of reasons why your project is bound to fail, even before the start; the fact you share the vision with them is enough reason for them to help you bury it before the vision is birthed.

You hear stories of how that project can never succeed in this part of the world, what do you do in an increasingly negative world, how do you sustain the energy of enterprise development when family and friends are growing increasingly frustrated about your future career path, when all voices around you are telling you to get paid jobs and you see your friends on paid jobs doing excellently well?

Don't disconnect from the BIG PICTURE; nothing happens by chance in this part of the world; there is no happenstance or luck. Every successful person, product and idea is a culmination of determination, persistence and positive pictures being played in the mind; everything that happens in the natural world starts from the spiritual world.

A person who is spiritually blind, dead and buried is totally frustrated in the natural world. There may be days when you think your set goals cannot be achieved. Don't forget to shoot for the moon; even if you fail you will land among the stars. Don't settle for less, don't short-change yourself in life; there is nothing that is impossible for you to achieve in life. If you can imagine it, dream it, work at it then you can achieve it.

I am tired of hearing stories of frail people, whose strength deserts them in the days of adversity. Who are run over by little challenges. They take cover for their lives when they are faced with life's unending battle.

No matter what hurdles you need to overcome in life, the journey might be so tough, and you feel your dreams are far from reality, but don't lose sight of the BIG PICTURE.

Though the vision might tarry, it might seem slow, wait for it, it will come to pass at the appointed time.

OUR DIVERSITY MAKES US UNIQUE

The world we live in is a global village and the only factor that makes us unique is our diversity. The world is such a large place that every human has a culture, a way of life, core values and principles they hold dear to their heart. To function in a global village, you must be easily adaptable to change. Many people suffer from culture shock and depending on the development index or infrastructural development in their new country of settlement, they find it very difficult to adapt to changes in their unfamiliar environment. Truth be told, it is not very easy to adapt to underdevelopment or overdevelopment depending on which side you fall into.

Taking a cursory look at the world economy, I can infer from the rapid development which the Asian Tigers have undergone in recent years and the passion of their government to invest in the human capital development of its citizens, are the major factors the Asian Tigers are now playing a dominant role in International Trade and its increased contributions to the Gross Domestic Product of the World.

No matter how much you conform with and cling to old ideas, exposure to new ways of life, attitude, response to emergency, time management and trivial things such as orderliness can go a long way in helping to change the way we think.

A British man who wants to marry a Chinese woman will be expected to use a different approach, something slightly different from his own culture; he will have to learn her culture, what is obtainable in her part of the world, and vice-versa.

I remember vividly how I felt exasperated engaging all my muscles in a bid to learn the Chinese language, and I began to appreciate the unique ability of every country. Diversity is a combination of the ways in which people are different. Living in a global environment challenges us to develop cultural intelligence; you must not just be interested in knowing the culture of the other nation but its practical application to your very life.

Having access to up to date information on global issues and events is also a major factor that can help improve our way of life. Information is available at the speed of thought on the world wide web; to stay ahead of competition we need to be informed, to avoid being deformed.

Perception of other cultures based on behaviour of citizens should not be a benchmark to destroy their heritage. The fact that some behavioural patterns might be a moral issue for people in your country does not mean if the same patterns are exhibited in other countries, the citizens are bad people, but it can be attributed to diversity and an unusual way of perception. That is why it is vital to develop an elevated level of cultural intelligence.

Next time you think of the disaster victims in Haiti, the Chinese for their ability to create something out of nothing, or you are looking at visiting the United Arab Emirates, always remember that our Diversity makes us Unique.

DISCOVERING THE BRAND "YOU"

Before they called him Man of God, he was first a man before God ordained him a prophet in the house. So, when you see a Man of God who has committed a sin and people are castigating the grace of God upon his life, remember he was first a man before he became a prophet. The truth about the human nature is that we are all prone to sin, but God's grace is sufficient for us all; we all have a point of weakness and strength; no man can lay claim to perfection. Apostle Paul was so anointed, but he had a constant thorn in his life, he cried to God to take it out, but God told him the pain comes with the grace.

Is there anyone out there who has been asking perpetually, why is my own like this or what do I need to do right to be like Mr x,y,z? I make bold to tell you that everyone has personal problems they deal with in the four walls of their bedroom or residence, your president, governors, senators, consultants, chief executive officers, role models, pastors and other public figures do have daily issues which confront them as well. They are confronted daily with the same societal problems, invest under the same economic system, suffer from the same infrastructural problem and suffer the same health issues as you do. There is none that can be equated to God; he is the only one who can lay claim to perfection.

In your quest for self-discovery, I will advise that you retain your identity. No man has ever survived being a photocopy of another; do not live above your means to increase public rating and perception. If there are successful people within your community or close circles, please rejoice with them; do not spite anyone because of their achievements. Like I emphasized in the previous essay, God can bless everyone at the same time without heaven feeling any loss of resources.

Do not be afraid to pursue your dreams, be humble and show love to all mankind. You must learn to cheerfully give and consciously bless others. Remember it is the Lord who owns the times and seasons of our lives; do not despise the days of little beginning. Though your beginning may be small, your latter end shall greatly increase. You must be the standard that others want to follow; do not short circuit the process to get the result.

The race is not always won by the fastest runner, the strongest man does not always win the battle (Goliath is an example), and intelligent people do not always come top – dare to make a difference. Make humility your second nature, do not hide your gifts and talents – they are your password to standing before kings and not mere humans.

Attend to your personal development; getting a good education is one of the antidotes to a life of poverty. The difference between the rich and the poor is a function of the level of information at their disposal. Stay informed to avoid getting deformed, stay abreast of events on the global stage. Test your knowledge and be open to criticism. No man is an island and we need others to survive. Be good to people on your way up because you may meet them on your way down.

You must discover the Brand "You", when no one else believes in you, you have to keep on fighting and believing in yourself. Do not despise the days of little beginnings, always remember that you cannot by-pass the process and achieve the result. Celebrate your small victories and little accomplishments. Investment in your brand is key, it might be attending a short course or maybe just researching on better ways of getting things done; look at the way the Biggest Brands in the world are run, they still budget millions for their Research and Development because the mindset is to be forward thinking and future oriented. If you are to be a listed on a Stock Exchange; would anyone be willing to stake their funds on you; would your Life and Brand be worth the risk. This is the time to go back to the drawing table and begin to see yourself as a Brand, don't underestimate your gifts and talent. Keep on pushing yourself no matter the limitations, no matter how dark the nights might be, Light comes shining through in the Morning.

The people who have their names written in Gold are those who were willing to pay the price in order to get the prize. Pay the price in the morning and afternoon period of your life so you can reap the fruits of your labour at a ripe old age (Night). The morning period is very important in the life of every man; it is the foundation to a great future. Let your foundation be strong.

As you continue your Journey to self-discovery, make honesty and integrity your watchword and be proud of who you are. YOU ARE TRULY SPECIAL.

THE ANALOGY OF IMMUNITY AND WHITE BLOOD CELLS

In Nigeria, the President, Vice President and State Governors enjoy Immunity from all form of prosecution while occupying Public Offices to counter disruptions that numerous litigations might foster on the Business of governance. Having some form of defence mechanism may not be a bad idea after all in a country with a chequered history of corruption and money laundering. Public Office holders who have been entrusted with the Commonwealth of the people have brazenly looted and stashed the wealth into private accounts because they know they are immune to prosecution at the time of committing the offence.

In the human body, the white blood cells are the soldiers that help us fight every form of sickness and disease. They are the soldiers that repel bacteria, viruses and germs from entering the human body. When the body is low on white blood cells, that is an invitation to disaster as the body loses its resistance and immunity to external forces.

The two examples above are an indication that we all need some form of immunity against the attacks of the enemy. If we do not stand for something, then we will fall for anything. An unlocked house with treasures will be broken into if there are no adequate white blood cells in the form of security to protect the house against vandals. It takes a conscious effort to build up our immune system against the camp of the enemy. Our immunity stems from the Word of God and living in consonance with the Will of God. The devil is only able to thrive in an environment where every defence mechanism has been destroyed and all the White Blood Cells have been neutralised.

In Ephesians 6:12; The word of God states "For we do not wrestle against flesh and blood, but against principalities, against powers, against the rulers of the darkness of this age, against spiritual hosts of wickedness in the heavenly places" (NKJV). To win the battle against the Enemy camp will not be by Theory or knowledge of science, neither will it be by human wisdom and intellect. Verse 13 to 18 of the same chapter explains the white blood cells that we need to resist the attacks highlighted in Chapter 12. Therefore, take up the whole Armor of God that you may be able to withstand in the evil day, and having done all, to stand.

14 Stand therefore, having girded your waist with truth, having put on the breastplate of righteousness, 15 and having shod your feet with the preparation of the gospel of peace; 16 above all, taking the shield of faith with which, you will be able to quench all the fiery darts of the wicked one. 17 And take the helmet of salvation, and the sword of the Spirit, which is the word of God; 18 praying always with all prayer and supplication in the Spirit, being watchful to this end with all perseverance and supplication for all the saints.

The only way we can trample upon scorpions and serpents without them hurting us is highlighted above. Building up our immunity against the schemes of the devil will guarantee us total victory.

A NEW DISEASE UNCOVERED: DON'T BE LEFT IN THE DARK

From the research laboratory of intellectual rights activist, a new disease that is spreading so fast and has been tested to kill faster than the dreaded Acquired Immune Deficiency Syndrome (AIDS) has been discovered.

From New York City, London, Rome, Paris, Glasgow and Johannesburg to the hub of activities in the West African region Lagos, this disease leaves a devastating effect on the carrier and never leaves them the same. I introduce to you a disease which has killed millions of people, turned the wealthy into top rated church rats, leaving various consequences worldwide based on the level at which it is displayed.

I introduce to you this killer disease named Ignorance. In Spanish it is called la ignorancia, in Italia, ignoranza, in French it is known as l'ignorance and the Chinese call It 无知.

In the early generations in Nigeria, there was no information on genotypes and the consequence of marrying sickle cell carriers, thus many parents lost their children to the cold hands of death which they believed was caused by some supernatural force and the child was called Abiku (Still-born). In my generation sickle cell carriers are advised to marry other genotypes apart from theirs and two AS genotypes are advised not to marry because of the possibility of giving birth to a sickle cell child. See the difference between those days and now; a lot of lives that were cut short due to ignorance would have been saved; however, due to lack of adequate information that was the story then.

On a flight from Lagos to London, a young man poured his salt and pepper into his cup of coffee because the air hostess told him he could consume all the food items handed over to him. I watched from afar as the young man drank his self-made concoction with good facial expressions to match, but I can imagine the royal rumble and pain he was experiencing within. See the hurt ignorance can cause.

I remember how stupid I felt when I discovered how I had wasted valuable travel time in the past asking people for directions to my destination when I had a GPS map on my Blackberry device that had all the information I required each time.

It does not matter what name it is called in your region, Ignorance is a deadly disease and the only antidote is getting access to the right information.

Many potential billionaires have lost opportunities to hit the goldmine because of the lack of adequate information. The major difference between the rich and the poor varies as to the quality of information at their disposal.

Some quotes on the subject matter:

"If you think education is expensive, try ignorance"
– Derek Bok

"Nothing in the world is more dangerous than sincere ignorance and conscientious stupidity."
– Martin Luther King, Jr.

"I say there is no darkness but ignorance."
– William Shakespeare

"The ignorance of one voter in a democracy impairs the security of all."
– John F. Kennedy

The above quote from John F. Kennedy also shows how we have allowed people to pervert our mindsets by telling us our votes will never count. The day voters gain invaluable knowledge and know that only their votes can put people in elective office, democracy will begin to thrive in our country.

"People always fear change. People feared electricity when it was invented, didn't they? People feared coal; they feared gas-powered engines... There will always be ignorance, and ignorance leads to fear. But with time, people will come to accept their silicon masters.
– Bill Gates

Do not be afraid to ask questions; do not be petrified to source for the right information. Together we can make the world a better place if only we have access to the right information.

LETTER TO MY SINGLE BROTHERS (BACHELORS)

Now I understand the full meaning of the word "life is in phases and men are in sizes". As we seek to move to the next phase of our life by throwing the phrase "self" into the trash can of history, I enjoin you, my single brothers, to choose responsibly. Remember, he that finds a wife, finds a good thing and obtains favour from the Lord. Nature abhors a vacuum in any form and when I look at the rate my friends are running to the altar, you need to plan for the journey ahead; if you did not sign the oath of celibacy. My generation is looking for fathers who are responsible enough to keep the vows they swore to on their wedding day; my generation is looking for men of integrity and honour who will not compromise when faced with temptation. Remember that life is a large marketplace with various wares on display in wholesale and retail, there are varied sizes, shapes, height and character on display; we have lots of boyfriends in our society but few husbands; many boys but few men; the same way we have so many girlfriends but few wives.

I write this letter to you, my single brothers, as we look for a way out of the solitary confinement that bachelorhood seems to offer. Do not let anyone delude you that sex is the major recipe served in the menu card of marriage. Marriage entails a higher level of responsibility; we need men with the ability to respond during crises and challenges. My single brothers, when the priest tells you that the two have become one, it has a deeper meaning which transcends beyond the surface and can be looked at in the context of submerging your willpower. We must cultivate the habit of dying to self and consciously minimize fault finding in our partners.

My single brothers, in your search for a life partner you must consciously look for a priceless jewel who believes in your dreams, vision and is ready to help you run with it. Beauty is temporary and will utterly fade; good character must not be negotiable and should be the standard as you make this journey anew.

My single brothers, in as much as the society has placed so much emphasis on expensive weddings, and divorce suits litter our law courts, don't be deceived to live above your means or budget for a wedding you will then spend your lifetime repaying the debts. I have heard various testimonials of single brothers who married with seven-digit figures and lived a life of penury thereafter. After your entire guests have left for the day, they barely remember if they attended your wedding (almost a wedding per weekend is the norm on the rosters of many families).

My single brothers, marriage is not a boxing show where your wife is turned into a punching bag. Women are to be treasured – please handle them with care. I enjoin you to trust her and love her like you love yourself. Help her to maximize her strengths and pursue her dreams. In the days of adversity do not despise her, let her breasts satisfy you and do not seek refuge in the home of the harlot.

My single brothers, the fear of the Lord is the beginning of wisdom, your choice of a life partner must fear the Lord and reverence him, a praying wife is the bedrock of every home, she shields her home from every attack of the enemy, this is a necessity when compiling the stats required in a life partner. Throw away the garbage being thrown into our faces that you must be made (cars, houses and other Mills & Boon fairy tales) before you can marry. There is a blessing attached to marriage; please partake of it. Two is better than one in all ramifications.

I will round up on this note. Be the standard she wants to emulate daily, spoil her with attention (women value it more than food), make her proud of you and be enthusiastic about her dreams and passion. Celebrate her success and don't be threatened if she is more successful.

As the next generation graciously calls you Daddy x, y, z, I hope our generation will have defined the very essence of fatherhood.

LETTER TO MY UNBORN CHILD

Daddy had you in mind even before you were born. Guess what! He wrote this letter many years ago as a bachelor when he was not even engaged to your mom. God says, "*Before I formed you* in the womb *I knew you*; *before you* were born. I sanctified *you*; I *ordained you a prophet* to the nations." So, don't be afraid to pursue your dreams. I tried all within my capacity as a youth to be a change agent in my own season, and I pray you will be greater than me in all facets of life. Daddy loves you so much, so he has been planning for your arrival even before he married your mom. Dad has a mental picture of the school he wants you to attend, up to your university education and he has been working towards securing your future without much ado. Dad believes so much in education; Grandpa always told him how much education was good for him even though he was a natural entrepreneur who believed more in business than education. Dad fell for Grandpa's bait and he became a firm advocate of education. Daddy attached some of his write-ups where he emphasized the difference that education makes in the life of every individual. Dad coined this quote: "To have a secured future, you must be willing to pay the price in order to get the prize". Dad wants you to pay the price to get to the top; the majority are always at the basement; only few people make it to the top.

Dad has the heart of a lion and is humility personified; he was choleric to the extreme and combined other temperament types to bring out the best in him. Dad was gifted in the skill of writing inspirational stuff; he read little but knew plenty, a gift he ascribed to the power of the almighty God. The world as you will get to know is a beautiful place. Show love to everybody you meet in life, even your enemies. Do not be afraid of negative circumstances but show immense character when faced with life's challenges. Dad had his own share of challenges, but Grandpa stood solidly behind him and Grandma was the best mother any child could wish for.

My dear child, do not wage war or strife against anyone for your dad is a peacemaker. Be a blessing to the poor; Dad got that from Grandpa and it became part of his life. Believe in your dreams; make positive confessions, even if life does not give you what you want always – never give up! Let honesty and integrity be your robe always, your mom can testify to this. Grandpa always said even in the face of death we should always say the truth. I admonish you to stand for the truth and be a model to your generation.

My dear child, be careful of the minute details of your life, the little decisions you make from the time you become aware of your surroundings will invariably determine your destiny, lean on God always and do not lean on your own understanding. He has been my source and my closest friend.

Dad enjoyed exceeding grace from the throne of mercy; he saw the hand of God multiply his little efforts in numerous ways. Therefore, Dad tells you, my dear child, that God's grace and mercy is your Key to a life of supernatural breakthrough.

This letter was written by your dad (Tolu' A. Akinyemi) on the 22nd of June 2010. Keep it as a treasure and let the words that I speak to you birth in you a new life.

LETTER TO MY SINGLE SISTERS (SPINSTERS)

I write this letter to you, the spinsters of my generation, knowing full well that you are unique and priceless in every way; without you the world would be a boring place (imagine men toasting goats and cows) so we appreciate the women folk for the fun and happiness they bring into our lives.

Your presence in the life of a man makes up for the imbalance and completely emphasizes the mind of God that it is not good for man to be alone, SO YOU MUST UNDERSTAND THAT "GOOD THINGS DO NOT COME CHEAP". My single sisters (single means unmarried), the first thing I want you to know as you seek a life partner is that you should shun desperation in the quest to get married; forget what friends, family or society will say. Marriage is between two people and the opinion of others will not count when you eventually marry your life partner. You must be wise enough to separate the wheat from the chaff so as not to make a wrong choice. Don't be carried away with the man who has a wonderful plasma television, but I would rather prefer you choose the one who has a good vision – with a good vision he can buy many television sets for you in the years ahead. A woman got married at age forty after many years of waiting on the Lord, yet she married a liability. I have heard stories of men who rented cars, clothes and other accessories when they went to visit their in-laws, they deceived their bride to be and for the spinsters who swallowed the bait you can imagine the lifetime of agony they would be subjected to. A wise man said, "Marriage is like having Cable TV and staying glued to CNN for the rest of your life", so I bet you don't want to miss out on the beauty and blessings of marriage by signing on the dotted lines with the wrong man. You can only fulfil your life's destiny, if you live a fulfilled marital life.

My single sisters, there is nothing worthier than being faithful in your relationships; women lose their self-esteem the moment they keep jumping from bed to bed, so don't trade your future away for momentary pleasure.

My single sisters, I agree with you that we are in the 21st century, and most ladies are now career oriented and have thrown the age-long adage that the woman's place is in the kitchen to the recycle bin of history. The people who are capable of leading successful lives are those who have been able to balance their lives effectively without any form of casualty, so if you are career oriented, do find time to cook for your husband, time permitting, and manage your home by investing your time in its growth. You will be shocked that many marriages crash due to tiny details that were not effectively thrashed out. If your potential life partner is threatened by your success, pay packet and career advancement, please feel free to show him the exit before going to the altar.

My single sisters, there is nothing impossible so far we believe, but I want you to thrash the belief system that you can CHANGE A MAN from your sub-conscious. If he is a fraudster, womanizer, drug addict, bottle addict, woman beater, please flee; it helps you reduce your prayer points.

My single sisters, no successful marriage was built on the foundation of pity so if you are still in that relationship because you pity his situation or circumstances, that criteria cannot sustain lifelong happiness and fulfilment.

As I was driving home from work some years ago, a woman became involved in an argument with another woman whose husband almost bashed their car. The woman's husband slapped her and told her to shut up. I was disgusted and angry at the same time. There are better ways you can get the message across without hurting your wife in full public glare.

My single sisters, if he has no vision for his life please flee, if you have been dating for the past five years and he has not for once mentioned marriage to you, run away! If he slaps and beats you occasionally and blames the devil for his actions, run with your shoes in your hands. If you cannot really lay hold on his source of income, please run. If honesty, trust and integrity are missing from your relationship, don't waste your time, run for your dear life – these are the main ingredients of every sane relationship. If he questions your every move and he is excessively possessive and jealous, it is better to be wary. A man barred his wife from picking up any calls after 6pm; I bet strange things are happening in marriages all over the world.

My single sisters, one of the qualities that a woman can possess that will make a marriage collapse early enough is a nagging spirit. Men despise women who nag. Support his dreams and life's vision, show him love through all seasons, remember the vow is for better for worse, don't use sex as a bargaining tool and give him an excuse to cheat. Be his mother, wife and his happiness, celebrate his successes and encourage him when he is down. If you are more successful, don't ridicule him and subject the crown to disdain. Remember, God ordained the man the head of the home, so don't take him for granted. When you eventually marry your life partner please value him by keeping fit and staying in shape, you need to look good and alluring all the time and I pray that my generation will produce more women who can stand with their husbands through all times and seasons.

LETTER TO MY CREATOR

As a living being who has enjoyed tremendous grace from the throne of mercy, I am appreciative of the fact that you deemed it fit for me to be alive today; it is not by human ability; human permutations and configurations could not have sustained me till this moment. All I want to say is thank you Lord, for creating me as a living being, not as a dog or a cat. Who can question your authority? No one. Thank you for your spirit that abides in me, thank you for everything you have done for me. I would have been an empty vessel, but you fill me up with goodness all the days of my life.

If all the hairs on my head become tongues, it is not enough to praise your name. I remember the days of old, the days when the future looked so bleak, the days of spiritual warfare and the never-ending battles, I remember the sleepless nights, the worries, the heartaches and the moments my soul was deeply troubled. You kept on assuring me that the troubles were not meant to consume me, that I will not suffer any shame or reproach and that your mercies will speak for me.

I thank you for the present days. It is a proof that you can turnaround anyone. You said you will have mercy and compassion on whom you will, it is not of him who wills neither of him who runs but you oh Lord that shows mercy. I have been around long enough to tell every living being that my God is real, he defeated all my enemies, every handwriting of ordinances and evil reports was thrown into the recycle bin of history.

I thank you, Lord, for my gifts and talents, for the gifts of revelations, you reveal unto me the deep things that ordinary eyes cannot comprehend; when I sleep you comfort me with your words – little wonder I wake up revelling in thanking you. I can only imagine why you choose to love me, even when I am undeserving of your grace.

You are my shield, my shelter, my comfort, my father, my sweetheart. You order my steps in your word, you give me wisdom to write, to think, to see into the future. My enemies are resigned to fate when they realize you called me into the world to fulfil your purpose on Earth. I am special; you washed away all my sins and gave me reasons to believe in myself. People ask me what makes me happy all the time, write almost every day and smile even amid trouble; I am always quick to tell them you are my password. You are the secret of my success, you are my life; little wonder I am addicted to you; how I revel in praising and worshipping your name always. You are my source; the day I forget that you are the pillar that holds my life, then I am ready to come crashing down from the hilltop.

When people see me early in the morning, jogging on the streets with my headsets clutched to my ears, I am only jamming your praise; I am only staying connected to heaven's frequency 24/7.

I love you, Lord, I love you with my life. I discovered I am a billionaire the day heaven gave me the spiritual cheat sheet; I cannot be POOR for the rest of my life, I have access to divine facility from my father who cannot be broke.

Thank you, Lord, for these times and seasons of my life. I am very grateful. You calmed the storms all for my sake; I walked through the fire and I was unfazed. You made me a treasure, a royal priesthood and a chosen generation. Who is man to question you?

You are the potter and we are the clay, you determine of what use to put all vessels. Is there anyone out there who is troubled by the circumstances of their life, who has asked God numerous questions, but the answer seems far away? Put your trust in God; he will never fail you. I am a living testimony of his goodness; the rejected stones will come back as the chief of the corner.

I write this letter to you in gratitude, there are one million and one names I want to call you Lord, a million and one things I want to thank you for, some puzzles and mysteries I need answers to, some dreams I could not interpret that I am waiting patiently for you to guide me through. This space will not be enough to send my message across but as usual, I go back to my sanctuary and I say Thank you to the King who says and never goes back on his word, and The King who talks and happens as he says it.

PART 3

WHO ARE YOU?

Many people are suffering from identity crises; there is a trend which has been the norm in recent times. When a new business is launched, we see a whole lot of people copy that same idea and thereafter we witness the herd mentality. For most people it is not their wish to infringe on the intellectual property of others; we see people lay claim to be what they are not. A lot of people have become entrepreneurs by circumstance. We need the character and strength to thrive in a dynamic world; we have all got our unique talents and gifts which is the only reason no other person has our characteristics. If you ask me, who I am? I should be able to communicate my life's vision statement in plain terms to the understanding of the layman.

Our life has different definitions to different people – that is the reason a man like the late Gani Fawehinmi will be tagged an activist, politician, senior advocate of the masses, philanthropist and a legal icon. Gani Fawehinmi means different things to a lot of people but when Gani Fawehinmi was alive he would tell you he was an advocate of the masses.

Christ asked this of his own disciples, 'Who do men say that I am?' They all gave him different answers, a prophet, a teacher and so on. Jesus asked them then directly, 'Who do you say that I am?' Peter said to him, 'You are the Messiah, the Son of the living God.' Jesus then responded to him, 'Flesh and Blood has not revealed this to you, but only my father in Heaven.' Jesus was saying to Peter, nothing on this Earth has revealed this to you, no miracle that I worked, no logic that you have followed to reason it out, no sermon that was preached to you, no book you read but it was revealed to you in Spirit.

There is a difference between who people say we are and who we really are; people might have tagged you a failure, but who do you say you are? You might have been tagged a victim but if you believe you are a victor that is what you really are.

STOP AND SEE

Are you running your life on auto-pilot mode and you seem not to be conversant with happenings in your environment? In moments like this we need to stop and see and probably take a switch to the manual mode; when we stop and see it helps us rid our lives of a life filled with activities that has no major achievements.

Imagine a Governor of a state who uses a helicopter on all his official trips. How will he stop and see the infrastructural decay in his state? The Governor will not be able to relate to the suffering and needs of the governed. In this essay, I will call stop and see the speed bumps that we normally encounter in our day to day lives. If those speed bumps were not on the roads, a lot of road users might have died. Most times, we want to have everything in life at the snap of a finger, a life without troubles, and the good life, and whenever we encounter a speed bump along the way, we believe God is not fair to us.

A lot of times that we face difficulty, it is a message from God to his people to reduce the activity, stop and see me help you out of this tricky situation. The speed bumps are also there to keep us on track with our state of humanity, for someone who has been lost in the world, a significant event that happens in his environment is all he needs for sober reflection and to evaluate the circumstances of his life.

No matter how desperate a company wants to get a contract, they will stop and see the benefits in the contract for them, calculating the projected costs and expenditure before laying their hands on the plough.

A lot of times, we are expecting manna to fall from heaven. Most people want the big break in business, they want the million-dollar deal, but my question is have you stopped to see the opportunities in your environment, have you stopped to see if what you call crumbs today will not eventually become bread tomorrow?

An unemployed graduate who has been looking for a job for a while and eventually gets one where they will not be paying him according to his potential and says he won't accept the job because of the meagre salary on offer. Stop and See that the work experience and on the job-learning will be a big boost to your Curriculum Vitae.

When we stop and see, we learn to become patient and think through situations before acting. When we stop and see, it enables us to act based on a solid premise. You think your father has the biggest mansion in your State – "stop and see" that there are better and bigger mansions in your State.

The speed bumps are not there to kill you; they are there to slow you down so you won't be killed by the speed. Take a break, stop and see, and watch your life turn around for good.

YOU WANT THE GRACE, DON'T THRASH THE PAIN

Grace is the divine favour toward man; the mercy of God as distinguished from his justice. Also, any benefits his mercy imparts; divine love or pardon; a state of acceptance with God.

When we see people at the top, I mean the pinnacle of the ladder in various fields of endeavour, there is always this tendency to covet the product and despise the process. Before you get the best value from precious ornaments, there is a period of pruning, when you see a metal that is smitten in fire; the metal is going through that process, so it can bring out something of value. Before you get something of value from anyone there is always a process to undergo; when you see someone, who has been so visibly blessed by God don't think their lives are perfect – Grace comes with the pain and the pain is one of the reasons why the grace is evident. Without the test there can be no testimonies, without the PRICE forget the PRIZE and the quality product we all see on display went through various production processes before getting the result that we seem to cherish.

Grace is achieving supernatural result with minimal effort, so before you wish that thorn in your life away, remember it goes hand in hand with the grace. We all want the blessings, the miracles, the anointing, we want to be the next big celebrity, but can we pay the price to get the prize, can we endure tough times so we can enjoy the glory ahead? Don't let your focus be on the pain you are experiencing but let your focus be on the GRACE of God that is upon your life.

Apostle Paul was a great teacher who had the GRACE of God in his life, but there was a constant thorn in his life to remind him of his humanity. He prayed to God to take it out, but God told him without the pain there won't be the GRACE.

I have heard of great teachers of the word who have a constant infirmity in their family and ministry, many may ask, is this not the man who has been going around town performing miracles? Why has he not been able to find a solution to whatever limitations that have been confronting him on the home front, without the thorn in their lives? Maybe that power of God may not have been so glaring.

I have learnt to live with the GRACE upon my life and take the PAIN as a period of pruning, so I can be better. Can you imagine a life without problems? A life without limitations, whatever PAIN you might be experiencing in your life has an expiry date; you will see the last of the issues that bring you to your knees.

Life is filled with contrasting TIMES and SEASONS, so if the present-day reality does not look like what you really want, be patient and keep trusting God, for he is our ever-present help in times of trouble.

HEAVEN OR HELL

It has now been a kind of routine to be constantly reminded of these two after-life destinations depending on your place of worship. Heaven and hell is real we are constantly told.

I bring a different message to the one that has been echoed in times past. Let no man judge you based on your beliefs, actions, attitude, for there is none who can lay claim to perfection. The holy book says in John 1:8 if we claim to be without sin, we deceive ourselves and the truth is not in us. My God is not interested in those who pre-judge you, he is not concerned about the death of a sinner, but he wants all sinners to come unto repentance. So, the fact that you drink, smoke or fornicate does not make you an object for condemnation. Remember the parable of the lost sheep – the shepherd left ninety-nine sheep and went in search of the missing one not minding what would happen to those he left behind. You are as important in heaven's dictionary as the pastor in your fellowship or a big-name preacher in your country.

Always remember that our walk with God is personal in nature; you should be least concerned about the happenings in your environment. I repeat let no man Judge you, we are all humans and there is no man who can lay claim to perfection. Apostle Paul with all his anointing still had a point of weakness, a thorn in his flesh that kept him in constant touch with his humanity. He begged God to take it out, but God told him that the grace comes with an element of pain.

We are all mortals and we go through the daily hassles of life, thinking, planning, sourcing for daily bread, decision making and all other issues that affect our humanity. In Christ Jesus lies our strength. Forget the vain philosophies and imaginations of humans; we are all weak in different areas and we have issues that we deal with and confront daily.

Live your life peaceably with everyone; no man has the criteria or formula for the salvation of your soul. Study the Word of God and live your life on its precepts; there is no short cut to success. Remember no one said it will be easy, they only said it will be worth it. In times of trouble and challenges, call on God – he is the only one that can save and deliver us from seeming troubles and every form of oppression. All the 'do's that you need to make it to the kingdom of heaven are in the Bible and all the "don'ts" in the Bible are the surest way to hellfire.

Every man for himself, we will all stand alone on the last day and account for our deeds on Earth. Make the right decisions and let's do it right. When there is life, we have hope for a better future and to live in eternity with our Lord Jesus Christ.

LOVE BINDS US TOGETHER

This essay is dedicated for February 14; St Valentine's Day, the annual ritual and permanent feature that has been part of our syllabus since our teenage years when we became aware of our sexual qualities. In as much as it is a day to show love through the exchange of gifts between loved ones, many young girls have swallowed the bitter pill of losing their virginity due to ignorance or the value attached to the day. Like sheep being led to the slaughter slab, many lose the very essence of their humanity based on a single day that has come to be widely associated with immorality in some certain countries.

To the young girls out there, sex is not love and love is not sex, God is love and the greatest commandment from God to Man is Love. As exemplified in Matt 22:36-40 ("Teacher, which is the greatest commandment in the Law?" 37 Jesus replied: "Love the Lord your God with all your heart and with all your soul and with all your mind.[a] 38 This is the first and greatest commandment. 39 And the second is like it: 'Love your neighbour as yourself.'[b] 40 All the Law and the Prophets hang on these two commandments."

Love binds us together, it is the very essence of our humanity and a natural quality that we must embrace and show to make the world a better place. The world can be indeed beautiful for someone out there when we quit hating and learn to love. The greatest expression of our humanity lies in John 3:16 when Jesus

Christ gave up his life for our sake, he died that we might live, he did not have to collect bribes to die for us, he bore our pains on the cross; what greater show of love can man enjoy than this awesome gift to humanity.

Without Love there will be no blue skies, without Love the world will be in turmoil and darkness.

As we drown in the euphoria of the day, we should remember the message is not just in the gifts, not in the virgin girls who will become part of statistics, not in the physical showing of affection, but in the number of lives we continue to impact while we are here.

THE RAGING INFERNO

It was a day you will forever wish not to remember, a day where treasures were destroyed in the blazing inferno, all was lost but there was life; he lost it all, everything he had worked for in his life.

The true measure of a man is not where he stands in moments of comfort, not his level of right standing with God in the days he can afford three square meals, not the days he can fly on first class tickets between Lagos and London, but I mean in the days where the future is uncertain, when everything seems to be lost and life looks like a ship without a rudder.

Most people find it very easy to praise God because they are living the dream, a life without hassles, but what do you tell a man who has lost hope in life, who feels there is nothing really to live for, the clothes are rioting with one rickety shoe that knows the major routes in the city.

What do you tell a man who is despised by neighbours, family and acquaintances, a graduate who has been consumed in the inferno of unemployment, a woman consumed in the inferno of childlessness, a businessman hounded by banks and other creditors? The only solution to this raging inferno is thanksgiving. Give thanks to God, with an understanding that the present situation is not a determinant of your promising future.

If what makes you brag is your fat bank account, your classy wardrobes, or the array of cars in your garage, let me tell you in all sincerity that is a false perception of life.

A young couple watched in agony, as their baby strapped to the seatbelt on the back seat of their car cried out in agony as she was consumed in the raging inferno caused by a truck without brakes. It was a sad day. If only we could turn back the hands of time and delete this day from our calendars.

I tell you in good faith, life is a battlefield and no matter the issues you are facing headlong and it seems the inferno that started as a small fire does not want to abate, don't lose hope, it's a moment to give thanks.

A newlywed couple on their way back from the wedding reception had their joy cut short when overzealous security officials killed the groom by accidental gunshots.

It was a sad day, a day you will forever wish had not happened.

A lot of people have lost loved ones, lost their businesses and have a gut feeling of anger and hatred towards life; they have felt short-changed by a system that tends to reward corruption and fraudulent acts above diligent work.

The only secret to living a good life is to develop an attitude of praise and thanksgiving.

I will end this essay with a message from a chat with a friend of mine. She said, and I quote: "it feels really good when you are not worrying about anything and you just trust him knowing everything is going to be good and perfect since he didn't bring you this far to leave you."

GOD'S DIVINE MERCY

As humans we are expert in running to breast the tape, we tend to be impatient most times, many people are masters in the game of hustle hoping that if the first seed does not pay off the second might bring the harvest. Let me share a secret with you: Life does not reward you for activity, rather you earn a reward for accomplishment. It is not about your skills, neither is life's success measured based on your knowledge. If you also think age is the prerequisite for the attainment of your goals and aspirations, then you are totally wrong.

Some think it's about qualifications, so they litter their Curriculum Vitae with various qualifications in the hope that they will get the better life. So, what is the key to getting the better life? What is the key to having a desirable future? How far can we go when aided by our human intellect?

I have observed something else under the sun. The fastest runner doesn't always win the race, and the strongest warrior doesn't always win the battle. The wise sometimes go hungry, and the skilful are not necessarily wealthy. And those who are educated don't always lead successful lives. It is all decided by chance, by being in the right place at the right time. (Ecc 9:11 NLT)

If you have been thinking why Mr A has been blessed and you who seems to boast of better qualifications finds it very hard to make a head-start, it is not shared based on human permutations and talent. Talent is not enough criteria for life's success. It is not about activity – the labourer exerts more energy in his work but earns less while the man behind the desk earns more based on his intellectual capacity. Some think it is about their class of degree, so they pay lecturers to pass through university, but the truth is, it is not about first class, second class or third-class grades, it is not how far but how well; better is the end of a thing than the beginning thereof. (Ecc 7:8 KJV)

God was talking about making his mercy available to Moses (in Romans 9:15-16 NIV): "I will have mercy on whom I have mercy, and I will have compassion on whom I have compassion". It does not, therefore, depend on man's desire or effort, but on God's mercy. There is a grace that makes us be in the right place at the right time. Life at times presents us with many questions yet we have few answers; always remember that there is little you can accomplish in life no matter how much you are desirous of success, fame, wealth, qualifications, love, peace and all the other good things that we seek in our daily pursuit of survival.

There is a God who can turn our little efforts into great gain and bless the work of our hands; he does not bless based on human timing and expectations. We must accept the fact that the race is not based on our strength but there is a God who controls the natural world from the supernatural.

POLYGAMY DICTATES THE PACE

The world has been turned into a polygamous enclave with all the infighting that has been the hallmark of our everyday life. There is fierce competition in the boardroom and in the workplace, the pull him down syndrome among colleagues who are expected to work in harmony; there is competition for admission to colleges and universities, everything has been politicized and in the quest to hit the limelight, to make the big leap into the world of glamour, in the bid to earn money, power and respect, people literally do not mind the skirmishes involved, the battles to be fought and won. The battle to get rich or die trying has also consumed a lot of lives; many have signed covenants with the devil using their life as collateral, many have dined with satanic agents and others have traded their birthright for a plate of porridge.

The citadel of higher learning has not been left out in the corruption that pervades the system. Payment of money to lecturers in countries with known systemic failures and in countries that seem to be advanced, many people who seem to be intellectually low outsource their coursework in a bid to get higher grades. The political system has felt the most impact of the competition that has undermined the value for human lives; it's a system of grab and share with life presidents who have been in power and are not willing to relinquish the same, especially in the African Continent and Arab World.

Citizens are daily sacrificed for the selfish interests of the political class, election rigging, and killing of opponents seems to be the norm, all in the name of sharing the national cake. Politicians without clear ideas and manifestoes to effect change spring up daily; all they want is to rig their way into power.

The competition has found its way into the family system, we have seen siblings wage war against each other all in the name of sharing family inheritance; instead of making their own name in this highly competitive world all they want to do is laze around and live on the leftovers of their late patriarch; we have seen an increase in legal battles amongst siblings fighting over inheritance and the high rate of divorce seems alarming.

The fierce competition has also made people adopt fake personalities, not living their real lives but trying to deliver a different view entirely to neighbours and those around them. The truth is no matter how fake a product is, it can never be an original. The truth is, even with the competition and challenges that confront us daily, we can still make our life and living worthwhile.

The Competition is an avenue to harness your potential and develop hidden gifts to bring out the best in you. Don't make decisions because everyone is doing it; always remember that greatness is in you and you can truly make your Life count.

THE OPPORTUNITY IN LIFE

The people who make the most out of their life are those who have made it a responsibility to make use of their opportunity as it comes. People who the world classified as nothing became people of value based on their willingness to convert seemingly half chances into clear cut goals.

We all have a chance to make our life and living worthwhile, the difference between our life's outcome when we do our stock taking will be in the opportunities that we had, and we utilized and the ones we simply over-looked because it came as a problem and not an opportunity.

Life is golden, death scary and daily living could be a herculean task once we are in utter darkness and unable to fully grasp our opportunities. Never discount any factor in life; we must always live consciously in the knowledge that our time is our life. What about the pessimist and optimist? The only difference between them lies in their perspective; they looked at the same thing on the same level but saw things differently.

What do you see as a challenge today? Who takes the blame for your failures? What changes do you want to effect and get results? Everybody has the chance to make a choice. Where you will be in twenty years' time will be a function of the choices we make today, including being alive or dead.

Everyone might have talked about second chances – what if there was no other chance for a trial, and what if that opportunity was the only one we had? Will you still be able to take your chance as it comes?

A football player who is invited for a two weeks' trial from a club in Nigeria to Manchester United with a clause for possible sign-on will do all within his power or even above to impress the manager, he will see that as an opportunity to hit the limelight and hence make the most of his chances. Even if he has a hamstring injury, he will see it as a chance to move into the big league.

The analogy of the football player is also what we need to replicate in our life, making the most and best use of our chances. We need to make conscious efforts to grab our opportunities and turn it into measurable results.

Among the 36 State Governors in Nigeria, each one of them can forever etch their name in GOLD, they have the chance to build infrastructure, provide good healthcare, and other gains of governance as provided in other climes; they could also loot the treasury silly and be charged for corruption.

Whether the Governors will have peace and become a hero after their tenure is totally dependent on the decisions they make while in office, or whether they will be moving from one courtroom to another is within their jurisdiction.

Make the best use of any opportunity that life presents to you today and remember it is not too late to effect change in areas where needed. Time is Life, Use it wisely.

BETTER IS THE END OF A THING

When you look at the contraption and configuration of the world, there is the concept of the now, the present, man's desire for immediate gains at the detriment of future happiness. We all want to have the best on offer at the tap of a finger? I guess as humans we are not to be blamed if we desire to make a head-start without much ado. It is the desire of many people to have abundant wealth, be successful, have a blossoming career and make the best grades in class. That has made the world we live in a habitation of the dragons, politicians killing each other and maiming citizens all in the name of political power. Armed robbers lay siege on innocent people like a prowler that feeds on its carcass. Many have sold their soul to the devil all in the name of being among the high-fliers in society.

What is the essence of a great beginning and a bad ending? Let's imagine Usain Bolt on the tracks competing for the 100 metres Gold-medal in an Olympic championship race; he will rather have a bad start and a good finish, not the other way around. People are wont to be disgusted about a lengthy process, we all want to attain excellence, but my question today is: How many of us are willing to pay the price?

In a chit-chat with a friend of mine some years ago, she said she couldn't marry a man who was not rich. That situation abounds with a sizable proportion of the women folk, they are on the look-out for the readymade suitor, but what if he is rich today or looks rich and becomes poor in a few years' time? Will the lady walk out based on a change in fortunes? That's a food for thought.

I would like to do a brief evaluation of Matthew 6: 33 "but seek first the kingdom of God and his righteousness, and all these things will be added to you". In my own summary, when we seek first his kingdom, we will put extra effort into making the end glorious; we must be uncomfortable with mediocrity and dormancy. At this stage whatever your hands find to do, do it as if your life depends on it. This is a season to water all fruits and crops, don't be resting when you are supposed to be planting or else in the days your contemporaries are harvesting you will have to make do with whatever the consequences of our past actions might be.

No matter how bad the present might be, always remember that the glory of the latter will surpass the former, lay hold on the divine, the supernatural; whatever circumstances or situation that might seem like a turbulent storm with no end in sight, always know that God is able to calm every raging storm. No condition is permanent; the one whom the World has despised and mocked is coming back as the Chief Cornerstone.

I CAME EMPTY, I WILL GO BACK WITH PLENTY

Like a baby in the rush of blood, with tender and loving cries, he came into the world, innocence radiated out of his untainted eyes; not knowing evil or any of the corruption that has been a part and parcel of the world, he started his journey. In emptiness he came, not having a foreknowledge of family, clan or tribe he made the journey into the world.

The whole community is in festive mood at his birth, it's time for a party and the whole area is agog and in joyous mood with his family at the new addition to the family chain. At least many are certain that the party will assure their folks of a dinner for their household and melodious dance-steps to the rhythmic music of the popular gospel artist who has been scheduled to perform. Forgetting their sorrows temporarily while gyrating to the loud music as it echoed out of the giant loudspeakers in the compound.

He started the struggle for survival, the chase and pursuit of emptiness, the partaking in the filthy lucre and the amassing of wealth as if he will be here forever. Then he thought aloud, I came in empty handed, why am I so desperate for power, money and respect, why did I dine with the devil all in a bid to belong with the power-brokers in the society? What is the gain of this whole-world, another voice said but almost everyone is doing it, why should I be left out? All the governors in the country are looting our treasury and trample on people's rights without any accountability to the people they govern, many youths are involved in drug trafficking, and Internet fraud in a bid to eke out a living due to the lack of employment opportunities. Then another voice said: are you willing to make the difference and be the change your generation desire, maintaining your integrity and not engaging in anything that will drag you into disrepute? His thoughts in disarray, the young man looked jolted and perplexed at the thought of living upright in a morally bankrupt world – if I can't beat them why not join them?

As he looked to sit on his chair to listen to the network news, then came a news flash about the death of a childhood friend, who had died early that morning in a car crash. His friend had just got a contract to build a refinery in banana republic, a country noted for its large oil deposits, but which had been the bane of bad and oppressive leadership and hence still crawling when they should be running among the league of the developed nations.

The news jolted him, and he realised the futility in the world – his friend had mansions, private jets, skyscrapers and a yacht, he was among the high-fliers and power-brokers in society because of his deep pockets and vast connections. His lifeless body badly mangled on the highway in a pool of his blood. The young man was devastated and now understood the futility in placing your trust in humans – do not store up for yourselves treasures on earth, where moth and rust destroy, and where thieves break in and steal.

But store up for yourself treasures in heaven, where moth and rust do not destroy, and where thieves do not break in and steal. For where your treasure is, there your heart will be also. (Matt 6:19-21)

THE PROFESSOR IS IN TOWN

It was a display that was a total ridicule to that which he claimed he possessed, his resumé was excellent and was every employer's choice as the words were carefully chosen and well crafted, the qualification he possessed was in high demand which made the young professor a darling of every HR department in town. His performance contrasted with his self-acclaimed ability, his presentation was simply shallow in the exact words of the panel and the integrity of his doctorate questioned. He had just brought that great citadel known worldwide for its lofty standards into disrepute and the young man felt depressed at the insipid display.

The professor went into a self-evaluation mode and called to question his decision to study a field that was not of interest to him; he had a flair for management while his parents felt he would be a perfect fit for an international health officer hence his decision to take a deep plunge into the international health systems, a decision the young man regrets anytime he reflects about his educational pursuit. He was only able to manage fair grades throughout his masters' degree programmes but his deep research earned him a seat on the doctoral train.

The decision has only thrown his life into disarray and he is simply finding it difficult to cope with the challenges and demands of a programme he has never been interested in but chose to undertake because he wanted to satisfy the demands of his parents.

Author's Notes

A lot of youths today have been unfortunate as they have not been living their own lives but that dictated by their parents or family. Parents at times have an ego that needs to be massaged among their committee of friends hence they want to have a medical doctor, an accountant or an engineer as a son or daughter. Hence lots of children find it difficult to do courses that align with their passion and dreams. This could have a catastrophic effect on both the parents and children as you have people who are not really interested in their career because it was forced on them.

In as much as the role of parents in the life of every child cannot be questioned, I would advise parents to help their children by identifying their areas of strength and what they are passionate about and carefully helping them to choose a course that will be profitable for them.

Parents can also assist their kids by not comparing Romeo to Juliet; all children can never be the same, and they have all got different destinies and life's assignments. Give your children the confidence they need to excel while they are young. Help them believe in their abilities and support them in areas where they seem to be weak.

IN THE PURSUIT

I was grocery shopping many years ago in a One-stop shop close to where I live. As I was about to step into the store, a young man bolted away with a big juice container and I joined the other store attendants to give him a hot chase, we caught up with him and retrieved the juice from him. Lo and behold we went back without laying a finger on him. He even threatened us to come close to him and bear the repercussions; I was stunned, flabbergasted and shocked at his conviction. Someone who had just stolen, walking away freely. My mind took a detour and imagined the scene occurred in Lagos. It would have been the height of insanity for him to have done that same thing in the city of Lagos. With a system that metes out jungle justice to petty thieves, it would have been suicidal for him to contemplate stealing or at best stealing a jar of juice.

Using the analogy above as an illustration depicts the moral of the essay. There are a lot of factors that can influence the level of a man's thinking; the environment we live in has a major impact on our pursuit. Some people have been so used to mediocrity and indolence that they are simply not in pursuit of anything. No goals, no vision and let me state probably No life.

I have seen a whole lot of people who had big and lofty dreams, they were passionate, full of life and had business ideas that would make Richard Branson green with envy, but the environment killed their dreams.

I believe literally to succeed in life, we must either be in pursuit of a vision, dream or clear-cut ambition or the vision, goals and ambition is chasing us to act, to dream, to shun mental laziness and incapacitation that has been the bane of many people.

In one society, someone steals a jar of juice, he is caught, he drops it and walks away freely, in another society, someone steals a jar of juice and he finds himself in the burning furnace. Whenever a person is tempted to steal their mind flashes a picture of the consequences of their intended action and does a brief calculation as to whether it will be worth the stress, pain and trouble.

The environment we live in does play a significant role; it's a determinant of how our lives will turn out eventually. In a system where nothing works, you fuel your own generator, construct your own roads, pay your medical bills, pay for your security and literally provide all the basic infrastructure for yourself – you cannot afford to laze around, you must always be in pursuit of excellence or you will retire to mediocrity.

Don't stop dreaming, you need to raise the bar on your aspirations; always stimulate the giant within you to action. Remember nothing moves until you move.

SHE RIPPED MY HEART

"Integrity is doing the right thing, even when no one is watching."
– C.S. Lewis

Like a sledgehammer pierced through the heart of its victim, the young man was in a state of confusion and disbelief; it all seemed like a dream, an illusion and his heart was begging for answers to a million questions at the same time. He was sweating profusely despite the air-conditioning system in the room and his heart shuddered each time he remembered the events of the last few minutes. He was the latest victim of a heartbreak and the only question in his heart was where has integrity gone to? Where are the ideals of motherhood? The agonies of his wife's sleazy affairs rattled him, and he had been the scorn of neighbours' gossip for his failed attempt in making his nuptial arrangement work.

As he analysed the full impact of her scandalous activities on his life, he looked at the seeds of his union and tear drops like the morning dew rolled down his cheeks as he stared into the ceiling in utter bewilderment at his misfortune.

His mind flashed back to the events that led to the union – he had been taken for a ride and he cursed the day he'd exchanged the marriage vows with the corporate harlot in the banking hall.

He had been taught that marriage was an institution of honour, he had gone into it with lofty expectations and was dealt a ruthless blow which came crashing down like a pack of cards with no second chance or a reprieve.

Author's Notes

The truth is even when you feel it is done in secret, I see all things; I know all things, even the deepest secrets that are beyond the reach of the human eyes. There is a God who knows the deepest secret of every man. The marriage institution is meant to be a noble one and not an object to be ridiculed by the antics of small minds.

There is a general occurrence trending worldwide, all those who commit adultery within this institution lose their covering, that edge of fire that is supposed to be a form of protection for their marriages.

What do you do in a world where infidelity seems to be the norm, in a world where Men find it comfortable to have a mistress outside? In a faltering society where people easily flaunt their sexcapades without any form of respect for that noble institution they chose for better or worse.

Marriage is a covenant, an agreement, the coming together of two different people who have chosen to die to self and live together as one. Respect the wedding vows, respect your partner; there is great gain in patience and ability to cope with the weakness of your partner.

The fact that cheating is a common trend in relationships is not an excuse for you to indulge in it; you can be the difference and role model in a society where we are experiencing a dearth in our values system.

LESSONS FROM MY FATHER

I decided to write some of the lessons I learnt from my father. As I ruminate on the major part of the lessons, I discovered a whole book cannot contain the lessons I have learnt from my father since I knew my left hand from my right. I am sure you will learn a few lessons from my father as I also did.

My father taught me that Time is life, I should use it wisely; he always emphasized the fact that we only know today, no one knows tomorrow so we should make use of every opportunity that comes our way in Life.

My father taught me that education makes the difference in our world – to enlarge your sphere of influence get an education; he always said you must seek knowledge to the extent that you will be able to function not just within your locality but on an international level.

My father taught me that we can truly succeed when we celebrate the success of others; he always enjoined us to show love to our neighbours and not to envy any of our friends or neighbours when they succeed.

My father instilled the fear of God in us, he made us understand early in life that a life without Christ will eventually spiral into a life filled with crises. He taught us how to be thankful in advance and stirred up our faith through positive confessions; he always confessed everything he wanted in life in the hope that it would come to pass. He is an optimist to the core and always inspired us that we can be whatever we want in life if we work hard at it and commit our ways to God.

My father taught us that integrity is very important in life, he emphasized to us that we should be trustworthy and honest in all our endeavours, he taught us that there is dignity in labour and he believes so much that life is in phases.

My father taught me that to rest at the night time of our life (Old age), we must sow the good seed early in life, and he always said it is foolhardy to start resting in the morning when you should be ploughing and tilling the land. (Investing to have a beautiful future.)

My father taught me how to be an original and never a fake, he taught us to cut our coat according to our size, he taught us never to live above our means; he always emphasized against indulging in any lifestyle that cannot be sustained in the long run.

My father taught me how to be disciplined, focused and set priorities in all I do. I learnt how to come home early for he despised staying outside at night. He always said most of the evil perpetrated happens at night – armed robbery, police shooting at sight and most of the accidents with fatalities and even death.

My father taught me how to be a responsible father; he is a role model, a father of many sons, a prophet and his words are always etched on marble. I remember there were times I memorized and wrote some of his words down, so I would not forget.

My father taught me how to be humble, he taught me that we are nothing in this world and we should live within our capacity always. Don't envy your neighbours who are successful or who seem to be successful. Remember the sky is large enough for all birds to fly without any harm coming to any one of them.

Above all, my father taught me how to dream, he taught me never to give up in life, he taught me that tough times never last but tough people do. I learnt from my father that success is not a function of background.

LESSONS FROM MY FATHER 2

A truly gentle and wonderful man; you touch the World in a simple but wonderful way
– Rume Daniels

It has been great honour learning from a man of immense character like my father. I remember the days gone by and your principles and beliefs system all ring true in my heart. Your words of wisdom are propellers, food for my soul. Even when distance separates us, I am protected by the covering of your prayers. In moments I felt like giving it all up, you gave me the impetus to forge ahead and pursue my dreams. How I love my father.

There were days I felt like being a local champion, but you gave me the opportunity to pursue my dream on the international stage and you were there to always challenge me and never settle for anything less than being the best. You taught me the principle of God's mercies and grace, even in the dark nights; you were like a shepherd who heralded me out of the storms.

I celebrate you today and always, for who I am today, I owe it to God Almighty and my father, you told us we can be anything we want in life if we paid the price and believe in God. You taught me that to trust in humans is futile, as our breath is in our nostrils and we do not have any power over our lives. I remember those days when we take every issue to God in prayer as you made us understand your absolute trust was in God.

Thank you for being a friend, pastor, mentor and shepherd, thanks for the immeasurable love that can only be found with great men. You have been a blessing to everyone around you and your words of wisdom have been profitable to many. As I celebrate your life through this essay, I pray that God Almighty will continue to bless and increase you in knowledge; my prayer is that the glory of God will not diminish upon your life. I rejoice that God has been true in your life – your life has been a testimony that it pays to serve the Lord. I pray that your good works will outlive our generation.

WHO'S YOUR PAWN?

After Adam and Eve had eaten the fruits of the forbidden tree in the Garden of Eden,

9 Then the LORD God called to Adam and said to him, "Where are you?"

10 So he said, "I heard Your voice in the garden, and I was afraid because I was naked; and I hid myself."

11 And He said, "Who told you that you were naked? Have you eaten from the tree of which I commanded you that you should not eat?"

12 Then the man said, "The woman whom you gave to be with me, she gave me of the tree, and I ate.

Many people in our generation also operate on this kind of level, they are always looking for a ready pawn for their seeming failures and weakness, and they fail to admit their errors due to ego problems or a show of strength.

Who is your pawn?

Ask the unemployed graduate with a second-class lower degree and he will tell you it is his failure to make a second-class upper degree that is responsible for his lack of job, ask the unemployed graduate with a second-class upper degree and he will tell you that it is his lack of connections that is responsible for his lack of job. Every human has the potential to create an imaginary pawn, the event or person that can always be their excuse when answers are demanded from them for their seeming failure to achieve certain objectives.

Yinka Ayefele, a popular gospel artiste in Nigeria, became very famous after sustaining a spinal cord injury. He could have made the accident his ready pawn, an excuse to hit the streets either as a corporate or local beggar. He evaluated his situation and dug deep into his arsenal; he chose to be a victor and not a victim of the circumstance life has thrust upon him.

Ask the man who beats his wife the reasons for his actions; it is the devil. Ask the rapist; it is the devil. Ask the armed robber, when he is caught; it is the devil. Ask the poor man and he will tell you a long history of how his generation is so wretched and his lack of opportunities is the cause of his failings or in the alternative, there must be a fiery witch or wizard in his hometown who is working against his success. Ask the student who has an exam but chose to be on Facebook or Instagram; if they fail the exams the pawn is either the lecturer or the questions on the paper had not been taught in class.

I look forward to the day men will begin to take responsibilities for their lives and stop looking for who to blame for their misery. Learn to turn every seemingly challenge into an opportunity, be in control of your life; there is a limit to what the government and the society can do to help you.

Your background is not a determinant of your future success. Even if you are in doubt the most powerful individual in the world few years ago, the former president of the United States of America Barack Obama was a victim of a broken home. He did not declare any pity party neither did he for once brood over his circumstances. From his humble beginnings he metamorphosed into a man the world cannot do without.

You alone have the choice to be the hero from Zero, forget the pawn, stop the pity party and blame game. When you are in dire straits and everything seems at a crossroad imagine the possibilities and you will be surprised how much of a success you will make out of your life.

SURVIVAL, DISCOVERY OR REALISATION

At which point does a man reach the stage of optimum satisfaction, as economists infer that optimum satisfaction is a point of full satisfaction, the stage where man is not in delusion, in the chase of building empires and castles in this temporary planet.

At the point of the search for means of survival, we have several reasons why the chase for wealth is essential and not self-seeking; every human wants to make the best out of life, become successful with good standing in the society.

Hence, the chase begins; at the stage of survival everyone is in the same race, bankers, lawyers, editors, politicians, students, artisans, pastors and all other professions or calling.

The stage of self-discovery helps us to channel our energy to where we can function easily and make the journey much easier. Until we reach a stage in life where we discover who we truly are, we tend to waste away our potential, the talent within has no capacity to reproduce itself on an equal or a larger proportion. The graveyard is an attestation of this fact; a lot of talent goes to waste before they reach that point of self-discovery in life. If you are not yet functioning in your own stage of self-discovery, do not put your life or talent to waste. Imagine a man with innate abilities in artistic drawing working in a field alien to his passion – it will be a life of struggle, until he discovers himself, until he learns to pull out of his comfort zone and follow his passion.

Another stage where humans tend to get stuck in life is the stage of self-realisation. At this stage, we have no more lifelines, we have little or no chances to make new choices that can define the very essence of our life. At the point of self-realisation, we evaluate the turning points in our lives, the opportunity cost of all our decisions and the alternative forgone. At the point of self-realisation, we can only wish to have done things differently when the opportunity came up.

In all my days and years spent on the surface of the earth, I discovered that man does not really have a stage of total or optimum satisfaction, the quest for new challenges and opportunities in a world where we have a taste for the latest models in town thus building up an avalanche of unnecessary items in a bid to satisfy our unending wants.

Either you are in the stage of survival, discovery or waiting for the point of realisation; always remember that optimum satisfaction should be the goal, the stage where we can truly look back and opine without fear that we have truly lived.

Some people lived while others existed. The outcome of your life will be a function of the choices we make today. Remember that your time is your life: Use it wisely.

VALUE WHAT YOU HAVE

When purpose is not known, abuse is inevitable
– Myles Munroe

I will also say when the value of a product or person is not known abuse is inevitable. Most times in life, humans tend to take what they have for granted, we tend to underestimate the value of the most important things and people in our life.

An employed graduate does not know the value of that job until the job is lost; the man who has a house does not know the value of his home, until there is a fire outbreak.

The woman who has children does not know the value of her children till the moment she meets a barren woman who is desperately praying for the fruit of the womb. The educated person does not know the value of that education until you meet the street urchins and those who have had their brains twisted because of lack of education.

We must learn to place value on what we have always. You will never know the value of your car until you are caught up in the rain when you are without it. You will never know the importance of your family, until you meet orphans and kids in a motherless home. You will never know how precious it is to have parental guidance and counselling, until you meet those who have lost their parents. The spinsters and bachelors who are ready for marriage will know the value of relationships better than those who still have plenty of time to play with.

It is a common trend for people to underestimate what they have, but the truth is what you despise is what others are longing for and will forever treasure once they get it. The woman who has a husband who treats her with respect will appreciate him better when she meets the woman who is emotionally abused by her husband daily.

We only appreciate the need to back-up our phone until we have lost it. And many people take the trivial things in their life for granted – we think it is normal to go out in the morning and come back at night, but many people leave their homes and never come back. Most times we lie in bed, we think it is normal to sleep and wake up; many people lie in bed to sleep and breathe their last.

You will only understand the value of good health when you visit the hospital and you meet lots of people who are desirous of health but cannot get it. I read the story of twin brothers, one lived a wayward life and the other a righteous life. The wayward guy committed a crime and the righteous brother gave up his life in his stead; the wayward guy realized the value of life when his brother died in his place and decided to live in righteousness.

The political office holder does not understand the value of the cries of the electorate, to render service instead of looting the treasury until he has been booted out of office through their votes.

My last bit of advice: value what you have when you still have it because it might be too late when you have lost it.

THE TIME IS COMING

The time is coming when our eyes become dim, the days of sagging breasts and frail bones. The days when intelligent people become dim witted, the days when nothing makes sense again. The days when we feel like running but there is no strength in our frail body. There will be a time when the most beautiful woman in the world, even when nude, is unattractive to a man.

The time is coming when we become slow in thinking and understanding, the days of poor memory, inability to recall events and the days when there will be no more struggle for survival.

The time is coming when the lure and desperation is ended, the time of stiff bones and a dead cold body. The time when we are desperate for help even in a bid to do the petty things. There is a time when our joy is derived from our children and grandchildren.

Time is life so please let us endeavour to use it wisely; there is a time and season for everything under the Sun.

The days when applying make-up only makes a woman look like a ghost. The time is coming when boys will become men; the time is coming when the chicken is coming home to roost.

The time is coming when the chase for the allures of this world will be ended, the dreams, goals and aspirations will all be gone with the wind, the worries, anger, troubles, lamentations and happiness depending on which side of the divide you belong will be ended.

In our entire search for the riches in this world, in our quest to fulfil destiny, let us remember all the time that we are only here for a while. It profits us nothing if we gain the entire world and lose our soul. The devil is moving about like a roaring lion, seeking for whom to devour. Make your life count, for how you spend your seconds determines your minutes, how you spend your minutes determines your hours, how you spend your hours determines your day, and how you spend your days determines the outcome of your life.

For every hand of the clock that moves tick tock, your life is also moving in a similar fashion. We cannot relive the times, it is impossible to turn back the hands of the clock; make use of every opportunity that you get in life. In Economics, Ceteris Paribus means all things being equal – in life all things are not always equal, so don't elect to do tomorrow what you can do today.

It is not by struggle or human ability, always remember that it is not of him who wills neither is it of him who runs but of God who shows mercy. As we celebrate our birthdays let us remember that the more we celebrate the shorter our stay left on Earth. Let us make our life count and our days purposeful.

DO NOT BE UNEQUALLY YOKED

When you miss out in the choice of a life partner, you have entered the bus popularly known in Lagos as a one chance bus. I remember asking a close pal of mine few years ago why people are averse to tying the nuptial knots these days; most of the folks I knew then were still bachelors and spinsters. I asked him with no sinister intentions in mind what the root cause of this problem might be. Could it be attributed to lack of finances, the bane of unemployment or lack of business acumen that could translate to cash? Or we have lots of boyfriends and few husbands, lots of girlfriends and few wives, or people are just dodgy when it comes to taking up responsibility? I guess there is no definitive answer to my question, but I think understanding our timing also matters a lot in this game of the heart.

Back to the main discourse, I can be so anointed, tongue talking, devil bashing and spirit filled but if I miss out in my choice of a life partner then I have sentenced my destiny to a life of frustration, heartache and unending pain. I have seen a lot of great people – men with potential, women who are at the top rung of the ladder – endure a life of unhappiness due to their choice of a partner. To live in misery, marry the wrong partner, I do believe that a broken courtship is much better than a broken marriage, so it is much better to take the flak for a broken relationship and move on than endure it and sign a deal with the mother of all frustrations.

Behind every successful man there is a successful woman, a motivator, a queen, the one who makes him feel he is the best and discover his abilities even when things go awry, the one who is always there to support and counsel him, the woman who is ready to stand by her man notwithstanding the circumstances and situations over time.

A woman who will always be faithful to her husband and respect the wedding vows which she consented to. You want to see a great wife, trust her, zip up, cheating and lying is a NO-NO do not be threatened by her successes but rather help her nurture her dreams and potential. You must always appreciate and not take her for granted. Behind that successful woman there is a king, so when you abuse her physically and emotionally, then we see the beast in the woman.

Whatever your reason for waiting in your quest to be married, do not forget that the God factor is very important. I have been privileged to have lived and been brought up by great parents who understand God's mandate concerning marriage.

If I were to be a woman, my choice of a life partner would be a God-fearing man (Lover of God), humorous, fun to be with, who does not smoke, who detests the bottles, maybe red wine on occasions (doctors recommend this for the heart). I would rather marry a man with a vision and not a man with a television, a good vision can buy you lots of television. I would rather be under the tutelage of a man who hears from the Lord. Maybe my parameters might be high, and maybe I have also been lost in my chase for vanity as some people are wont to say. Maybe it's all fantasy, but there are a few fantasies that can happen in our time.

And as a man, what do I really want in a woman, what are my standards and parameters? A woman that is broken, a woman that is thirsty for the Lord.

No perfect being, none is perfect, only God is.

AUTONOMY AND AGENCY

I had the opportunity to talk on the subject matter in a staff training many years ago and the main point I spoke about was do we have control over our life.

Most of the things and events in our life we have absolute and full control over and my highlighted points are thus:

TIME

Every human being (Old, Young, Rich, Poor, Man and Woman) has an equal allotment of twenty-four hours to be used daily. Whether our time is being used wisely and profitably depends on us. When you can effectively manage your time, then you have been able to manage your life effectively.

DECISIONS

We are a function of the decisions we make, we have absolute control over our lives when we can make wise decisions in our daily living.

CHOICES

The choices we make also go a long way to determine whether we can exercise control over our life or not; every human being has a chance to make a choice. The choices we make today will invariably determine our future outcome.

ATTITUDE

We have control over our attitude, our attitude determines our altitude. We can choose to always be happy and make happiness our state of mind no matter the situation and circumstance that we face in life. We can always trigger happy-moods and stay out of being moody or depressed.

If someone upsets you, can you still be happy? Difficult but possible. When you allow other people to determine your moods through their behaviour towards you, it invariably means you have ceded control of your life to them and they are the pilot of your life.

Charles Swindoll said, and I quote, "Attitude to me is more important than facts. It is more important than the past, than education, than money, than circumstances, than failure, than success, than what other people think, say or do. It is more important than appearance, gift, or skill. It will make or break a company...a church...a home. The remarkable thing is we have a choice every day regarding the attitude we will embrace for that day. We cannot change our past...We cannot change the fact that people will act in a certain way. We cannot change the inevitable. The only thing we can do is play on the one string we have, and that is our attitude. I am convinced that life is 10% what happens to me and 90% how I react to it. And so it is with you... we are in charge of our attitudes."

Your attitude is your life: when you have a good attitude, you have a good life; when you have a bad attitude, life becomes chaotic.

PERSPECTIVE AND BELIEFS SYSTEM

Another thing we have control over in life is our perspectives, the way we see things, our outlook on life. We can either be an optimist that sees the silver lining in the dark clouds or a pessimist that sees difficulty and impossibility in every situation that they are confronted with. You have control over whatever myths you choose to believe.

THE THINGS WE CAN'T CONTROL

We have no control over our birth. We all came to the knowledge of our existence, we had no foreknowledge of the family we were born into or the sex we will be at birth or the day we will be born. We had no control over the choice of our father and mother; we also do not have control over our death, for death is the destiny of every man.

We do not have control over whether we will wake up whenever we sleep. We also do not have control over our ageing process – once we were young, now we are old; these days I feel so old at the speed and frequency the hands of the clock are moving. One generation comes, and another goes – that is the bane of mankind.

MY NAME, YOUR NAME, OUR NAMES

Bartholomew, Adil, Alexandra, Kenny, Antonia, Clark, Adeola, Tim, Mabel, Oluwanifemi, Aaron, Foziah, Dipan, Evelyn, David, Peter, Paul, James, Fred, Temidayo, Eugene, Adenike, Johnson, Sarah, Barth, Adedeji, Rabiu, Funmi, Austin, Melissa, Deborah, Linda, Daniel, Hayley, Lauren, Lisa, Navid, Katie, Mustapha, Amaka, Ayo, Barth, Eugene, Max, Jake, Yvonne, Kenneth.

What is the big deal in a name? Why the fuss about the name we give to our children? Why do parents and family rack up different names for us at birth? If it was just for the cause of identifying kids, then I am sure one name is just enough and we are good to go. I tried to envisage a world where we all exist without names – this scenario will be very funny and could be detrimental and that will be the peak of identity crises, not the one people suffer these days when they fail to realize who they truly are and try by living other people's lives.

I remember after Barack Obama won the race for the White House, many parents named their new-born babies after Barack Obama because they believed the name signified luck; when President Goodluck Jonathan of Nigeria assumed the office of the president, many Nigerians changed their names to Goodluck especially on Social Networking sites, as it was widely believed that the president's name brought him luck and has always brought him luck all of his life.

A Yoruba proverb says, our name is like a shield and gives us direction in life. The truth is that our names are also powerful mechanisms and carry a message in whatever we do. An example of the power that a name carries, when you mention the name of Jesus every knee will bow, and every tongue confesses that Jesus Christ is Lord. The Bible says in Proverbs 18:10 "The name of the Lord is a strong tower, the righteous runs into it and is saved". The example of the power in a name can be signified by the enormous power that is in the name of Jesus.

The reason why people change their names from that depicting oracles and changing it to Godly names is because we believe our names is a true reflection of who and what we truly are. Your name gives power to your personality; it could also reflect the circumstances of our birth in the family we were born into.

You are whatever name you call yourself. If you believe you are a success, then no man can withstand you or the anointing of God upon your life. If you believe you have bad luck and nothing good can be achieved in your life or your family, you also get the same result. Always remember that whatever names we call people around us, they eventually live it out.

I am very mindful of the name I call myself, I am a new creature and all old things have passed away, which also reflects in the name I call myself. You can have dominion in whatever you do; you can be a partaker of the good in the land, if only you remember that you are what you say you are.

THAT WE MIGHT HEAR HIM

God is still in the business of speaking to his children, and when I say his children, I mean every one of his creation. We are all wonderfully and fearfully made and the thoughts of God towards us are of good and not of evil. Most humans are unable to hear God all the time because they have their minds tuned to this temporary world. Why have we shut out the voice of the father from penetrating into our inner minds?

All my life, I have never struggled to hear the voice of the father, he speaks to me daily, he ministers unto my soul and gives me instruction all the time on which way to go. Before any major event happens, he reveals unto me the deep secrets that the ordinary eyes cannot comprehend.

There is no big deal in hearing the voice of God and being in sync with his will for our lives in every season. The same way we hear and understand the instructions of our parent, that is also the same way our relationship with God should develop. When you know the will of God for your life, you cease to live a stressful life, you are free from struggles, pain, backwardness and stagnation. Many people experience stagnancy because they have not been hearing from God or they would rather carry out their own objectives rather than carry out God's plan and purpose for their lives.

When you hear God and know his plans and purpose for your life, everything becomes easy and the things that seem as a high mountain to the ordinary man become mincemeat for you. Even when there is a bad patch, a temporary glitch and a failure in any aspect of your life, you will come to the realisation that whatever situation you are going through is not your permanent stop, the pain must be experienced before you can count your gains, the trial and tribulations before your testimony and the mess before the message.

I am always joyful and revel in the gift of revelation that God has given unto me, even when in dire straits, I remind him of his words and promises to me. Even in the darkest nights, in the moments when everything looked bleak and life really was at a crossroads, his words came in handy, it birthed a revival in my soul.

The truth is, God is not a man that he would lie, neither the son of man that he will repent whatever he has said concerning your life might tarry and seem slow in happening, but please don't grow weary in your faith, wait for his promises and his word will be established in your life.

Just imagine the possibilities of knowing the plans of the father for your life; it is simply mind-blowing and breath-taking.

GRACE!

I feel excited writing about the grace of God that has been made available to every mortal being. Grace is available to all humans to enjoy dominion on Earth, while we have the ability to live in the palace and partake of God's inheritance.

According to the free dictionary, Grace is seemingly effortless beauty or charm of movement, form, or proportion. Grace is a favour rendered by one who need not do so; indulgence.

It is also a temporary immunity or exemption; a reprieve.

Many times, we engage in a struggle for survival, our mindsets have been configured to fight for the basics of life. We fight for food, shelter, resources, good jobs and we have forgotten the place of God's grace. All we pray and ask for is crumbs, we are happy to live a normal life; we are encouraged to be normal so all we do is short-changing ourselves because we rely on our intellect. After all, as far as we can eat three square or round meals why do we need to ask for more?

Grace is the secret to supernatural living; God's grace is sufficient for us to function on this earth.

Why are you trying to run the engine room of your life based on your own ability and intelligence? Your human brain is too small to help you navigate through this difficult terrain. It is grace that helps you to stand before kings and not mere mortals; it is grace that took Joseph from the prison yard to the king's palace.

Someone needs to say a silent prayer today, Dear Lord, do not take me to a place where your grace will desert me.

You cannot achieve anything in life on your own. Based on our strength we are weak and vulnerable to life's many dangers and weaknesses, but God's grace is sufficient for us, his strength is made perfect for us in weakness. The truth is we are humans and there is a limit to what we can achieve in the context of our power and imagination; people who think it's about who and what they know are only living in a fool's paradise. The race is not always to the swift nor the battle to the strong, remember it is not of him who wills neither of him who runs but of God who shows mercy.

But for his grace, we would all have been consumed in the raging storm of life. His grace kept us from imminent dangers and gave us right standing with the father.

Isaac enjoyed so much grace that he sowed in the land of Gerar during the famine and he reaped in the same year a hundred folds. Grace confounds the imagination of humans – in natural circumstances you cannot plant crops in a time of famine and expect a harvest.

Grace denotes effective divine power in the experience of people. So whatever endeavours you lay your hands to do, ask for God's grace with an understanding that his grace is all you need to achieve all of your expectations effortlessly.

WE CANNOT ALL BE FOOLS

I asked my friend who claims to be an unbeliever the reason for his decision – he told me he was an ardent believer in Charles Darwin's theory of evolution and he has not been convinced enough there is a need to believe in God.

The truth be told, all the billions of people who wake up every Sunday and go to the nearest worship centres cannot be fools, the Muslims who worship on a Friday are also not idle people; the other religion groups cannot all be idiots and jobless people. The fact is we all attest to the fact that there is a spiritual being who controls the universe. So, I find it appalling that some set of people run their lives based on their ability alone.

If religion was total falsehood, I am sure there would have been a part of the world where people do not have any religious beliefs as a bloc not the sparse numbers of atheists and closet atheists who attest that there is no God, but most people believe there is a supernatural force that controls the universe. There is a supernatural that releases blessings to the natural in varied proportions.

I probed him further, so if you have any problems, who do you call upon? He answered no one. Your brain is too small to act as the engine room of your life, human ability can fail, the natural factors are also not constant, your intellect can only take you to a point in life, so when the big issues arise how do you resolve them?

Don't be deceived by vain philosophies, as the world is filled with people who have varied opinions and diverse views about creation and the theory of evolution; don't live your life based on vain imaginations; there is indeed a supernatural force that controls the universe. From time immemorial you can check out the antecedents of people who doubted the power of God and mocked him – they did not live to tell the story.

Who is man to question the maker? I asked my friend who was responsible for his creation and he said he was created by his father and mother, but the truth is the world is such a large place with different personalities and you don't expect everyone to follow the same route.

Jesus Christ died that we might live; he paid the ultimate price just because of you and me. Don't make his blood spilled on your behalf of no consequence by living your life anyhow; you cannot afford to misbehave or do it your way. Our Life is a script and we are all actors in this world, we are all going to play our part and leave the stage someday, so make your life count and make a conscious effort to do it right.

If at the end of my life, I discovered I was a fool for believing in the gospel of our Lord Jesus Christ, I would rather be the fool after death than be a double fool for not believing and not having a wild card entry into the exclusive club of his children.

PART 4

ORDINARY MAN, EXTRA-ORDINARY GOD

There is a wow factor that adds the extra into our ordinary nature and makes us distinct among our peers and contemporaries. Many times, in life we think that life's success is guaranteed by the extent of our struggle, how often we can cut corners, how good we are at hustling, family background and other factors that the human faculty can easily understand and dissect. But the truth is the supernatural controls the natural; to experience good success in the physical you must be in full control of the spiritual. Why do you think some people never seem to succeed in life no matter how much effort they put in?

As humans we are mere mortals created out of dust for such a time as this. I realized that because God knew us before he formed us and knows every little detail about us, I came to an understanding that the race is not always to the fastest, nor the battle won by the ordinary being, so there is a God who puts the sugar and honey into our tea that makes the supposed high mountain become a plain ground. So, when it feels like we are down and out, and everything seems to be at a standstill, never give up or lose hope. The only choice we have in moments like that is to run back to our source, the God who can suspend natural factors to work in our favour.

It's not about who you know, your level of intelligence or your social status – grace makes the difference. As humans there is nothing spectacular about us, we have no control over our lives, there are no guarantees we will wake up the next day when we sleep but there is a God who gives us a sense of accomplishment in all our efforts. There is an extra-ordinary God who puts the special effects into our lives and instil us with the swagger (ability) to confront life's troubles.

He said in his word in Romans 9 that he will have mercy on whom he will have mercy upon, so it is not by human permutations and calculations. He is the God that lifts us up again after a terrible fall. When people question you and really think you cannot rise again after the fall, the God who adds the extra into our lives is simply saying that I am the God of a second chance and his ways are simply different from the ways of man.

Why not join the winning team, why not dine with this great God? When you are in his team you can never be a loser. You can never achieve anything on just your own ability, nothing worthwhile can be accomplished within your own power, but to enjoy the extra benefits of fruitfulness, promotion, academic success, business and career success, marital bliss and good moral values for a good life, you must tap into the extra that comes from this great God.

I AM PERFECTLY IMPERFECT

Can you imagine what life will look like if we are all perfect beings, no flaws, no weakness, no pain and nothing that moves us to cry, nothing that brings us close to and keeps us in constant check with our humanity, a life without issues and difficult moments, a life where we get all we ever want at the click of a button, no long prayer requests.

Many people find it very tasking and highly insurmountable the high mountain called their weakness, so instead of confronting it headlong, they ultimately plan to flee from it. Someone said he is a married man, my weakness is single ladies and I find my wife very boring hence an extra-marital affair is my next priority. No one is perfect, no not one and we either have the choice of running away from our weaknesses or turning them to focal points, when we can smack our chest in confidence and utter once a weakness now my strength.

We can have gifts that make us peculiar and feel so anointed but the pain is there to keep us in constant check with our humanity, so the grace comes with the pain. I was a guest at an interview panel of a multinational company many years ago and they were asking me what my major weaknesses were. I reeled out weaknesses that were strengths in some way, I am a goal getter and I don't give up until I accomplish my mission, I thrive under harsh economic and business climates; and they were quite impressed with many of my glorified weaknesses that were strengths in disguise.

When I say weaknesses, I am talking about weaknesses where you look around and say, no more person. (Yoruba proverb) If this man can do this then the entire mankind has lost it. The truth is, so far, we have the human nature in us, do not expect perfection from any man, please forget titles. When I hear stories of a Man of God who was involved in any form of activity that might bring the kingdom of God into disrepute, I first remember that he was initially a man before he accepted God into his life. As humans our breath is in our nostrils and our level of resistance can be broken and shattered and the seeming perfect man who can do no wrong can simply fall like a pack of cards.

Now the truth is we can confront our weaknesses, so don't live all your life in captivity of this monster called weakness. I understand the fact that if temptation has not come our way this does not really make us to be above board – you can gain control over your supposed frailties and turn them into strengths. People always tend to criticize when they have not been faced with the realities of life but always remember that you can always produce value from every negative circumstance that you may encounter in life.

GREATNESS: HIDDEN IN SMALL PACKAGES

Have you ever encountered great people before? Most times the criteria for achieving greatness does not lie in the physical statistics of an individual, neither is it a function of family background, family name or heritage.

Every great person I have seen had a story; they paid the price before they got the prize. Most times I have heard heart rending tales of people who moved from grass to grace, from poverty to opulence, from unknown figures to role models the world cannot do without. Most people think that the criterion for being great is a function of family background, educational qualifications, connection in high places, certificates acquired, level of intellect – but let me shock you a bit: have you not seen professors who live in squalor? Or people who were bequeathed with wealth, yet their lives are in a perennial mess.

If greatness was shared by human beings, it would have been very normal to use the above statistics as a prerequisite for being great. We could have added the fluency and command of the English language, probably we could also have added family inheritance to the list, but all the above requirements are nought, it does not have any bearing on your life neither does it count towards your future success. Your present-day situation is irrelevant to the future, so why do you worry yourself over friends who are ahead of you? Life is a marathon and not a sprint.

There are different vessels in my father's house, gold, silver, bronze and clay – greatness does not always come with the familiar packages, and it does not always come with the standard of humans; it is always outside of the usual expectation and not a tick-box activity. When my God decides to use you as a vessel of impact for your generation, you do not necessarily need any qualifications; when people commend me for my writing skills, where do you get all that great stuff from, I pass all the glory to God because I know that if it was by human qualifications, I am the least qualified. There are times I wonder if it is normal for me to write without a script or plan of action, in most cases the essays I write about come as an idea, a thought or the Holy Spirit drops it in my mind. I pick up my laptop and begin writing.

Commitments do not even give me the opportunity to read as many books as I would love to, so almost all my writings are divinely inspired. I am sure some of my friends never expected me to follow this path, but I can boldly say that it is the almighty God that is the secret behind my writing skills.

Is there anyone reading this who has been frustrated with life and thinks there is no hope for tomorrow? The truth is don't ever give up on God, my father is still in the business of doing miracles, no matter what your package may look like. He is not concerned with the beauty, dress sense or eloquence of the package; he decides to have mercy on whom he wills.

ADVICE TO SINGLES ABOUT TO MARRY

Life is in phases and men are in sizes. A lot of my bachelor friends are bidding bye-bye to the singles club and going to the altar. There is always that next stage when we all must take that bold step and begin a new chapter in our lives. As pastors admonish couples on their wedding day, marriage entails a lot of responsibility and strong character on the side of both parties, patience is key and of importance. There will always be disagreement but the ability to settle it amicably is a hallmark of a good union. A man is not supposed to make his wife a punching bag or to use her to show off his boxing skills; a good union can only thrive in an atmosphere of love and good understanding between the couple. Marriage is not to be endured but to be enjoyed.

This is a quote from a picture of Barack and Michelle Obama in the early 90s: "All a man needs is a patient woman to stick by and watch his dreams fall into place and to quit nagging". Do you think she knew he would become the president of the United States at that time? I don't think so, but she stuck with him and his Volkswagen Beetle anyway.

Even an incurable optimist will have his mind polluted if he gets married to a nagging wife, the persistent moaner, all she does is complain, never sees the blue lining in the sky – so in making a choice of a life partner you need to be sure you can cope with the weaknesses of your partner.

Don't marry your partner out of pity; you cannot sustain a good marriage on pity. A failed relationship or courtship is better than a failed marriage. As new couples you need to help your spouse nurture his or her dreams, believe in them and help to water the seed of greatness in them. As partners you need to help them understand that they carry a lot of value and can be all they aspire to be in life.

Rome was not built in a day and Life is not a bed of roses. The foundation of every good marriage should be built on love and integrity. Always remember that you must stay true to the wedding vows. The citation "For better for worse, for richer or poorer, in sickness or health till death do us part" is not just a citation but a covenant between couples. Successful marriages are not made in heaven but are attributed to the conscientious ability of couples to suppress their own will. At times they die to it and give their partner's will dominance.

To everyone getting married, it will be a union to remember for you all. Your Union will be fruitful with lots of beautiful children, your future together will be bright, and you will not regret getting married to your spouse.

TIME IS LIFE: GET BUSY

I would have avoided this essay like a plague if my time had not been used wisely. Let's look further than the solidarity and goodwill messages for the grace to witness a New Year. We all know a living dog is better than a dead lion, but when we examine the statement carefully the living dog has it usefulness. Our time is a valuable resource and should be such. When we waste our time, we invariably waste our life. Every second, minute and hour of the day that we spend should be treasured as time once lost cannot be regained.

Time is fundamental to our very existence as humans, shared in equal measure and proportion to all mankind so there won't be disaffection or complaints that it's because I have less time than the other fellow out there being the main reason I failed to achieve my life's goal. How we use this resource will invariably determine the outcome of our lives.

Life does not reward you for activity but rather it rewards you for accomplishments. Life will not reward you for the gifts and talents you have but the gifts and talents that you have which you put to good and effective use. So, the next time you see anyone in your chosen field of endeavour who seems to be doing well and all you do is criticize, I would advise that you stop in your tracks and put your own gifts to use instead of bashing the seemingly successful people.

Time is Life, Get busy. In all thy getting please make yourself busy. A busy man is an expensive man. When you are busy you will be accountable for how you spend this resource and make your life worthy of emulation.

When I say Time is life, get busy, I am not saying get busy with activities. There is a major difference between the man who wins the Olympic medal and other contestants, so it's not the participation that matters but accomplishing results. If we self-reflect on our life in the last one year, would you have experienced growth in every area of your life within this time frame or you are just moving in whatever direction the wind blows.

Stop chatting away your future if that relationship is not going to add value to you. Go for associations that will increase you and give your life a semblance of hope. Always remember that when there is life, there is hope. There are No permanent situations; after the night comes the morning. We complain all the time about bad investment vehicles, about unaccountable governments, but sincerely speaking, if your life was an investment vehicle would anybody be willing to stake their funds on this investment vehicle or will you be a bad investment to put funds into? This is a food for thought: let's do an evaluation of our lives and look at how we can effect a CHANGE in areas we need to. In every season you must have a PLAN B if your present plan does not work out; you need to look at other ways of making your dream a reality.

It's a time to move from being a dreamer, a time to stop living an illusion but a time to work and effectively turn all your dreams into reality. TIME IS LIFE, GET BUSY, FRIENDS.

THEORY, CONVENTION, PERMUTATION AND CALCULATION

We have natural laws and super-natural laws, we are also aware of some known theories, conventions, permutations and calculations. I have heard stories and testimonies when natural laws were suspended in the lives of people, human calculation was pushed aside and the impossible became possible.

As humans we are always quick to draw conclusions based on our reasoning; 1+1 will always be equal to 2. Most times we tend to limit ourselves, our God and what God can do in our lives.

Don't be angry when people draw conclusions based on what they can see, if only they can see what you see. Even when our eyes of understanding have been shut and we cannot comprehend or see God in that situation, always remember that God's ways are not our ways, his ways and thoughts are entirely different from ours.

I remember an assignment, a major project that I had invested a significant part of my life to achieving and I only saw myself as just good enough. I was living in the good enough mentality until the measurable results came in; I saw that I had been limiting myself in more ways than one and excellence was not far away.

The natural law says you need a connection to get a decent job; you need to know people to make a head start in life, but these laws have been broken in the lives of many people and yours can also be an exception. I remember a prayer session for a mentor of mine in the early nineties and the pastor kept praying, God said in this city, you will have many houses. My mentor and his family could barely mutter Amen because in the natural, it was impossible, their situation as tenants was quite bad and here was a pastor prophesying about being the owner of many houses. It seemed like a mockery because their calculation was based on their own thinking, their own theory and convention. They could not see beyond the present because the future looked bleak.

Truth is, there is no lasting situation the same way the morning comes after the night so there will always be temporary setbacks, slight hitches, situations that seem insurmountable and problems that seem like a giant. There is a limit to how far you can travel on your human imagination; there will be situations and circumstances that might test you to your limits and what may look like the best is to curse God and die.

Forget the ways of man, in the natural you might have been written off, you might have had many failures than your successes. Always remember that people can be myopic in their reasoning and there is a limit to how far people can see as we have limitations and are in no way perfect.

Always put your trust in God, in the supernatural and watch natural laws, theories, permutations and calculations suspended on your behalf.

FRIENDS LIKE ENEMIES

I dedicate this essay to all friends masked in the garment of enemies, I dedicate it to those who laugh in your presence but scorn you in your absence. I dedicate this essay to all the rumour mongers, backbiters, gossips, those who engage in idle talks, I dedicate it to the PhD holders, the masters in the art of the pull him down syndrome, the champions in the game of if we can't surpass him then let's destroy him. Most people see their enemies as a demon that needs to be destroyed, their nemesis, but ideally the best sucker punch you can give to those who plot your downfall is to become a success right before their very eyes.

After the creation of mankind, the creator of man himself saw that the heart of those he had created was evil and desperately wicked. Hence, I will not be amazed if the picture of the world in your mind is grim, dark and shocking. A world where joblessness is at the zenith, resentment of the success of others abound, it's an odd and bizarre world. The secret to success that many are not aware of lies in the celebration of other's people's successes, so eschew all form of bitterness and envy, rejoice with those that rejoice and watch your harvest season come.

A word of thanks for these same people called our enemies, those who see no good in you, those who are constantly plotting evil against you, for without you our lives would not have been on a turbo-speed, accelerating towards excellence and hiding under the shadow of the Almighty God.

One final truth, except the Lord builds the house, the labourers are only wasting their time, the interpretation of this passage is no matter how much evil is planned against you, there is a God who knows the beginning and the end, there is a God who knows the times and season of our lives, he is the potter and we are the clay, he knew you right from your mother's womb, that is the absolute truth, knows your life's story and knows about every little detail in our lives.

To the man who says what is he or she doing that I can't do, she does not know how to sing, dance or write, he or she was not the best student in our class, so I can also do whatever he or she is doing better, my answer to that is, Romans 9:16, It is not of him who wills, neither is it of him who runs but of God who shows mercy. |Even so, it's not about skill, intellect or ability; God's way is different from the ways of man so dwelling on some unused gifts is just a way of crying over a bleak future.

The world will become such a better place if people had foresight, if people can grow up and work at their own successes and stop looking for an imaginary hate figure, someone to blame for their failures and weaknesses.

On a final note, a big thank you to those who constantly plot our downfall – without friends in the cloak of enemies we would have no challenge and drive to become better persons.

RESPONSE MECHANISM

In recent times, most of my mentoring opportunities have been offline and I have been doing my best to be abreast of tackling issues and challenges in people's lives as they happen.

I have discovered that everyone has their own challenge, their problems, the pain that keeps them in constant touch with their humanity and bring them to the knowledge that we do not possess any supernatural power hence we appropriate powers we do not have to ourselves.

It is not what happens to us as individuals that matters, but how we respond to what happens to us ultimately. Thus, it is the response mechanism that we adopt that is the big deal. Issues abound everywhere; the human nature comes with a lot of frailties and imperfections.

That is the truth, so our perspective to the issues that confront us is a significant factor – how do you deal with bitterness, how do you deal with a failing marriage, a future that lacks a clear-cut direction, how do you deal with the challenge of falling behind your colleagues' achievement wise? Do you adopt the victor or victim mentality? Some people are masters in the blame game, good at organizing pity-parties so people can commiserate with them, but every one of us have the chance to make a choice, and invariably the choices we make will determine the outcome of our lives.

It is better to have a solution focused mind-set than dwell on problems and limitations that we encounter in our daily life. Anybody can experience failure; the problem is not that you failed but are you willing to learn from your failures and mistakes and have a brand-new start.

Check out every remarkable story – without doubt there was a rough patch; there was a process, the pruning stage before the result. One of the major differences in our life's result also has to do with our perspectives on issues, to life, to our environment. Some people feel the reason why they have not made a head-start since graduating from the university is because the government has not provided employment opportunities while others used that as a springboard to put their talents and gifts to beneficial use. Now you can see what I mean when I said it is not what happens to us that matters but our response to the issues.

The optimist and pessimist had the same glass in their front, but their perspectives differed – the optimist saw the glass as half-full while the pessimist saw the glass as half-empty.

In conclusion, many people live in seclusion because they find it difficult to live with the hurt and pain caused to them by others. You have a choice to be masters in this game of life, you have the choice to develop the attitude of winners and dominate your circumstances and situations. It is not what happens to you that matters but how you respond to what happens.

FIRST THINGS FIRST

It is very important in life that we learn to do things in order of their importance. Always remember that life is in phases and men are in sizes. Don't choose to do tomorrow what you can do today.

In the 21st century, people are wont to follow the fad, what's trending et al, and are lost among the crowd. Don't base your decisions on what everyone is doing. We must consciously plan our lives for effective results. Always remember that Life will present you with opportunities for advancement and self-destruction; it depends on which path you choose to follow.

There may be times we might feel tempted to take our eyes off the goalpost and forget about our life's vision because of some temporary bliss. There are people who live in the make-believe world and those who truly live their dreams. We must learn to live within our means all the time – enough of the fake impressions and fake lives people tend to live these days to massage the ego of people around them.

Many people take each day as it comes thinking tomorrow will take care of itself and worries, but you need to have a concrete plan and a practical step of turning your plans into reality and deliverables measured.

Do not put the cart before the horse, first things first means make hay while the sun is shining, sow your seed in due season so harvest time will not elude you. The winner is the man who learns to make use of every opportunity positively – what if there was no second chance to have a GO at your dreams? What if there are no opportunities to right the wrongs of the past? I just imagine what life will look like. Everyone can have a brand-new start, make a difference in their life and always aim for the top.

Don't despise education and continuous life-long learning; no man is an arbiter of knowledge. We must have minds that are receptive to information and learning. First things first means you will not live with regrets in the years ahead based on the things you failed to do with the opportunities that you had.

I will conclude with some advice to men and women alike; to the men, you must make yourself too relevant to be ignored, pursue your dreams and life's vision, always remember that you need a solid vision to take on responsibilities and face life's challenges. A blind man cannot lead a family, community and nation.

To the women, following a man without a life's vision or a man who has a sleeping or dead vision is like sailing on a ship without a rudder. Always remember to do the first things first then Life will be worth living.

THE OPINIONS OF OTHERS DON'T DEFINE YOU

I remember in my first few classes in economics in Senior Secondary School, we were taught various definitions of Economics in those early times. As I came to grapple with the definitions of economics, and an understanding of what the different authors expressed in their definitions, there was no superior definition to the other, yet different opinions nevertheless existed.

The same conclusions are seemingly true about humans. The fact that different people have varied opinions about us does not in any way make one school of thought superior to another. I remember different authors in economics had their definitions, some narrow and others broad, based on the variables and factors considered before reaching their conclusions.

Despite the multi-dimensional nature of economics, authors expressed their thoughts based on available information at that point in time. Thus, whenever I read criticism of narrow definitions of economics before there was a generally acceptable definition that became the reference point in the subject matter, you could see various definitions based on the thinking pattern of authors and the school of thought they belonged to.

Given that humanity exists, there will always be difference in opinion held by various individuals about you. From my knowledge on the workings of life, you cannot begrudge anyone based on the opinions held about you. They either base their judgement on limited information or wholly ignorance. Most times people criticize because they have not been in situations and circumstances beyond their control, with little or no opportunity to salvage an already hopeless situation.

I have also been guilty of the same in times past when I based my judgements of people on what I heard and never really got to know them to establish whether those views were true or not. What I discovered eventually was that we should not live our life based on the opinion of others. We are too distinct as humans to be lost and submerged in the ocean of the crowd.

Who do people say you are? When we die, we hear contrasting views on our personality, we are viewed in diverse ways by different people. My next question is who are you? People are inclined to hold and have different opinions about you, but it does not matter what they say: what really matters is who you are.

The major problem plaguing our generation is lack of knowledge; it is not a crime to be ignorant. Ignorance becomes a crime when knowledge is not sought as a panacea to cure our seeming ignorance. Some have missed life-long opportunities based on the fact they failed to seek out additional information to compensate for changes in time.

Your life is yours to live; only you can define it.

THE RELIGION CARD

Through my interaction with people of diverse cultures and varied backgrounds, I have come to an understanding that it is not just about waving holy hands in fellowship and claiming to be born again, or by speaking in tongues that brings us into fellowship with God. A lot of people are just religious in nature and play the religion card, people who don't even know God show love to their neighbours.

What is the essence of your prayer, faith, and titles (born again, tongue talking, spirit filled) if you have no love in your heart? What is the essence of waving sanctimonious hands and doing a lap dance when you have no love in your heart? The truth that many people lack the foreknowledge of is, "Man judges the action of their fellow humans while God judges the heart", so if all you do is live in bitterness towards a fellow human being, then you still have a long way to go.

Imagine David living with us at this present age and with his many sins; he would have been sentenced to death by hanging, that's the plain truth, but since God is not man, David was a man whom God had a special interest in his case, so despite all his seeming failures and weaknesses, he was a man after the heart of the Lord, he knew what can turn God on, he knew the soft spot of the father and so many other things that made God have mercy on him.

A lot of people face judgement from people right, left and centre. If human beings were to be God (a pitiable situation), it would have been terrible, bad, mean and many other despicable adjectives will be used to describe the ascendancy of man to the throne of God.

So the world does not really care what your strengths are, whether you were a student pastor or a senior pastor, nobody is bothered whether you are prophet, apostle, doctor, evangelist whatever you call yourself, let's forget about the religion card, the world is not interested whether you are Christian, Muslim, all the world needs you to show is love and not judgement.

Always remember that God is love and God's ways are not the ways of man. The thought pattern of God is different from humans, so it is in our best interest not to harbour grievances towards any man in our heart.

Our actions, lifestyle, attitude and behavioural pattern we exhibit should give us away as true believers not by the number of services or end of the month prayer meetings we attend. People should be able to say he is worthy to be emulated based on actions and not by the religion card.

We need to despise being religious and embrace living the life of a believer that it might be seen that our lives truly reflect that which we claim to profess.

EXCELLENCE: A BARRIER BREAKER

The life-long ambition of every man should be the desire to pursue excellence; you must as a necessity despise mediocrity and being second best. Excellence distinguishes you from the crowd, irrespective of family background, inheritance or circumstance and situation. We must continually thirst and hunger to achieve excellence. The spirit of excellence sets you before kings and not mere mortals; having a spirit of excellence breaks us free from the pangs of poverty, lack, unemployment, failure in business and those who crave for excellence are always desirous of increasing their knowledge bank, not drowning in the ocean of their mistakes, and making the best of every life situation as they happen.

According to the free dictionary, Excellence **is** the state or quality of excelling or being exceptionally good; extreme merit; superiority and an action, characteristic, feature, etc., in which a person excels.

It is always easy to blame our seeming failure on external factors, the government, a well-connected uncle or cousin who failed to help us, a dormant economy and other factors that we find very easy to use as the pawn depending on our life's situation.

Ecclesiastes 9:10 says "Whatever your hand finds to do, do it with all your might, for in the grave, where you are going, there is neither working nor planning nor knowledge nor wisdom".

There are people from extremely poor backgrounds who made it to the very top due to diligence, resilience and consistent commitment to daily improvements, so your life outcomes are extremely dependent on what you settle for. You must develop a never say die attitude, conquer your fears and learn from your past mistakes to get the best from life.

You must always question yourself periodically – what am I doing presently that I can do differently to get the best results? You must challenge yourself always to move from where you are to where you want to be. Excellence is a journey and we must daily strive for it, so it is not a destination.

We have many impediments that can be a clog in the wheel of our progress, but an excellent spirit helps us not to take our eyes off the bigger picture; with an excellent spirit we can always be in line with our life's vision.

There is really no point in pursuing a dream and not showing any or enough commitment to follow it to its logical conclusion to make a success of it.

Even so, to take the lead, have an EDGE, please show enough commitment towards excellence in all you do. Pay the price so you can get the prize; never settle for less when you can be the best. Don't go to bed expecting tomorrow to take care of its worries when you can make your life and living a worthwhile experience.

As you make a commitment to make excellence your co-traveller on this journey, the result is freedom from limitations and the ability to break free from every barrier that's a seed of mediocrity.

WRITE YOUR STORY

What we say is what we get; through our words we shape our world. There is a lot of pessimism and sanguinity in our world today and it all depends on which side of the divide you choose to stay on. Many people have come back from the brink, when they were written off, and, like the heroes at Chelsea football club during the 2012 Champions League final, wrote their names among the folklore when history is recounted.

We are the pilot of our aeroplane (destiny) and whichever technique we use to navigate our lives will produce results. As a matter of urgency, to be in tip-top shape, we must consciously choose the people we listen to. There is a difference between someone telling you that difficulty abounds in a field of endeavour and believing the fact that difficulty abounds. In the past, I have written about achieving your dreams even in the face of difficulty and all those wonderful motivational tips to get to the topmost in this increasingly competitive world.

Currently, I am breaking barriers and making in-roads to places where ordinarily people feel it is impossible. Write your story, carve your niche and make your life count. Who says your association is irrelevant, you cannot have an unusual story in the company of mediocre people? Do not discount the God factor: to be the best, you must trust in God foolishly knowing that he is able to bring out an object of value from the dung, the waste, where people had said nothing good can come from thence, testimonies will abound.

The only person who is permitted to stop you from reaching for your goals is you. Champions fall and rise again. If you want to fail, please feel free to fail forward. With our humanity comes a lot of mistakes; even in the days of adversity, do not despair. Whatever you are good at, keep pressing on; do not trade away your future dreams because the present contrasts with what you have always wanted. Believe in yourself and do not give up. If you weary not in well doing, in due season you will reap if you do not faint.

You can be the best in whatever you choose to do; even though the past has been bitter, the future can be better. You can choose to step up from obscurity into the limelight, from being unknown into a world changer, to a person the world cannot do without – it all depends on us, the sacrifices we choose to make today for a better tomorrow.

Don't stop believing, keep pressing on. As I am re-writing my story through the help of the potter who moulds us and forms us into vessels of honour, I pray that you will be relevant in your sphere of influence.

DEVELOPING THE CAPACITY TO SEE

Many people today have been blinded by situations and circumstances around them; there are a lot of negative events that has impacted on our ability to see positivity amid the failings in our World today. For some individuals all they see is problem, lack, increasing prices of commodities, Joblessness, failure even when things tend to be positive they prefer to stay negative to be on the safer side. Remember that what you see is what you say and what you say is what you get. Our words shape our world and define the very essence of our lives.

The fact that the present is not what you want is not a determinant of the future – tomorrow holds lot of promises and testimonies. Always remember that the promise is yet for an appointed time, so even though it seems slow, please wait for it. The time to stop dwelling on the problems and the things that are not working is nigh; we should focus our energy on the positives, the things that are working. Instead of seeing problems it is better to focus on the solutions, no matter how long the night might be, the morning will come to herald a new beginning.

My prayer today is that the Lord will open our eyes of understanding to see that the things which we think are problems and limitations, the reasons why we give up easily and too soon are the tests we need to pass before we give our testimonies. We must develop the capacity to see that not all problems are caused by witches and wizards, lest others take advantage of our vulnerable state. Our life is a sum of the decisions and habits that characterize our daily living.

We must come to an understanding that the hurts of the past should not make us bitter but better people. We must come to an understanding that the God who gave us the vision is also able to supply the provision. We must learn to put our total trust in God even when situations and circumstances are not in alliance with our desire. Don't stop seeing that wonderful and glorious future, keep working at the fulfilment of your dreams. Always speak words of affirmation of the good things life can offer into your destiny.

Even when things don't seem right, there is a God who makes all things to work together for our good. Always remember there is no problem without a solution, there are no permanent situations and predicaments, there is nothing called impossibility. The first step is to develop the capacity to see, envision the future, then begin to say words of affirmation to yourself. All we need to do is to develop capacity to see beyond the present and give motion to our vision, matching our faith with works, and watch God make our life a testimony for all to see.

THE ARCHITECT, FASHION DESIGNER, POTTER AND THE DESIGN

A designer whether an architect who is responsible for the final design of a building or a fashion designer who is responsible for designing various attires can also be likened to the Bible verse of the potter and the clay. The designer can do as he/ she pleases with the object at hand and can make one design very glamorous while another design not as good. Jumping off from this dimension of the architect and the construct, to our roles as individual designers, in truth, the potter has a bigger role to play in our lives in moulding us as he deems fit, either as unto honour or dishonour. But we also have a role to play in whatever becomes of our vessel – either we become honourable or dishonourable vessels can be attributed to our very own life, the decisions we make, the activities that fill up our daily routine, the kind of investments we make into our lives will determine the shape of what the final construct will look like. Many people heap together the mistakes of their lives and form a monster called destiny, so the final shape of our construct is what we call destiny, it is a sum of our life's decisions, the habits, the people who inhabit our close circles, our mentors and those I will call the influencer group in our lives and the important things that make up our very life.

You can only get as much output as the level of your investments, so if you want a vessel fitted unto honour, you will need to invest a lot of effort, time and resources to get the desired result. We need to begin to understand that even though many people want to hand over total responsibility of their lives to the potter in moulding them to become vessels unto honour, we need to play our part by making the work of the potter easier; an architect is responsible for design, planning and supervision of structures, so as individual designers you can rock the boat of your design so early if you fail to plan; living everyday as it comes will only churn out a shapeless design. Therefore, if you want a brilliant design, the kind that will be the cynosure of all eyes as we see when models' catwalk on runways in different fashion shows in the world draped in different apparels showcasing the level of investments each designer has put into their product. Check the activities that occupy our day, how we spend our time, our values, our aspirations, and the other visible items that are predominant in our lives' fixtures' list.

Drawing inspiration from the architect and the fashion designer, they don't just sit back without any input yet expecting to get results. In essence, "Don't ask God to order your steps, if you are not willing to move your feet". Remember that you are the Chief Responsibility Officer of your life, take charge so your life can be a testimony and come out as a brilliant design.

THE ANALOGY OF THE SPRINTER

On your tracks, get set, the gun booms and everyone begins to make a dash for the finish line. The configuration of life brings differing results on desired pace towards the finish line. Assuredly, I say unto you, the race is not to the swift, so whoever said the fastest runner at the start always wins the race is giving us a make believe or at best a misconception of the true facts. Our destiny in life is different, life comes with a lot of twists and turns, a lot of beautiful and awry moments, good seasons may go bad, but always remember that our finishing line is at best very different.

Usain Bolt will always sprint towards the finish line in a One hundred and Two Hundred Metres dash but anytime he chooses to compete at the eight hundred metres, one thousand five hundred metres and Ten thousand metres, he has to develop a new strategy, a new approach altogether; he has to start working on techniques for the long distances, he has to forget about being the fastest runner at the starting blocks. He will begin to focus his energy on gathering momentum when it matters, conserving the energy for the last lap of the race.

The analogy of the sprinter is to let someone out there know that we all have different finishing line and races to compete at, hence when you see someone in a sprint, a dash towards the finishing line, there is no need for comparisons – some are in it for the short haul while some others are in life's races for the long haul. Always remember that being at the right place at the right time, gunning for opportunities, taking our chances and being decisive in the choices we make are all valuable indices in our life's outcomes.

The analogy of the sprinter considers the place of preparation, for we know that athletes train hard year in year out, work hard in the gym to stay in shape and maintain their fitness levels so also it applies to us. Life is not a casino, it does not function on guesswork nor does it favour perpetual dreamers. Do not despise the place of preparation – you want a favourable life outcome, be prepared. Success will only come when opportunities meet preparation. You desire the prize, pay the price.

Today and tomorrow are different in all ramifications, though the promise might seem slow, delay does not equate to denial in anyway. Don't forget the long-haul sprinters suffer from fatigue, some suffer injuries along the way while others are draped in sweat before they cross the finish line. In all circumstances, keep your eyes on the end goal and final prize. Life is in phases; men are in sizes with different races and allotted space. Remember we are in this race called life for the long haul; there is no stopping you if you are prepared to make use of the opportunities that are available to us.

FINISHING STRONG: A SEQUEL TO THE ANALOGY OF THE SPRINTER

Life is 10% what you make it and 90% how you take it
– Irving Berlin

You can start whichever way, but the most important thing is that we are in life's races to stand out and be outstanding. We tend to be calculative when we feel we are not gathering enough paces from the starting blocks of life but like I pointed out in the analogy of the sprinter, it is not about your start but how well you finish. Life does not reward mediocrity and people I will call the also-ran. There is no delight in coming to the world and leaving without engraving your footprints on the sands of time.

Many people have resigned themselves to accept whatever circumstances and situations life thrust at them as destiny, but we all have the capacity to change our lives. It starts with the right belief system and a can-do attitude. When you are in life's races for the long haul, you will come to an understanding of Ecclesiastes 9:11 NLT: "I have observed something else under the sun. The fastest runner doesn't always win the race, and the strongest warrior doesn't always win the battle. The wise sometimes go hungry, and the skilful are not necessarily wealthy. And those who are educated don't always lead successful lives. It is all decided by chance, by being in the right place at the right time".

Finishing strong is not about being the swiftest in the race, it does not have any correlation with our background, it has no relationship with the kind of spoon we were fed with at birth, whether golden, silver, wooden, plastic or muddy. Finishing strong has a lot do with our mental capacity, our ability to stand when the easiest thing to do is join the bandwagon of those who find an object of blame for their woes and gleefully take the chance to start a pity party.

To finish well, we must develop inner strength to trudge on. Nobody has said life was indeed a bed of roses. Before athletes participate in tournaments, whether minor or major, they invest a lot of resources to get to the levels of champions. Success only comes to those who are prepared to get it, if we want to finish strong, we must know the secret of positioning. Whenever I watch Roger Federer and Rafael Nadal slug it out at major championships, I see that their results have a correlation with their positioning on the court. Specifically, we must be conscious of our positioning in life, we must be overtly mindful of the places we are par time, because Ecclesiastes talks about being at the right place at the time. Positioning has to do with the opportunities that we make use of in life, the chances that we take, the choices we make, and our thought process, which are all important prerequisites that determine the course of our life.

You might have had a slow start, but keep your focus on the finish line, it is all about finishing strong.

UNRAVEL YOUR HIDDEN GEMS

There is something peculiar to every individual, a treasure, which I will refer to as hidden gems that the world needs to see. We cannot afford to come to the world and live carelessly. Our life is a gift that has been committed unto our hands, hence we must endeavour to live a life of purpose. Our individuality infers that we are distinct and there is a unique ability that we have.

The world needs to see us unravel and spring forth; there is so much in you to offer to the world. Be bold to face your fears and courageous to conquer new grounds. We all have extraordinary talent and gifts. It is time for you to write that song, record that album, write that book, register for that short course, start that business, learn a new sport, learn a new language, map out that vision and travel to a new country. You can't afford to live a mediocre life when you are a king set for the palace. All you need to do is open your inner mind to the endless possibilities that will spring up when you unravel your hidden gems.

A quick story to spur you on, after writing my first book 'Dead Lion's Don't Roar' which touched so many lives, I picked up another dimension which was accepting spoken word events invitations and using words as a medium of impacting a greater number of people. Thus, the dimension enacted was that the first hidden gem was unravelled, and this led to the discovery of another talent which hitherto would have been dormant if I was happy to just be a passenger; an onlooker in this journey of life.

A lot of great ideas, songs, inventions and creative minds have departed the world with all their ideas. They did not Unravel that treasure and share with the World before they closed the curtains on this chapter of their lives.

For some others, the hidden gems have been Unravelled; however, they choose to do nothing with their gift and talents. Let me remind you that the world needs to hear your roar, don't just be part of the statistics, make your life count and coming to the world a worthwhile adventure. You must know your life's purpose as abuse is inevitable when purpose is unknown. It is time to come out of obscurity and become celebrated in your endeavours.

Let's tell ourselves and young ones (the generation next) that we can be master over many things. You just don't have to be master of one. You can be brilliant at one thing but there is no harm in being exceptional and having mastery over many things. So, having an illustrious career does not harm your chances of harnessing your gifts and talent. You can write, sing, dance, paint and be good at sports – that is truly fantastic. But there are other remarkable things you can also do and be exceptional at. Do not place a limit or lid on yourself, there should be no ceiling of limitations.

The world awaits your legacy; there is a gift in you which generations to come will forever be grateful that you unravelled. Untie that hidden gem; loosen up as it is time to flourish. Your story will be heard all over the world as you choose to unravel your hidden gems. The world is your oyster, go forth and conquer.

EDUCATION MAKES THE DIFFERENCE

This essay is to encourage the career minded, the people who are desirous of life-long learning and continuous personal development. Some people have great arguments while Education does not seem to hold water, that's good for them. However, if you are on the path of education. You must always stay educated, if your Curriculum Vitae as it stands today looks the same as it was five years ago then that's a cause for concern. We must constantly seek to improve ourselves, go on that short course, write that professional exams you have always desired. If you think Education is expensive, try ignorance. - Unknown. The best people in our Organisations are those who are constantly learning, always seeking ways to improve processes.

Education means we need to evolve. Insanity is doing the same thing repeatedly and expecting different results. It could either be in your career, professional life or Organisation. Look at the great companies/Organisations of yesterday that have entered the history books and now renowned as a previously great Organisation with enormous potential to conquer its sector however they are now part of our business lexicon to remind us of their once historic feat. Evolve means you must change with the times, it means you must understand that every year and decade come with it's new in-thing and you must make yourself and Organisation relevant to partake of the benefit of change. Evolve means we must be willing to learn current ideas to improve our art, brand, and Organisation. Evolve means we are flexible and open to change. Evolve, Change and be flexible, it could be your key to a whole new World of great attainments.

Also, education does not need to be all about going to school but it's about keeping yourself abreast of developments and happenings in your sphere of influence. Books are written to keep us informed to avoid being deformed, so educating yourself might be reading books, watching the news on television and investing in your knowledge bank account. An old Chinese proverb says, and I Quote, the best time to plant a tree was 20 years ago, the second best time is now.

In Nigeria, Peak as a brand is synonymous with Quality and renowned for its Leadership through the years. Using the Peak example as a case study for the importance of education and self-development; many people either in their Career or Leadership when they get to the top relax with a mindset that they have arrived. They stop doing the things that took them to the top of their industry and profession. The passion and hunger that took them to the top is lost and they fail to evolve and innovate. Peak has always been at the top of the Dairy sector and has remained the market leader in most of the segments they trade in. The Peak Story was truly inspiring for me and I have always been challenged by this to embrace continuous learning and improvement. My final admonishment, in whatever you do please reach for your Peak. Don't settle for less. Embrace self-development and continuous learning. I would close with this; Education truly makes a difference.

THE ANALOGY OF POWER AND TIME

We all have the power to move mountains, whether dead or hibernating power; we must make a conscious effort to ensure we activate that power within. It is hard to tell how far we can go in life when we break the barriers of ignorance. Investment in knowledge and information gives us the wherewithal to confront our personal demons. We only pay for our ignorance in life, the moment we have access to adequate information, we become free to explore our world.

When a person can decree a thing and whatever they decree is established, they move from the realm of babies feeding on milk and can start cracking the bones, which is the realm of fully grown adults. My people perish for lack of knowledge; what we spend the most part of our life craving for is within our grasp, every one of us has within us enormous potential and abilities to rule our world.

There is nothing called impossibility, we only call it impossible because we have not been able to overcome that difficulty. The ingenuity we wish to exhibit is either inborn or can be acquired through investment in information. In recent decades, people have broken the limitations posed by differences in race, age, gender and equality is the norm in most parts of the world. Either black or white, what the world pays you for is your expertise, the added values you can bring to organisations. What this says is, there is no time to waste, no time to start moaning about how unfair the world has been, when you waste the days, your waste your life. There is no joy in counting the days if we don't make the days count – our time is our life, we ought to use it wisely. There is no way to regain lost time; everyone gets this resource in equal proportion.

When the chance to make choices comes your way, do not despise the days of little beginnings; there are opportunities that do not seem like the big deal, but greatness is always hidden in small and unfamiliar packages. Therefore, we must have an inner eye to spot the unfamiliar packages, the gold wrapped around in dirt and mud; you want to be great, to be at the pinnacle of your chosen field, so don't be afraid to start small. To succeed, there must be a desire, a will and putting all resources towards the achievement of our plan.

In this season, we must be conscious about our thought process – success only comes to those who are prepared for it. Our opportunities must not be lost due to our lack of preparation. Remember, we have just got one life to live. We must make it count.

IF YOU ARE A STAR

A star has been conditioned to give light and illuminate darkness. Even in the darkest of nights when the STAR shows up, darkness has no choice but to give way. It does not matter how your life has been conditioned up till this moment, the STAR in you will always make a way for you. A STAR is not limited or hindered by factors that limit ordinary humans. The STAR in you will place you before kings and not mere mortals. The candlestick has the capacity to provide light and darkness literally bolts away; it might take time before the STAR in you comes out but if you are a STAR, your light will shine forth. You will be too blessed to be hidden, too prosperous to be forgotten.

A STAR is a threat to the kingdom of darkness, because STARS illuminate so much the evil that darkness represents is quickly forgotten. Do not worry or be distraught if your STAR has not shined up till this moment, it might seem slow in coming but STARS represent a reprieve in this dark and evil world. A STAR is conditioned to lighten irrespective of country of nationality, skin colour or background, it is not a function of who you know but the capacity that you carry within.

Are you content with being a local or community champion when you have been conditioned for World domination? A STAR is always the centre of attraction because all things begin to fall in pleasant places. The number of years you might have lived in oblivion becomes inconsequential when your STAR begins to shine. You need to understand that you are more than the present;

a beautiful future lies ahead, you are not a slave but a STAR. As a STAR, you do not have to worry about protocol and standing order; the same way the protocol of darkness is broken when the STAR shows up, that's the same way protocol and standing order will bow for you.

If you are a STAR, the situation and circumstances that limits ordinary people will not be permitted to limit you. The problems that happened to others that made them give up too soon will be your own stepping stone to the ladder of success. Let us repeat these words of affirmation together, I am a STAR and I represent illumination, darkness and all that it represents is not permitted in my life. My life will be an attraction for all to see, I am a success and not a failure. Irrespective of my background, I begin to enjoy WORLD DOMINATION. My light will shine so bright that darkness will not be able to comprehend, and I begin to prosper in all that I lay my hands upon.

DELAY DOES NOT MEAN DENIAL

There is no harm in waiting for the promise; the fact that we have the assurance for wonderful things in life and they are not forthcoming does not mean they will never come. What about being an eternal optimist, developing a possibility mind-set and believing that nothing shall be impossible to them that believe.

Many times in life people give up too soon, so they abort the promise before its delivery. Like I tell my protégés and friends, I don't mind waiting for the promise, even though it might seem slow, I believe that it will surely come to pass. A lot of people have been "missing in action" in life. Susan Boyle, a British singer who came to international public attention when she appeared as a contestant on the TV programme Britain's Got Talent on 11 April 2009, was missing in action for a whole forty-seven years, she was unknown until (takes a deep sigh) she sang "I dreamed a dream". She rose to international fame and in Britain Boyle's debut album was recognised as the fastest selling UK debut album of all time selling 411,820 copies, beating the previous fastest selling debut of all time, Spirit by Leona Lewis. I Dreamed a Dream also outsold the rest of the top 5 albums combined in its first week. In the U.S., the album sold 701,000 copies in its first week, the best opening week for a debut artist in over a decade. In Italy, it was the first album of the month in the Italian No. 1 Account by a non-Italian artist ever. In only a week, it sold more than 2 million copies worldwide, becoming the fastest selling global female debut album.

For some people, they cannot afford to be missing in action for five years never mind forty-seven years. The fact that the promise seems so slow does not mean it isn't going to happen. You must believe in yourself, have a good self-esteem and keep saying positive words of affirmation to your future.

A lot of people experience delay in life, delay in getting married, delay in getting the fruit of the womb, delaying in experiencing academic success, but my advice is that no matter the problem you might be facing, don't give up. The truth I need to bring to your knowledge is, when it's your time for success, there is no stopping you. The sky is wide enough for all birds to fly in, so the fact that Davido is reigning in the entertainment industry in Nigeria does not stop Whizkid from shining.

We must also be careful of those we allow to speak to us; some people are champions in sowing negativity into situations. The fact that it's difficult for Ade, Alan and Alex does not mean you will find it difficult in life. Do not be limited by dogma, tradition or live your life based on public opinion.

I have tasted the goodness of our God, he has done remarkable things in time past, so I always give praises for all he has done in the past, the grace to function in the present and the beautiful future ahead. Through your time of waiting, I pray that the Lord will give you the strength to keep forging ahead.

It's not over until you win.

THERE IS TREASURE IN THE TRASH

Many a time in life when we find ourselves in dire situations and circumstances, we are wont to think that condition and incident has the final say over our lives. Darkness gives way when the illumination of light takes over; there is no permanent condition in life. The fact that something has not been done does not mean it's impossible. Even in the trash, the mire, the dung, treasure abounds. Your passion is your permission. What are you saying concerning that situation in your life? Are you hopeful of a better outcome or you have given up too soon?

In a bid to get an object of value from the ground, the digger goes to great length, covered up in mud and earth to achieve the aim; it will suffice to say that treasure abounds in the trash. The scenario that fits the description of deriving an object of value from trash can be explained succinctly by the production process in developed countries where various products are manufactured using recycled products. Recycled products are wastes, trash, and our dustbins that are now being used to manufacture valuable products which are sold for cash. Some products are manufactured from 100% recycled items while some others are manufactured with less. So, whoever thinks there can be no treasure in the trash should have a re-think.

Greatness is hidden in small packages. Even when all our desires are yet to come to reality, we must continue to dig deep, and build our inner strength so we can keep standing in the days of adversity. Even when Nathanael thought nothing good could come out of Nazareth, Jesus Christ the messiah was a Nazarene. And whenever people let you feel that you are worthless, always remember that one man's trash is another man's treasure; you carry a lot of value on your inside.

To be in the trash is not the problem, being stuck in the trash is the ultimate problem. We must pray that the Lord will open our inner eyes, that even when we are in the trash that our eyes of understanding will be enlightened that we might spot the treasure (opportunities) always. To move from the place of trash to a state of treasure, we must have a vision, goals and aspiration. To move from the place of wishful thinking to getting results, we must as a necessity not live each day as it comes but we must take responsibility for our lives. We must learn to be at the right place at the right time, and always make use of our opportunities.

Whenever we find ourselves in murky waters, we can decide to pick ourselves up and discover the treasure that abounds therein.

WONDERFULLY FLAWED

Great people with immense strength of character, individuals who lived with a purpose in their own season, but they were flawed, herein our flesh lays our weakness. There are no perfect people; our humanity makes us imperfect beings. Jacob was a cheater, Peter had a temper, David had an affair, Noah got drunk, Jonah ran away from God, Paul was a murderer, Gideon was insecure, Miriam was a gossiper, Martha was a worrier, Thomas was a doubter, Sarah was impatient, Elijah was depressed, Moses stuttered and Zacchaeus was short.

This essay is to challenge anyone who has made mistakes in the past and people believe your past is what defines your future. The truth is, no matter how flawed the past might have been, the future holds lots of promise. Stop trying to be who you are not, we only have one life to live so we have the chance to turn things around; be yourself and remember man's judgement is not God's judgement, man judges your action while God judges the heart. In Mark 8:27-29 (NIV) Jesus and his disciples went on to the villages around Caesarea Philippi. On the way he asked them, "Who do people say I am?" They replied, "Some say John the Baptist; others say Elijah; and still others, one of the prophets." "But what about you?" he asked. "Who do you say I am?" Peter answered, "You are the Christ."

Jesus asked the disciples who men said he was because he had an understanding that man's opinion about us will always differ. Imagine these great people I talked about in the first paragraph, despite their weaknesses and frailties, God found them worthy to be used for his glory, so I live each day knowing that I am flawed, I have made mistakes, made wrong choices and in all these, I am wonderful, I am blessed and God's goodness and mercies abide with me everywhere I go.

No time for pity parties, there is nothing new under the sun, you might have failed in the past, but the truth is you will not be the first or last to fail so the best bet is to pick yourself up and have another shot at success. Don't let anyone tell you the lie from the pit of hell that something good cannot come out of your bosoms. We are beautiful but imperfect people. Some people live under the illusion that there are perfect people out there, people who are above board but as long as we live everyday with breath in our nostrils we are just mere mortals; only God is perfect, above mistakes and without sin.

Remember that he who Christ has set free is free indeed; don't live your life in captivity by your flaws. God does not call the QUALIFIED, he qualifies the CALLED.

BELIEVE

Nothing shall be impossible to those who believe. Before you have your mind focused on being a success in any of your endeavours, you must believe that you have the capacity to excel in whatever you lay your hands to do. We live in a world of stiff competition for places at the top; so many people have given up too soon. The fact that a feat is not easy to achieve does not mean it is impossible. When situation and circumstance around us seems hopeless, we must ignite the fire of belief in ourselves. Don't stop speaking life into that situation, keep saying it; through our words we shape our WORLD. There are times we have goals and aspirations but events around us can quell our desire for success; it does not matter what people around you see. You must as a priority give motion to your vision.

Even in times of dire straits, I never stopped believing in myself and the ability to pull through tricky situations. Remember it is not what happens to you that matters but how you respond to what happens to you. Life is in phases and men are in sizes, so whatever season you are in, I say REJOICE for your best is yet to come.

Irrespective of skin colour, nationality and background, standing order and protocol has the capacity to stand at attention for you. You must believe in yourself, when the good comes, embrace it, when the bad season comes do not be overwhelmed; always remember that there is a time and season for everything in life. Remember that even though we live in a physical world, matters of importance, mouth-watering deals and all that matters in our life is settled in the spiritual realm. We must be in control of our spiritual space, as humans we are wont to have moments of pessimism and doubt, times when we are weighed down by circumstances around us, but I admonish us that we should not waver. Life is fleeting, there are no permanent situations, everything that happens is but for a moment.

Always remember that the sky is wide enough to accommodate everyone, do not be envious when people around you succeed; to succeed in life we must celebrate the success of those who succeed. Always speak words of affirmation to yourself, be thankful for the present, and believe in your capacity to make things happen; even in the dark nights, you must see the silver lining up in the sky.

We must be optimistic and dwell on the good side of life, we are a product of our thought processes. If you think and believe it is possible then it is. Remember no one can stop you from achieving all your goals in life except YOU.

Don't stop believing.

PART 5

IT IS BY THE LORD'S MERCIES

Some people think Life's success is guaranteed by the national colour of the passport they possess, so they devise means to obtain either a red, blue or whatever passport colour they feel can give them more chances of being a success at all cost. My dear friend, it is not about your passport of nationality, the accent or phonetics that is evident in your pronunciations, neither is it a function of the Godfathers who are available at your beck and call.

The secret to life's success can be found in Romans 9:15-16, (God's Word Translation) For example, God said to Moses, "I will be kind to anyone I want to. I will be merciful to anyone I want to." Therefore, God's choice does not depend on a person's desire or effort, but on God's mercy. There are times we feel we have that charm and aura that makes us distinct amongst our peers and whatever we touch turns to GOLD, but the truth is we are capable of achieving our dreams, goals and aspirations in life not because we possess any unique ability or because we are lucky but because we are privileged to function under the mercies of the Lord.

When you try to carry out tasks based on your own ability, what you get is results based on your human effort; but when you come to an understanding that you are still standing by God's mercies, then you begin to operate on a different type of frequency altogether. When you sleep at night and you are awake in the morning, you need to understand that you are alive because God's mercies kept you; you embark on a short or long-haul journey and you arrive at your destination safely, always remember that it is by the Lord's mercies. Many people started that same journey but did not make it to their destination alive.

When you are studying towards a degree course, and you finish on time and finish well, you must know that it is by the Lord's mercies that you are able to finish at the right time and finish well. Not everyone who starts a project is privileged to complete it, so when you start a building or work-related project and you complete it, then it is not just mere luck but the Lord's mercies.

The moment we start living under the illusion that we possess a lucky charm, or we have good luck flowing in our direction, from that time failure beckons. In recent times, I have been reminded of how lucky I am, but I keep reminding people it is by the Lord's mercies – if God had not conspired to favour me then my best efforts would have turned to zero. There is a limit to how far we can go in life when we operate under our intelligence or ability but when you function under the mercies of the Lord, then you have the capacity to soar and be outstanding.

DEVELOPING INNER STRENGTH AND CHARACTER

In this season, when people are in the chase for loads of magic and shortcuts to get to the finish line, we need people of strong character, people who are not afraid to have their face mired in dust and earth and remain standing. People are shaken in the days of adversity; however, anyone can face adversity, but we need inner capacity to keep standing.

It is easy to criticize those who failed in times past or those who fall from a position of grace to grass. Even the strongest humans possess a form of weakness, a buffet to remind them of their humanity. To everyone who has experienced any form of delay in life, always remember that delay is not denial. The days of adversity are times when you need to re-examine your relationship with God; anyone can fail and experience bad situations, but we need to be resilient and have an understanding that tough times don't last but tough people do.

Inner strength and character helps you to stay strong even when situation and circumstances seem hopeless. No condition is permanent in life – the same way the dark night gives way for the dawn of a new day, so does the times and season of man change. Therefore, do not be dismayed if the promise is not happening yet.

In the season when the road seems to be rough, keep forging ahead, there is no stopping you. Keep hope alive and be optimistic because the future holds lots of promise. You don't have to give up on God because he has not given up on us. Everyone has their own season, their season to shine, and be in the spotlight. We must develop inner strength to understand the concept of waiting for our time, no matter how long it might take: believe, believe and believe.

Bad situations and circumstances is not our destiny, so keep the dream alive and don't let it die. Our life is a sum of the choices we made in the past, so there is no point forming a monster called destiny. Sometimes we experience problems and tricky situations in the journey of life; nobody promised us that our lives will be smooth sailing from birth to death but our ability to stand strong in the days of adversity will have a bearing on our life's outcome.

My concept of inner strength of character means even when I am waiting on God for a promise and it is not happening yet, I give thanks because I have an understanding that even though it tarries, whatever he has promised me will come to pass at the appointed time. Even in the storms I see God, because he can make a way, so for every test I see an opportunity for a testimony.

AWESOME GOD

There is a limit to how far we can go in life based on our human ability; truly there is a maximum capacity we can achieve on our own strength. Those who understand the dimension of the world we live in know that there is a deeper realm where the seal of approval either for good or bad is put on our activities on earth. Through our words we shape our world, no such thing as mere coincidences, the sum of our life, the choices we made, mistakes and obstacles are all part of the experience in life that gives us the mental alertness to reach out for our dreams.

There is no stopping you; we can always be the best, get to the top rung of the ladder irrespective of our race, colour and background. If the outcome of our lives or achievements is to be determined by flesh (Man), it would have been cumbersome and handled in a lopsided manner because man's judgement is flawed but there is a God who does not call the qualified but qualifies the called.

Our humanity does not make us immune from the storms, but we have a father who shelters us from the storm. We are weak and frail, but we have a God who is our strength in weakness. My faith and absolute dependence on God has given me wings to soar like the eagles because I have an understanding that God's goodness is not shared based on eloquence and finesse but life's blessings is a function of God's mercy. Paul might plant, and Apollo might get a pipe to water the crops directly from the

Atlantic Ocean, but if God does not give the increase, it becomes an exercise in futility.

In all things, always remember that you cannot be limited by the situation and circumstances that limits other people; you are a success and have the capability to achieve your dreams. Who has decreed a thing when the Lord has not said it; you can do all things and live a remarkable life provided that our total trust and dependence is on God.

There is a God who can dismantle the wisdom of man and turn to foolishness the permutations and calculations that have been made about us. My God thrives on impossibility, where man has said there is no way my God will cause there to be a turnaround for us in this season. In life, always remember that it is not about who got there first, or the most intelligent and educated, but it is a function of God's grace and mercy. It is not about the beginning but the ending – even as we give God the wheel of our lives, I pray that his mercies will be enduring in our lives.

WORDS FOR THE WISE

We live in a world filled with loads of PHD (pull him/her down) holders, a world where we preach love but have no love in our hearts. It is stale news how wicked and deep the heart of man is; Man's inhuman act to man transcends generations. The cruelty and all the pitfalls experienced in life are not beyond the knowledge of God. Weeping may endure for the night, but Joy comes in the morning.

As humans we are weak and frail in nature, we are prone to make mistakes because of our imperfect nature but we have a father who is our sufficiency even in weakness. We must learn to fail forward. There is no crime in failing and falling but there is a crime if we take that failure as the outcome of our lives. Whatever experiences and mistakes of the past are not a determinant of the future. There is no stopping you. The only person who can stop you from reaching for your dreams is you.

As humans, we have the capacity to be the best in whatever we set out to do, if we dare to believe in our dreams. We must be conscious of our thought processes – what do you think about? We must have a mind-set and beliefs system that embraces positivity, even in dire straits when it seems there will be no solution to a knotty issue; we must as a necessity choose to be eternal optimists. We must also be conscious of our association in our quest to get to the top. You must not be equally yoked with people who have their minds clouded with a negative beliefs system.

There is a group of people that I call "lamentation", all they see is the negatives, how A and B and C failed to accomplish a set goal hence they think we cannot also make it. We must be mindful of the kind of people we allow to sow words into our lives. The fact that Mr A built his first house in thirty years does not mean you will build your first house in that period.

Above all, trust in the Lord and the power of his might. There is little we can accomplish based on our human understanding, we must live our lives not on our arithmetic and calculations but with an understanding that there is a God who knows our times and season. Man's time is not God's time, and man's speed is not God's speed. Praise and thanksgiving is the key to unlocking supernatural blessings, so when we are tempted to murmur and complain about what we do not have, we should step into the garment of praise and praise the God who is able to meet all our needs.

GOD CAN RE-WRITE YOUR STORY

A lot of people have been brought back from the brink, the abyss, the dung and waste land but now have glorious testimonies. The forgotten individuals of yesterday have now become people the world cannot do without. Those the world labelled barren and unfruitful have experienced the joy of motherhood; those that were labelled failures have gone on to succeed in their endeavours. All these wonders have only been able to occur because of the Holy One of Israel who has the capacity to rewrite our story.

Who does the World (people) say you are, then I ask again, who does God say you are? Most times we choose to believe based on our current circumstances, but we must consistently connect with what the word of God says about our situation. Thus, when it seems as if there are seeming difficulties on our way, we must hand over that situation to the potter. God has the capacity to lift us up after a fall – who has told you that you cannot succeed when the Lord has not said so?

Everything in life happens for a reason. The reason why we face the tests is to share our testimonies, though sorrow comes in the night; but our Joy comes with the dawn of the morning. Have you heard stories that made you cry, and help you keep hope alive? I have gone to a stage in my life where I trust in the Lord absolutely and foolishly, it's so unreal but true. The more I give the wheel to God, the more I enter a dimension of grace that no human factor could have helped me to achieve.

Don't give in to negativity and pessimism. When people talk about the lack in the world, believe that your best is yet to come. See the abundance; see the light at the end of the dark tunnel. There is no impossibility to those who believe, and I must say this, you must trust in the Lord with all your heart to get the best from God. There is a limit to how far we can go in life when we try and resolve the issues of our life based on our own imagination but when we hand over our life to the potter, he revels in making us a delight.

I challenge people who have had amazing and strange stories, people who have given up too soon on God, those who tend to see the world as an unfair and cruel place to live in; it is not over until you win. Keep hope alive, always remember that as far as we are alive and have breath in us then there is no stopping you.

FAILURE AS A SPRINGBOARD TO SUCCESS

Most people think failure should not be permissible in our everyday living; we are wired not to learn from our mistakes. Many a time people prefer to learn from other people's mistakes but the truth about life is that there are times we need to learn from our very own imperfections. The disappointments and the nights we sit, and cry remind us of our humanity and make us realise we are prone to errors but more candidly using it as a springboard to ultimate success.

I have failed so many times, but my failures are the drivers of my success. In all my failures, I have failed forward. No pity parties, no time for attention seeking, in it all I have picked myself up ready to give success another shot. Your failures should not make you give up on life; they must always drive you to the point of success. There are times we feel like throwing in the towel and we believe that life is unfair, but when adversity comes knocking on your doorstep, you must look that challenge in the face and stand your ground.

No matter the dimension the raging storms might be, put your trust in the Lord, there is nothing he cannot do. He is capable of bringing back to life everything that has been pronounced dead in our lives. The world might have called you barren but who do you say you are? Speak that situation and circumstances back to life; the power to make your life a success is in your hands. Tough times never last but tough people do.

Another secret to be a success, is to see the end from the beginning. Do not see the darkness in the tunnel but the light at the end of the tunnel. Apostle Paul had a thorn in his flesh that reminded him of his humanity, he prayed to God to take it out, but God told him the pain comes with the grace. Do not despair if it seems like you are just hanging on and your mates seems to have progressed far ahead of you – remember the difference between the optimist and the pessimist is how they see things. The optimist saw the same glass of water as half full while the pessimist saw the same glass as half empty.

No one has said the road to success will be an easy one, but it will be worth it; keep forging ahead. Remember, success is who you are, and no man has the capacity to truncate your destiny. In the failures, please fail forward; our failures will be the springboard to our life's success.

YOU CAN CHANGE THE STATUS QUO

Everybody wants to change the World, but nobody wants to change themselves
– Anonymous

There are a lot of predominant norm that we tend to see as the status quo – we can't really change them, so we accept these factors as part and parcel of our lives. So many people have short-changed themselves and accept whatever life throws at them and form a monster called My Destiny or My Fate. It is not your destiny to be a failure, neither is it your destiny to be a second-class citizen.

There are people who have broken free from the barriers in society; barriers abound in every modern society. In truth, the majority are in the base, and limitations abound in every society of the world; competition for places in the top echelons of society remains stiff. But you can re-write your story – nothing happens to us by chance.

Who do people say you are? Who do you say you are? The fact that people have accepted mediocrity as a way of life does not mean that being a mediocre is the way to go. What is the effective way to change the status quo? You must consistently challenge yourself to be the best in whatever you lay your hands to do. The fact that most people have embraced mediocrity and are always singing the "whatever will be, will be" anthem does not mean you can't make a change from the prevailing status.

More often, people tend to follow the crowd. The fact that everyone around does not seem to break through does not mean you cannot have a head start over your contemporaries. You must consistently challenge yourself to be the best. Carve a niche for yourself in life; you must never trade the spirit of excellence for mediocrity, not now or ever. What can you do differently to get results? Who has said you can't make it or break through the limitations in the society?

Some people have tried applying for jobs and have given up hope; some others have stopped trying completely and accepted whatever their situation is as permanent. I bring the message of hope to you today, that you can break free from the status quo. You must not forget the place of education, education not as in the four walls of an institution but learning as life is a school; to stay relevant in this school, you must not despise a break from the norm to be a better person.

Someone is saying I think I am a failure; anyone can fail and most of the success stories we see around today have failed in times past, but they have broken themselves free from the limitations that failure can pose. The next time you fail, fail forward as Success is who you are; concentrate more on the learning points from failing and see as you experience a total turnaround in life.

WHAT IS RIGHT OR WRONG?

We live in a very complicated world that many people still find it difficult to understand and comprehend how it works. You hear of good things happening to bad people and negativity and dreadful things happening to good people. We see people trying to be the judge of other people's actions and they feel they are the standard bearers and they represent holiness here on Earth, but I have come with a message today that you alone can define what is right and wrong to you.

Don't live your life based on the definition of what is wrong or right in the sight of humans. Remember man will judge you by your actions but the Judge of all mankind will look at your heart. Remember that we are all mortals and no man is infallible; the flesh makes us weak even when we feel exalted and beyond temptation.

A lot of people go into a rage when they see a pastor who has passed judgment on, say, for example, adulterers from the pulpit and makes certain people in church feel like condemned sinners and then they discover upon his death that he had a secret wife or love children from different women and they begin to lose hope in the set-up of the church or the religious settings involved.

If people were judged based on their actions as many people think and are wont to believe, then there won't be any opportunity for a second chance.

The theme behind this essay is that man will judge you by your actions and crucify you based on your lifestyle, but God will pass his judgment based on your heart. Despite the many sins of David, taking another man's wife and sending the husband to the battle front to be killed, he still found favour with the Lord. Jacob got away with his brother's birthright and the Bible recorded that God loved Jacob and he hated Esau.

I encourage everyone reading this, that you must not live your life to impress anyone. The very thing that defines our human existence is that it is the person who wears the shoe that knows where it hurts. So that person you are trying to emulate might have a thorn in his flesh that constantly reminds him of his humanity.

You alone can define the standard by which you will live your life, you hold the aces and you can use all your lifelines favourably to your advantage. It is good to have mentors and role models and people you aspire to be like, but always remember they are mere mortals like you and their breath is in their nostrils.

Make your choices as the spirit leads you to act and remember that the one who cannot create you is not permitted to Judge you.

TRUTH OF LIFE: YOUR JOURNEY IS NOT MY JOURNEY

From my understanding of the dynamics of how life works, every human has a distinctive calling; we are unique in our own separate ways. There is a place where only you can fit in and my prayer today is that we will have the wisdom to discover our place in life. When we discover our place, we cease from struggle and all the limiting factors that are stopping others from excelling become a stepping stone for us.

Any time people who have an opinionated angle in their thinking pass judgement on how best you should live your life, I burst into a derisory fit of laughter. My inner voice comes out with hey buddy, you must understand that your life is different from theirs. If you weary not in well doing, in due season you will reap if you do not faint. Friends, I admonish you that you should not let the opinion of others determine your decisions in life and drown out your own inner voice. Even twins with all the bonding in the womb come out to become different people, moving on to different things in life.

In the past few months, the core of my message has been on timing; we all have our time to blossom, our time to shine, so I would like us to come to an understanding that the life we have is not a competition with other people. I spent the core part of my years under the tutelage of a great mentor who taught me to cut my cloth according to my size. The fact that Mr A is driving a Range Rover does not mean you should blow your savings on a Range Rover just for people to know you have arrived. Always remember that abuse is inevitable until the purpose of a thing is known – what is your purpose in life? Are you living your life in line with your vision or just living every day as it comes?

Even if your journey today is filled with all sorts and it seems as if you are not getting the desired results, run back to Galatians 6:9, somewhere along the line there will be a shift, somewhere along the line, there will be a testimony. Life is not a bed of roses and has never proved to be, for all it is worth, never give up on your dreams; even though today might not look like what you have ever wanted it to be, the assurance we have is that our future will be better than the present.

In conclusion, remember that my destiny is different from yours, so is my journey different from yours. Keep your eyes fixated on the finish line for that is all that matters.

TRUTH OF LIFE: SPEAK THE WORD

We can never get the desired value from a luxury product until we have a thorough read of the manual. To stay ahead of the negativity that pervades our world today, we need to constantly speak the word of God to energize our body, soul and spirit. When others are seeing a casting down for themselves, you must see a lifting up for your soul. When others see you as a failure, you must see the success in whatever you lay your hands to do.

I will share a personal experience with you. After resuming work in one of the "Big Four" Consultancy firms in the city, we were always inundated with stories of people getting sacked or who had been previously sacked for several reasons. Myself and a close friend who was also my accountability partner always spoke the word of God, we are unshakable and not sackable and we always said we will be the ones to sack our employer not the other way around... we both moved on to pastures new and sacked our employers.

On another occasion, I was behind in my productivity for the week and I told my team members that because of me something drastic will happen on the project and the next day, we had news that those who were behind in their productivity for the week would have their deficits carried over into the new week and lo and behold, the carryover was wiped off in the new week – talking about speaking the Word of God. My team members became very curious about knowing more about this Jesus that I was talking about.

When people call you barren, speak the word of God to that womb and make a declaration that your womb will bring forth life.

I have had people call me and tell me to my hearing that as far as they are concerned, there is nothing in this city, but I continue to speak the word of God to all that I lay my hands upon that they will be a success and not a failure. No matter the situation you might be facing, always speak the word of God. There is no circumstance or situation my God cannot turn around; people might mock you today but in speaking the Word of God which is life to that situation, people will also celebrate your destiny tomorrow.

Always remember that through the Words that God spoke, the World was formed. For you to truly live your dreams in the physical, you must take ownership of the spiritual. Nothing happens to us by chance.

Speak life to that situation.

TRUTH OF LIFE: ABSOLUTE TRUST IN GOD IS THE KEY TO THE NEXT LEVEL

We can only achieve little or nothing when we operate in the realm of our own wisdom, there is a frequency where we operate in another level when we put all our hopes on God believing in him that he is able to help us solve the riddles of our life.

We need to get to a point in our life when we come to an understanding that no matter how big the problem is, we serve a God who is bigger than our problems. When we put our trust in man, we live in uncertainty because people derive their breath from their nostrils; it is ludicrous to trust in man who does not even have any assurance that he can be alive to witness another new day. Trust in the God who can make a way where there seems to be no way.

When you live in an advanced world where you have no connections, no father or mother who can assist you in pressing buttons in high places then you will understand the importance of abandoning your life recklessly to the Lord. When there is an issue that stands like a mountain before you, trust in God; when you are in despair with no hope for tomorrow, trust in God; when it seems as if the sleepless nights and tears are unending, trust in God.

There is a God who makes a way where people have said there is no way; I serve the God who is able to bring peace to every storm. Proverbs 3:5 readily comes to mind, Trust in the LORD with all your heart and lean not on your own understanding; even when it seems our World is falling apart trust in God. God understands our life, our times and seasons, he knows about the load we bear, he knows our deep secrets and where the shoe pinches.

We all know it is not easy when you have no assurance that tomorrow will be better, when the light is not visible from our position in the tunnel but there is a God who is able to make our tomorrow better than our today. Stop dwelling on what you don't have, dwell in the presence of God who is able to bless you and your seeds.

Always remember that you can go to God with your entire burden and cares when you have nowhere to go, when it seems as if there is no way, trust in God. There is practically nothing my God cannot do, he is the God who turns the poor to the rich, he makes our life a beauty when the world has written us off. No matter what you feel the obstacle might be, trust in God.

From my personal experience and relationship with God Almighty, I can say with all boldness and authority that trusting in God has been the sweetest experience of my life.

GOD'S TIMING IS PERFECT

This has been the core of my message over the past couple of months to my friends and colleagues – many times we want things done at our own timing and we want quick fix solutions to our life's issues. But as humans we are quick to forget that there is a God who knows how our life will turn out to be. There is no mistake or missed chances with God, neither are there failed projects or never-ending circumstances in the sight of God.

We must come to an understanding that everybody has their time and season under the sun, a time to be born and a time to die, a time to sow and a time to reap; no matter how much we desire miracles to whatever issues of life we might have, there is a God who knows the perfect timing. God is not a magician; if you desire a testimony do not forget that success comes when opportunity meets preparation. God's ways are different from our ways and his thoughts differ from our thoughts. Five years in the sight of man is not the same in the sight of God.

Negative situations and circumstances come and make way like the dark nights; there is no permanent condition in Life. The poor people of yesterday are rich today and the oligarchs of yesteryears are the poor of today. God is the potter and we are the clay; he chooses to have mercy and compassion on whomever he wills. With this knowledge comes an understanding that there is practically no need to be desperate for anything in life; once you are prepared for your success, when your opportunity comes in God's perfect time then it will be unmistakable that the Lord has done it.

When it is God's perfect timing, everything will align to work together for your good. I have heard astonishing testimonies of couples who had to wait on the Lord for the fruit of the womb for more than seventeen years; they had the wisdom to understand Isaiah 40:31 "But they that wait upon the LORD shall renew *their* strength; they shall mount up with wings as eagles; they shall run, and not be weary; *and* they shall walk, and not faint". Don't live your life in competition with any human being; everybody has their time to blossom and shine.

No matter how dark the nights might be, there is hope for a better tomorrow. Don't ever give up on God, he is never too late. The fact that what you trust and believe him for has not come to pass does not mean it won't happen. The sky is large enough to accommodate all birds and when you see others succeed, there is no need for being bitter and resentful towards the progress of other people. To enjoy our own success, we must learn to celebrate the success of others.

CAST THE FIRST STONE

The parody of life is that people are wont to cast aspersions on the character of others – he who is without sin should cast the first stone. If humans were God, people like Apostle Paul would never have had another chance at redemption. It's a crazy generation, the Ph.D. holders have grown up, if I can't do it then I must pull him down syndrome is rife today. If you think you are blameless, holy and without sin, feel free to malign others for no cause.

Always remember in life, you will see people in the mould of Apostle Paul: individuals who have fallen but still rise, people who have made mistakes but are still standing. It is not their fault that they made those seeming mistakes, it is for the glory of the one who sent them. No one is infallible; as long as our breath comes from our nostrils then we are prone to make mistakes. Our human nature epitomises our weakness but remember there is no condemnation for those who are in Christ Jesus.

Let no man condemn you; God can re-write your story, like he did with the transformation of Saul to Paul, the same way God changed the name of Abram to Abraham; God is able to bring back the seeming dead things to life, dead circumstances can be turned around. Your past is in the past, you can have a brand-new future, remember that Jesus is the reason we can face tomorrow.

The heart of man is desperately wicked – who can understand it? The generation of people who laugh with you and mock you behind your back. He who God has blessed no scheme of man can derail; he who God has anointed for a purpose, then all attempts to bring him down becomes futile.

It does not cost a dime to show love, even to those who spitefully use you and persecute you. Many are guilty of casting the first stone, judging others just to cover up their own frailty and insecurity. Always remember that it is a beautiful but imperfect world; follow your heart and convictions. Do not be wavered by the negativity that permeates around. Remember that your story is for his glory.

WHOSE REPORT WILL YOU BELIEVE?

There are a lot of negative reports out there about the bad economic times, negativity pervades the clime whichever part of the universe you live in. You have a choice on whose report to believe – you can either stand on the report of God or you believe the report of the world. The world may call you barren, but the word of God says you will be fruitful, multiply and replenish the Earth. Therefore, it's up to you what report you choose to believe. A friend told me how she trusted in the Lord on an issue even though the situation was hopeless, but she chose to believe God's report and a helper came her way whom she never knew before and the seemingly high mountain became reasons for her to testify about the awesome power of God.

I remember before leaving Nigeria in 2010 for the United Kingdom, a neighbour of mine who had just returned painted a gloomy picture of the country, how things were hard, lack of jobs and racial discrimination – that was his report and I determined in my mind that I was only going to believe the report of the Lord. And since I got here, it's been from one open door to another, God literally made me relevant even in places where I could only have dreamt about. He gave me a voice and made me a source of blessing to lots of people around – instead of lack of jobs, he gave me more than I had hoped for. Thus, it pays to trust in the Lord, when all you see around is hopelessness and gloom, you might feel like giving in to the pessimism that abounds and begin to operate on the world's frequency. There is great gain when you allow God to take the wheel, believing in the fact that he will do more than you can ever think of or imagine.

Dear Friends, even when God gives you a word, always hold on to it, though it tarries it will definitely come to pass. I was in a prayer session with my brothers many years ago and God told me he will give me global impact. I never knew it was ever going to happen but to the glory of God, his word came to pass in my life.

Some years ago, the dilemma faced by most of my friends was the decision on which country to live in after their degree – even though there are many people who have degrees, but no jobs and they are thinking of the next steps. I admonish you all to hold on to God's word about that situation, the fact that the times is not favourable for the majority does not mean you will also suffer the same fate.

One of my pastors gave a testimony that before he married his wife, his family prayed about it and told him not to marry her because she won't conceive. He ignored the report of his family and believed in God's word, she gave birth after their marriage to three wonderful boys.

Dear Friends, there is no Life my God cannot change; there is no situation that my father cannot turn around. The things that are impossible to humans are possible with my God, so you might have lost hope in Life and you are living your life based on the report of the world, I admonish you to believe the report of the Lord. You might have been written off as a failure and despised that nothing good can come out of your life, don't worry or lose hope, put your trust in the Lord and believe only his report and he will surely make a way for you in the desert.

GOD NEVER FAILS

Life is not a bed of roses. I have passed through the thorny paths more often than necessary, through the stormy waters and the fiery furnace and there were times when I felt just like throwing in the towel. What is the point of this whole experiment when you put in more effort and get little result? But the truth is God's grace and mercies is sufficient enough for us; even at times when we do not deserve to be partakers of his inheritance, he never leaves us or forsakes us.

God never fails. If he speaks a word it will surely come to pass, if a man should promise you a thing, it is not one hundred percent sure he will keep his promise. A man does not have any control over his life, but God's words are life and they are eternal, never waver at God's promise no matter what you might be going through now, wait for it and it will surely come to pass.

God has been good to me, the promises and deep revelations despite my weaknesses and my frail human nature. At times we want to juggle our lives based on our own thinking and time, more like going beyond our speed limits, but the revelations and his word keep coming, he renews my soul daily and gives me grace to overcome every form of temptation.

Do not judge a book by his cover, do not write off anyone for my God owns the times and seasons of our lives. The fact that you fall does not mean you cannot rise again. The failure is not the problem; what you do with your life after the seeming failure is the big deal. I have experienced failure and scary moments, there have been times when I entered my cubicle and wailed before the Almighty God, "why me" I cried. He told me clearly that even though you walk through the fire, your feet will not be burnt.

Do not be afraid to put your trust in an unknown God. I have experienced him in all ramifications and I can say of a truth he has been faithful. It is not the beginning of a thing that matters but the end thereof. God promised us that the glory of the latter will be greater than the former, so your past might have been filled with many painful moments but always remember the future is scattered with lots of good news and testimonies.

My encouragement to the person reading this: it is not a function of location, skin colour or family background. When the book of remembrance of heaven is opened for you, he will surely overwhelm and make your life a source of strength to those who are weak in faith. God can turn an unknown man into a famous king.

Do not give up on God for God will never give up on you.

DOMINATING THE SPIRITUAL

The physical and spiritual space in every city in the world is dominated by supernatural forces. Put succinctly there is a God in every city. To experience a leap from where you are to where you want to be means taking charge of the spiritual space. Nothing happens to us by chance. We have the power to shape our future, we can move mountains in the physical realm but the shift, the change in circumstances, would have occurred in the spiritual for it to take effect in the natural world.

Many times in life people take for granted their spiritual space, we tend to focus most of our energies on our quest for survival, striving for food, shelter, clothing and all the beautiful things of life, forgetting that when you are the Lord in the spiritual, then every other little detail begins to align in the physical. Life becomes very easy when we are in control of our spiritual space, as we come to the knowledge that the supernatural is the gateway for dominion in the physical world. We must make concerted effort to guard the spiritual jealously.

To enjoy the flow of the supernatural, consecrate your totality to the God of Gods. Speak life at every opportunity; remember our words shape our world. You must be your own cheerleader, don't stop dreaming; don't stop pushing for your goals and aspirations. It is a world where negativity pervades every sphere. When everyone around is pessimistic about your chances of success, you must be an eternal optimist, always see life from the bright side. You know who you serve and call upon. Even when you are not seeing results, never give up.

Our association is also very important. We must carefully select the people we call our friends. Don't forget the concept of times and season; there is a time and season for every event under the sun. Don't navigate through life based on your wisdom and ability – on our own we are weak, as humans we are frail. Trust in the Lord with all your heart and do not lean on your own understanding; in all your ways acknowledge him and he shall direct your paths. (Proverbs 3:5-6). In the past couple of years, I have surrendered my spiritual space to the all-powerful God. I tried to push through on my own in ages past but in the few years that God has taken over the rudder, the sail of my ship has been steady.

Remember it's in your hands. When you are in the driving seat in the spiritual, then the physical becomes a walkover.

IT IS YOUR RESPONSIBILITY

People heap together the mistakes of their lives and form a monster called destiny, forgetting that it is their responsibility to make things happen. Before we play the blame game, take responsibility for your actions. Guard your heart above all else, for it determines the course of your life. (Proverbs 4:23 NLT) So when people speak negative words to you or about your future, it is your responsibility to guard your heart diligently against the scheme of the evil one. When faced with temptation, remember that it is your responsibility to flee from every appearance of evil.

Our association also has a major impact in determining the outcome of our lives – who are those that inhabit our close circles? Some people are always nagging and never tend to see the good in situations and circumstances and always see the negative in every situation. Remember it is your responsibility to see the morning after the dark nights.

It is our responsibility to shape our World through our Words, speak life to every situation. In hopelessness speak hope, in lack speak abundance, in sickness speak health and in barrenness speak fruitfulness. It is your responsibility to act as the cornerstone and Chief Accounting Officer of your life. No time for pity parties, what we are today is the sum of our life's decision. Our choices today are a key factor in shaping our tomorrow. Therefore, it is our responsibility to make wise choices.

It is your responsibility to stay alert! Watch out for your great enemy, the devil. He prowls around like a roaring lion, looking for someone to devour. (1st Pet 5:8) It is your responsibility to feed your soul with the Word of God. No other person is permitted to think and plan your life for you; the buck starts and stops at your table. When things are not working, it is your responsibility to look at the root causes and work out solutions. When we take responsibility for our actions we show that we are capable of responding to every situation. The moment we take responsibility for everything in our life is the moment we can change anything in our life.

Our past might have been filled with failures and seemingly insurmountable mountains, but it is our responsibility to make the future better than the past. It is our responsibility to be happy always and change the course of our life by having the ability to respond to situations as they occur. Always remember that we are free to make choices, but we are not free from the consequence of our choices.

Act responsibly and Take responsibility.

ANOTHER LEVEL OF GRACE

There is a realm of grace higher than the ordinary; this is the level where the super is added to your natural ability. In this realm you can build up and tear down, uproot and destroy as the need arises. This new level of grace, the ordinary mind cannot decipher; succinctly put, this level is unfathomable to small minds. When you operate in this new level of grace, you must understand that your capacity has been enlarged. In this new level, mediocrity is not an option, even though we are not immune from negative reports, we are not immune from the same problems that ordinary people encounter, but we have the power and authority to control what happens to us. In this realm, standing order bows for our sake and protocol is bypassed just because of the God who never fails.

In this level, there are three vital resources that we need to make our lives more beautiful than we can ever dream of or imagine. In this level, you must learn to trust in God, trust God in the same manner a little child trusts in the parents. Even in times that we sit and cry, trust in God. When you hear negative reports, trust in God for a good report. Trust God in the understanding that there is a limit to what you can achieve on your own.

Another vital resource is hope. There will be times that the best option available is to give up, admit defeat. I admonish you, dear friends, to keep hope alive. When there is life, there is hope; as the night gives way for the breaking of a new day you need to come to an understanding that keeping hope alive will lead to a whole new level of possibilities. No matter the situation and circumstances you are facing in life, I say this too shall pass.

Instead of fear have faith in God, you must never stop believing and dreaming of that wonderful future. To enjoy this new level of grace, you must have the confident assurance that no matter the size of your mountain, it has the capacity to become a plain ground. When you develop faith in God, it does not matter the size of your problem – all that count is the size of your God. There will be times when the spirit of fear creeps in and you may feel inadequate, not capable and have negative thoughts; in such situations speak life, let your faith come to work.

My soul, spirit and body are lifted whenever I uproot what God has not planted, such sheer gladness when you abide in this new level of grace; our lives become a testimony and like the candle set upon a hill cannot be hidden. Finally, I admonish you keep hope alive, trust in the father and have faith in God and watch God beautify your life and make you a standard.

LOVE GOD, LOVE PEOPLE

The irony of life is that most people profess their love for God but despise the works of his hands, his creations. It is only mankind who has had the luxury to be created in the image and likeness of the Almighty God. What a travesty to love God and hate his people, what an anomaly to proclaim your love for God yet your next-door neighbour lives in want and poverty. Love God, Love People is a very deep essay and it takes spiritual understanding to dissect the information therein.

It is unfathomable to hate people and love God; we have no choice but to love people and pray for them, even our enemies. There are many times I have prayed for people in my closet even when we have not been in contact for many years; that is the love of God and his creations.

In recent years, I have seen people who love God and are passionate about God but despise people. I try to decipher the point in loving God but despising people. When you love God, you are looking out for the good of others, when a brother or sister has fallen you are not trying to keep them down but help them back up. Many people who claim to love God are always looking to bring others down, spreading false rumours, gossips and other vices that do not edify the spirit of God they profess.

Most times people create imaginary enemies where there is none, I laugh in amusement whenever I intercede in prayers for those who we do not get along, and in those instances, I see the God in them and decide to love God as that is what we represent through our human body. The Bible enjoins us in Mark 12:30-31 to 'Love the Lord your God with all your heart and with all your soul and with all your mind and with all your strength.' The second is this: 'Love your neighbour as yourself. There is no commandment greater than these.'(NIV)

I grew up in a family filled with the love of God and people. I have seen my parents go to great lengths to make others happy, even in times of dire need. My father taught me that loving people could be as ephemeral as rejoicing with them whenever they succeed. There is no gain in being bitter against God's creation, you hurt yourself more in this process as bitterness kills the fabric of your soul and spirit. When you love God and people, you are on your way to becoming a better person.

Loving God and People should be our way of life. The way I have learnt to deal with spiteful people is through interceding for them in prayers. The answer to some of our prayers is not 40 days dry fasting and anointing service, just Love God and his people and watch God transform your life round about.

WHAT ARE YOU SPEAKING?

Let me begin by saying that your life reflects your words. I have observed a common trend prevalent in our world today: negativity has eaten deep into the hearts of people. A lot of people know a thousand and one reasons why things will not work out with examples that perfectly fit.

I have never been an advocate of a perfect life, a life without problems and challenges. I can say authoritatively that problems will come and there will be situations that will test us and shake us, but the choice to keep standing despite what life throws at you is entirely yours. My question today is, are the challenges of life breaking you or are you dismantling every road block mounted on your way to destiny?

Remember that the Bible says in Proverbs 18:21: the tongue has the power of life and death, and those who love it will eat its fruit. In my understanding, this succinctly put means the onus is on us to keep speaking life, abundance, promotion, fruitfulness and growth in all spheres of our life. When all you speak is negative then the results will also be abundance of negativity. Remember you cannot sow the seed of negativity and expect a harvest of success.

Many people desire a better life but at every opportunity complain of how difficult it is to prosper in certain economies, they nag about every situation and challenges they encounter in life but the only recommendation I can make for those who want to lead successful lives is you have the power in your tongue. Speak life into every dead situation, the world may call you barren; declare that you are fruitful, when people call you a failure, remember that success is who you are.

One of my major strengths that has kept me in continuous motion is the power of speaking. At every opportunity I speak life into my job, marriage, going out and coming in, my business, finances, spiritual growth, wife, family and friends. Dear Friends, nothing happens to us by chance, our world is created through our words, so before things happen to us in the physical, settle them in the spiritual. Whatever will be will not be if we do not allow it to happen, so close the book of lamentations and wear the garment of praise and thanksgiving.

The definition of people is of little importance as the opinion of others does not define who you truly are; what matters is what you call yourself. When negative reports come, do you accept that as the final word over your situation or do you speak the report of the Lord believing that God is able to overturn every negative situation and give you everlasting Joy?

Dear Friends, I admonish you to speak life and watch God make your life a testimony for the world to behold.

PART 6

TOUGH SOLDIERS, TOUGH BATTLES

The bigger the battles you face in life, the bigger your life assignment is. There is no perfect life, we all face challenges that might test us to the limit, which might shake us to our foundation. There will be nights that we sit and cry, there will be times when we are puzzled at the pain and we question the very essence of our human existence. I admonish you friends, do not waver at the depth of your problems; the tougher your life assignment is the bigger the battles you will fight.

In a military formation, the toughest soldiers are drafted to the high-risk zones because the military high command knows that the chances of success are quite high when the best individuals face the toughest of oppositions. I challenge you today to be a tough soldier; God has not brought you this far to give up on you. No matter the size of your problem, remember that your God is greater than any challenge or issues you might be facing in life.

Many years ago, I heard the Holy Spirit say to me that even when you walk through the fire, your feet will not be burnt, through the waters you will not drown. So, amid my battles I saw the Lord. Who are you seeing in your battles? Are you looking up to the Holy Spirit to comfort you or are you seeing the negatives? No weapon fashioned against you shall prosper and every tongue that rises against you in judgement has been condemned already.

Always remember that every challenge we face in life has an expiry date; this too shall pass. No matter the pain that might remind you of your humanity, God's grace is sufficient for you even in your weakness. I am not interested in the size of your battles, neither am I concerned at the size of the opposition, assuredly I say unto you those that are with you are more than those that are against you. The battlefield is a place of preparation, preparation for the future glory. Your face might be smeared in dust and you might be all bruised up, but you will laugh last.

Some things happen to us in life so that the name of God might be glorified in our lives. There are times we must wait upon the Lord, waiting for his promise. At times it might tarry, but it will come to pass. God will not allow a difficulty that is too much for us to bear to happen to us; tough times will come and go but guard your barracks against the wiles of the devil. During the battles, always see the Lord. There is no lateness in God's dictionary. At the appointed time the promise will come to pass.

We need tough soldiers, soldiers of Christ, soldiers of the kingdom, people who will keep standing amid the storm.

THERE IS A KING IN YOU

But you are a chosen people, a royal priesthood, a holy nation, God's special possession, that you may declare the praises of him who called you out of darkness into his wonderful light. (1st Peter 2:9 NIV) It is rather saddening that in our world today, people have lost their identity; the problems and challenges that we encounter daily have made us forget who we are. Remember that you are peculiar and distinct; we are partakers of the royal heritage of our Lord Jesus Christ.

Kings ooze royalty, they have the power and capacity to decree a thing and have it established. The time to stop playing the victim card is now; you are a victor and not a victim of the circumstances of life. There is no perfect human being; we are all beautiful but imperfect people. Never allow people to speak defeat into your life; the fact that some others have lost their identity in the kingdom and have allowed the society, the economy, their finances and job define who they are does not mean we should allow the tangible to define who we are.

The first step to living in royalty is to come to an awareness of your kingship; nothing happens to us by chance in life. Before anything happens in the physical, always settle them in the spiritual. As God's special possession, all that concerns us is already blessed. A king makes law, and nobody dares challenge the words of a king. We were all created in the image and likeness of God, so we are joint heirs with Christ.

In situations where you have been called a failure, I declare that you are a success in Jesus' name (Amen). The Lord God will bless the works of our hands; we are lenders and not borrowers in the name of Jesus. Your life is your kingdom; you must always be in control of the affairs in this kingdom. When the challenges of life beckon, never lose sight of who you are in the kingdom.

We have the capacity to re-write the story of our lives, so at every opportunity speak life, praise your way out of every situation – you are not a slave but a king. People might be lamenting about how difficult it is to survive in certain economies but the King in you will set you apart. We must endeavour not to sell our birthright to the devil; even in the face of negative reports you must continue to speak the report of the Lord on that situation. When the world says there is a casting down, you will rejoice and say there is a lifting up for your soul in Jesus' name.

Let the kings rejoice, let the kings revel in their royalty.

RISING ABOVE THE STORM

The storms of life are inevitable at some point during our sojourn in this world, they are constant reminders of our humanity. Life is indeed vain, vanity upon vanity all is vanity. Most times we love life when all is going well with us, but how we cope in the face of life's challenges defines us. The storms of life are not there to destroy us but shape us, to make us and not mar our future. There are nights we sit and cry, moments when the morning seems afar off, we look left, right and centre and there is no helper forthcoming; I admonish you to look up to God amid your storm. When all hope seems to have been lost, the all-knowing God is able to calm the raging storms. During that crisis, speak peace, speak life, this too shall pass.

The grace to rise above the storm can only come from God, not from our wisdom, intellect or ability. Only God has the power to calm the raging storm; our assurance comes from Isaiah 43:2 (NLT), when you go through deep waters, I will be with you. When you go through rivers of difficulty, you will not drown. When you walk through the fire of oppression, you will not be burned up; the flames will not consume you. Amid the storm, look up to God, the author and finisher of your faith, seek the face of God and hear his voice concerning that difficulty – one word from God is enough to calm you through the storms. There is no circumstance that is too hard for God to overturn; he is the all-knowing God. The God who makes a way where there seems to be no way; when people say there is no way God has the capacity to make a way for us.

A perfect example of a man who was able to rise above his storm was Job. Quoting from Job 2:9-10 His wife said to him "Are you still trying to maintain your integrity? Curse God and die." But Job replied, "You talk like a foolish woman. Should we accept only good things from the hand of God and never anything bad?" So, in all this Job said nothing wrong. (NLT) "I admonish you to praise your way out of that storm, speak the word of God into that situation. Remember, there is a time and season for every situation we might face in life. Amid your storm, say nothing wrong. To the person who is saying I have lost everything, assuredly I say this "You can recover all", lost time, lost opportunities, lost finances and every other thing you might have lost to the storm."

I admonish you that no matter the size of your mountain, give it all to master Jesus. You can rise above the storm; no matter the situations, never give up on God.

DO NOT BE TOO ATTACHED

We are all on a journey in this world and the only constant factor that applies to us all, young or old, rich or poor, tall or short, black or white, is life and death. In the last couple of months, I have tried to play back as much as I can remember my early days in this world. As a new-born we are not aware of anything in this world but during our life's journey, we become too attached to things of the world. I understand the fact that we are born into a family, we make friends, build relationships and the quest to lead better lives makes us fall in love with life and all its allures.

As passengers in this world, let us not forget that we are only here for a while. Our focus should be on eternity, as life is vanity. We came to this world with nothing and when death comes knocking we shall leave with nothing. Colossians 3:2) Set your minds on things above, not on earthly things. 3) For you died, and your life is now hidden with Christ in God. 4) When Christ, who is your life, appears, then you also will appear with him in glory. 5) Put to death, therefore, whatever belongs to your earthly nature: sexual immorality, impurity, lust, evil desires and greed, which is idolatry. (NIV)

Put your trust in God in all things. As humans we derive our breath from our nostrils, we have no power over our tomorrow. We cannot tell when we sleep at night if we will wake up the next day but put your trust in the God who never fails. The same way we had no say in the family we were born into or what gender we will be at birth, we will also have no say when it is time to meet our creator.

Let your affection be on things of the kingdom, let your life epitomise Matthew 6:33 which reads thus "Seek the Kingdom of God above all else, and live righteously, and he will give you everything you need". So, the first step is to seek God first and all other things you ever desire will be given to you. When you have God on your side, every other thing becomes a bonus. Good health, peace of mind, long-life, promotion, battles are won, storms are calm, and all the bliss that comes with life are the add-ons we get from being on the side of the Lord.

My prayer is that God will open our eyes to see how fleeting our days are and the wisdom to be attached to God and his works. Too much attachment to this world brings pain and tears but one with God is the majority. As we continue our journey, do not forget that we are only passengers here and from dust we came and to dust we shall return. My prayer today is that God will teach us to number our days, so we can apply our hearts to wisdom.

NO ONE KNOWS TOMORROW

Our times and season belongs to God, he is the all-knowing God, the God who knows our beginning from the end and our ending from the beginning. Through the hurt, pain and disappointment he will still be God. My father always admonished us, his children, never to put our trust in any man, as man has no control over his own life. That is the perfect truth: we have no power over our future, we can plant for all we can and water, but God is the only one who can grant the increase. The aces in this race belongs to God; there is little that we can achieve on our own.

As humans, we derive our breath from our nostrils. Our humanity represents frailty, one moment we are here and the next we are gone. Life is what you make it to be, tables turn, life will always continue. The poor man today has the capacity to become rich tomorrow. Life is a mystery, hard to understand and difficult to comprehend. Give it all up to the God who knows tomorrow; all that we are and have belongs to him. No condition is permanent in life; the night will give way for the morning at some point. Create your own happiness, make peace with the past and trust God for the future. When I reminiscence about life, the most crucial factor that comes to my mind is that all our struggles and sleepless nights are all for a better tomorrow.

Has anyone ever written you off? Do you look at the past and present and feel no good can come out of your tomorrow? Dear Friends, I admonish you to give your tomorrow to the potter.

He is the potter and we are the clay; only God can mould you and give you a better tomorrow. Because he lives, I have no fear of tomorrow for God is with me. Life may not be all rosy; no one ever said it will be easy; different people in the world with different experiences about tomorrow. Never write any one off in life. The man without shoes became the president of the most populous nation in Africa. Tomorrow indeed has no limits as long as you do not limit yourself.

Every new day we hear heart rending stories of people who had a new beginning and stories that move you to tears. They never knew what tomorrow had in store for them today. We have an assurance for a better tomorrow in the Lord. Only God can calm the raging storm, only God can restore unto us the years the locust has eaten up. As we continue our sojourn in this world, hand over your tomorrow to the God who has the master plan.

I wish you all a wonderful tomorrow.

ONE WORD FROM GOD

All you need in life is one word from God. Many times, in life we try to run our life based on our human understanding. Oh, what sheer joy when we live our life based on God's promises; when you hear from the Lord, then you are free from every form of anxiety and worry about what the future might hold. The Bible says in Hebrews 4:12, For the word of God [is] quick, and powerful, and sharper than any two-edged sword, piercing even to the dividing asunder of soul and spirit, and of the joints and marrow, and [is] a discerner of the thoughts and intents of the heart. (KJV)

One word from God can calm the raging storm of our lives. The Bible says in Habakkuk 2: 1-3 I will stand upon my watch, and set me upon the tower, and will watch to see what he will say unto me, and what I shall answer when I am reproved. And the LORD answered me, and said, write the vision, and make [it] plain upon tables, that he may run that readeth it. For the vision [is] yet for an appointed time, but at the end it shall speak, and not lie: though it tarry, wait for it; because it will surely come, it will not tarry. (KJV) No matter how long it takes for it to happen, when God has said it, it will definitely come to pass.

To navigate through this world, all you need is one word from the Almighty God; quit trying to run your race through your human wisdom. The Bible says in Matthew 24:35 that heaven and earth shall pass away, but my words shall not pass away. (KJV) That is the assurance we have in Christ Jesus, he can do what he says he will do. No matter what the world says about you, all that matters is what the word of God has said concerning that situation. So, when the world calls you barren, just quote what the Word of God says in Exodus 23:26 there shall nothing cast their young, nor be barren, in thy land: the number of thy days I will fulfil. (KJV)

The reality or present circumstances might look bleak but just one word from God is able to change your life completely. There is a limit to how far you can go on this journey; when you are at a crossroad in life, call upon the Lord who never fails. Dear Friends, I admonish you to trust in the Lord and the power of his might; there is nothing impossible for God to do. When you hear from the Lord, you operate on another frequency and level entirely. The challenges that ordinary people face that make them give up and declare whatever will be will be are the situations that you encounter, and you speak the mind of God concerning that storm – this too shall pass.

Always run with the vision, the revelation and word from the Lord. At the appropriate time in your due season, the Lord will make all things beautiful in his time.

DON'T PUT THE GLORY TO WASTE

We are all a reflection of the glory of God; we are the wonderful creation of his hands, his very own beloved. God created man in his own image and likeness, Psalm 82:6 "I said, 'You are "Gods"; you are all sons of the Most High.' (NIV). If ye are Gods then you have the power to decree a thing and have it established, do not allow the devil to mesmerize you and denigrate your destiny. In all situations, give thanks to the Lord. Speak the word of God into your life with the understanding that God's word can heal, deliver and transform you. You are a candle set upon a hill; you have the capacity to illuminate every dark place.

You are a carrier of God's glory. Put the glory to work, wear the glory as a garment and let it reflect in all your ways. Footballers go on the pitch with a winning mentality – never accept defeat in any sphere of your life. What people say about you is less important; the most crucial factor in the equation of your life is what God is saying. One word from God is all you need to live stress-free, so quit worrying about the future when you serve the God who knows the end from the beginning.

The glory has worked for me in numerous ways, it has distinguished me from the crowd, and living in the glory is a wonderful experience. A tenant who owns the title deed of all the properties in Manchester and is unaware lives like a tenant until the day he becomes aware, the knowledge of his new status gives him an aura, he walks majestically and begins to live in his own reality. We need to live our life in the awareness of his glory. Until you begin to put the glory to work, you will never know the value of that which you carry. 1st Cor 10:31 "So whether you eat or drink or whatever you do, do it all for the glory of God." (NIV)

Put away the garment of lamentations; you are not a victim but a victor; you are who you say you are. You deserve to be celebrated and not an object of pity. Many a time, people tend to complain about how difficult it is to break through in certain economies and climes, but when you are a carrier of God's glory, you need to speak life and not defeat into your life and circumstances.

I admonish you, friends, do not let this precious gift from God go to waste; put it to effective use.

THE PARABLE OF THE LIT CANDLE AND STARS IN THE SKY

The candle is designed for illumination, to give light amid the darkness. It does not matter how long a room has been in darkness when the candle is lit – darkness gives way for light. The same principle of illumination applies to the stars in the sky; they give us illumination amid darkness. I have recognised a visible trend over the past years: I am designed to illuminate, to give light, when I speak people listen; that is what the light that we carry does, no matter how long we have been on the periphery, the candle of our light burns brightly that darkness cannot comprehend.

Matthew 5: 14-16 "Here's another way to put it: You're here to be light, bringing out the God-colours in the world. God is not a secret to be kept. We're going public with this, as public as a city on a hill. If I make you light-bearers, you don't think I'm going to hide you under a bucket, do you? I'm putting you on a light stand. Now that I've put you there on a hilltop, on a light stand—shine! Keep open house; be generous with your lives. By opening up to others, you'll prompt people to open up with God, this generous Father in heaven (The message bible).

As the stars are designed for illumination, if you are a star your light will also shine. What others do and struggle to accomplish, you will do and achieve momentous results. Currently, a Spanish

El-Classico football match without Cristiano Ronaldo and Lionel Messi is incomplete because they are the stars in their team; when they are on the football pitch they can win matches for their teams single-handedly. This theory also applies to us as we are the light of the world, we have the capacity to shine irrespective of the conditions and limitations of life. A lit candle is not limited by the size of the room, neither are the stars in the sky limited by landmass or population; they will always give light.

When your candle is lit, standing orders will bow for you, protocols will be dismantled for your sake, the situations and circumstance of life that limits other people is not permitted to limit you. As light bearers, you are not permitted to fail; no matter how long it takes for you to be recognised you cannot be hidden for too long. From obscurity you will be sought out, no matter how hard and tough you think life has been, your light will shine, when you plant and water, God will grant you the increase. When a candle is lit, irrespective of the colour it gives light; this also applies to us, irrespective of your skin colour or background, the light of God will distinguish you from your contemporaries.

In this murky world, your light will always shine and when your light has shined, you lose nothing by helping others to shine.

THE PARABLE OF THE LIT-CANDLE: HELP OTHERS LIGHT THEIR CANDLE

A candle loses nothing by lighting others up. We must help others to get along in life as the sky is wide enough for all birds to fly. Celebrate the success of others; there is no point being bitter by the success stories of others but always remember that God can do exceedingly far greater than you can ever think or imagine. You attract supernatural blessings whenever you light up other people's candles; it is more blessed to give than to receive.

When you are shining help others to move ahead. Going back to Matthew 5:14-16 "Here's another way to put it: You're here to be light, bringing out the God-colours in the world. God is not a secret to be kept. We're going public with this, as public as a city on a hill. If I make you light-bearers, you don't think I'm going to hide you under a bucket, do you? I'm putting you on a light stand. Now that I've put you there on a hilltop, on a light stand—shine! Keep open house; be generous with your lives. By opening up to others, you'll prompt people to open up with God, this generous Father in heaven. (The Message Bible)

Do not be comfortable being the only success story among your committee of friends, in your family, community and neighbourhood. Jesus gave up his life that we may have life in abundance; as light bearers you must drop the tag of self but being selfless in all your ways. Our duties as light bearer is to give hope to the hopeless, speak life to those who are hurting, feed the poor and let your light shine amid the darkness.

Always look for the good of others, how they can move ahead in life. Remember tomorrow is a mystery, nobody knows what tomorrow holds. Do not despise people who are experiencing their days of little beginnings, do not join the bandwagon of the PhD (Pull him Down syndrome) holders. I admonish you, friends, God's timing is perfect for us. The candle loses its purpose when it cannot give light to everyone in the house; let your light shine amid the darkness. Be generous with your lives; be a source of Joy to those around you and the only result you will get is that your light will never stop shining. When you give your money, time and resources what you get back is double; for the seed you will receive the harvest.

When you light up the candle of others, in the days of adversity you will receive strength and capacity to overcome all your travails.

THE PARABLE OF THE TALENTS

Whenever I read the story of the servants whom their Master entrusted with talents before embarking on his journey in Matthew 25:14-30, I relate with that story as if it is happening in this present time. Whenever I see tombstones in a cemetery, what I see is thousands of talents that might have gone unheralded. Laid in those tombstones are chart topping pop artists, CEOs, creative writers, inventors and many more professionals that have left this side of the divide as unsung heroes. As with the servant who buried his talent, many of us have excuses for not fully expressing our innate abilities and potential.

Many of those people in the graveyard were laid to rest with all their dreams, goals and talents. Many people have readymade excuses for burying their talents and not fully expressing their potential. Quit making excuses about unfair situations and circumstances; never let anyone stop you from being whom God has purposed you to be. As long as we have breath in us, we will be faced with challenges, rejection and unfair situations. As with the servants with different amounts of talent, we will have friends and colleagues who are more talented than us and some others over whom we have more talents. Do not use anyone as a yardstick of your progression in life.

The fact that we fail is not the problem; failing and not dusting ourselves up is the main problem. Failing and dwelling on our failures is an impediment that inhibits many people from realising their full potential. Let me use an analogy of a very talented young man who arrives in a new country with dreams and ambitions but adapting to a new culture and way of life might either propel him to his dreams or inhibit him from the achievement of his dreams. If he develops his talent and uses his potential to full capacity, here comes the faithful servant; but if all he sees is failure, economic problems, and unfair situations then he might end up being an educated cleaner or caregiver.

Our talent is God's gift to us; what we do with it is our Gift back to God. Do not let your dreams be drowned in the ocean of rejection; the fact that you are not where you are supposed to be is because you are a work in progress. Keep making positive strides towards the achievement of your dreams. Your talent might be one, two or five, so please nurture that which the Lord has committed into your hands and more will be committed into your hands.

BUT FOR YOUR GRACE

We are what we are by the Grace of God. Many a time in life we want to get ahead quick and fast. If we had our way we would be on the fast lane all through our sojourn in this world. All that we are and have is by the grace of God. It is not because you are the wisest, the most brilliant or the best qualified that you are blessed; it is all down to the grace of God. There are many educated, super qualified and supposedly smart people who live in penury and want. Grace is not measured by the eloquence of your speech or your diction; it is given to those whom the Lord wills.

Grace sets apart and distinguishes the carrier from the multitude. We are alive, hale and hearty not because we are better than those who are in the intensive wards of hospitals with life-threatening illnesses, but we are simply enjoying God's grace. 1st Cor 15:10 But by the grace of God I am what I am: and his grace which *was bestowed* upon me was not in vain; but I laboured more abundantly than they all: yet not I, but the grace of God which was with me. (KJV)

Psalm 124:2 If *it had* not *been* the LORD who was on our side, when men rose up against us. (KJV) At every opportunity, I always wonder how life would have turned out for me if it was not for the Lord who was on my side. God's grace has been sufficient; his mercies are new every morning. With grace what you enjoy is pure and unadulterated love from God; you might look undeserving in the eyes of people but in God's sight you are a royal priesthood, a chosen generation and a peculiar people.

If not for the grace of God, life would have been tough. Even in the darks nights, God's grace has come through. Amid the fire, his grace has allowed me to walk through without getting my feet burnt. Do not forget the grace of God; it is an aura, a distinguishing factor that makes you the best in whatever you commit to do despite your inadequacies. When you are weak God's grace will give you strength, when you are oppressed his grace will speak out on your behalf.

But he said to me, "My grace is sufficient for you, for my power is made perfect in weakness." Therefore, I will boast all the more gladly about my weaknesses, so that Christ's power may rest on me. (2nd Cor 12:9 NIV) Even in your weaknesses and frailties, all you need is God's grace. I admonish you, friends, all you need in life is God's grace, to move from where you are to where you are supposed to be. Grace will make a way for you and celebrate you.

WORK OUT YOUR OWN SUCCESS

We are in the know that success comes when opportunity meets preparation. Hence, there is no need for rhetoric on how to achieve success. The world indeed does not owe us a living, so it is time to drown out the voices of excuses about how unfair life has been. I have heard many amazing stories of people who broke the barriers of poverty and rose to the peak and became success stories in their chosen field of endeavours.

The onus is on us to make our life all that we want it to be, so quit making excuses about the past – there is no point organising pity-parties and playing the blame game. People tend to blame others for their predicament, for some the economy might come in for the blame, while others put the blame on their background – if only they were born into a wealthy family, they would have had a better life. Assuredly I tell you, your background is not a reflection of your future. The past should be put in its place which is the past.

There is no magic formula to achieve success in life, but you can become all that God has purposed you to be if you have that desire to attain it. To achieve good success in life, you must as a necessity come to acknowledge that it is your own responsibility as the Chief Executive Officer of your life to work out your own success. Always remember that life is an individual affair and you are first and foremost answerable for your own actions and inactions.

Success is not achieved through wishful thinking or daydreaming; a lot of effort goes into the place of preparation. Before the athlete mounts the podium to celebrate their victory, day and night they are at the training ground working towards the achievement of their goals; they also invest a lot of time in the gym while adhering to healthy eating habits. To achieve good success, you must be disciplined and practise self-denial to make your dream a reality. Insanity is doing the same thing repeatedly and expecting different results. To be successful, you must carve a niche for yourself. You must be ready to let old habits die and say no to yourself even in difficult circumstances.

When all you hear is how tough the economy is and how difficult it is to make headway in life, I admonish you to take responsibility for your own success. Invest your time in value added activities, do not despise continuous learning; life itself is a teacher, the more we live the more we learn. Quit procrastinating. A lot of people tell me they will get things done tomorrow and when I ask them tomorrow, they tell me tomorrow, but the fact is they never get things done tomorrow. Remember that success is who you are: you will succeed.

CALL FORTH YOUR ISAAC

Now faith is confidence in what we hope for and assurance about what we do not see. This is what the ancients were commended for. By faith we understand that the universe was formed at God's command, so that what is seen was not made out of what was visible. (Heb 11:1-3 NIV) There is power in the name of Jesus to break up every chain, so whatever seems dead in your life can resurrect through the power in the name of Jesus. There is nothing impossible with God; speak your desires to life. I admonish you, friends, to live your life knowing that your God can bring to life every dead thing as far as you can imagine.

When the world calls you barren, call forth your Isaac to life. What you need is one word from God. In Abraham's old age God ordained him the father of many nations. 11 And by faith even Sarah, who was past childbearing age, was enabled to bear children because she considered him faithful who had made the promise. 12 And so from this one man, and he as good as dead, came descendants as numerous as the stars in the sky and as countless as the sand on the seashore. (Heb 11:11-12 NIV) Have faith in God and trust him to do what he says he will do. There is no point living in fear, when you can spice your life up with faith. Speak your expectations to life. Never settle for less or second best; it is the will of God that we are the head and not the tail.

After calling forth your Isaac to life, begin to live your life as if that which you hope for has come to pass. Start living in the

"When" reality and discard the "Ifs". Don't just have faith; put your faith to work. People might say it is easier said than done but remember that the power of life and death is in your tongue. Never ever lose faith in life and the accomplishment of your dreams.

When calling forth your Isaac to life, there are so many things you must ignore. You must ignore every negative medical report; the doctors might have called you barren, but the Bible says "and none will miscarry or be barren in your land. I will give you a full life span. (Exodus 23:26 NIV) Recruiters might say you are not qualified for a job role but God qualifies the called. Dear Friends, see what Mark 11:22-24 says 22 "Have faith in God," Jesus answered. 23 "Truly I tell you, if anyone says to this mountain, 'Go, throw yourself into the sea,' and does not doubt in their heart but believes that what they say will happen, it will be done for them. 24 Therefore I tell you, whatever you ask for in prayer, believe that you have received it, and it will be yours. (NIV). I admonish you, friends, this is the conclusion to this essay, faith in God, not doubting in your heart and discard every form of fear – what you get in return is that whatever you say will come to pass.

GOD DOES NOT NEED US AS HIS PERSONAL ASSISTANT

Many a time in life people tend to purpose in their hearts to let God have his way and take the glory but often we tend to assist God to make his will happen not in the best of ways. Faith without works is dead that we know, but if you are willing to trust God for the promise then you must also be ready to wait patiently for the fulfilment of God's promise.

As humans we want our expectations in a haste, so we begin to scheme how to make our dream come true, forgetting that God's promise is yet for an appointed time; if it tarries wait for it as it will definitely come to pass. If your desire is the promise of God, there is no point scheming to have what God will give to you on a platter of gold. Remember what the Bible says in 1st Cor 3:6-9, I planted the seed, Apollos watered the plants, but *God* made you grow. It's not the one who plants or the one who waters who is at the centre of this process but God, who makes things grow. Planting and watering are menial servant jobs at minimum wages. What makes them worth doing is the God we are serving. You happen to be God's field in which we are working. (The Message Bible)

Quit the scheming and plotting to make things happen in your life, let your investment be your works. God is still in the business of transforming the lives of his creations; even amid the storm when the future looks bleak and uncertain, hold on to God's word. The grass withers and the flowers fall, but the word of our God endures forever (Isaiah 40:8 NIV). "The things which are impossible with men are possible with God" (Luke 18:27). Man knows a thousand and one reasons why things will not work. As humans we conjure up excuses and think we are not good enough, so we think the only solution is trying to resolve the problems of our lives based on our human understanding.

I admonish you, friends, God does not need you as a personal assistant. Whatever you desire from the Lord, he is able to do exceeding abundantly above all that we ask or think, according to the power that worketh in us. (Eph 3:20) Don't involve God in cutting corners, do not manipulate your way to the top and come back to give the glory to God. People are in the habit of seeking God's face yet seek out other ways to resolve the issues of their life not knowing that they cannot resolve the issues of their life outside the tent of the most-high God. There is no need to be running from pillar to post; the answer to that problem is with Master Jesus. Remember, Heaven and Earth will pass away, but my words will never pass away. (Matt 24:35)

COMMON ETIQUETTE: A WAY OF LIFE

Common etiquette should be a mandatory requirement in our day to day lives. We should not always take the people in our lives for granted. When you offend people or have been in the wrong, learn to say sorry. Being sorry does not make you less of who you are or reduce your authority in any way; it truly shows you are emotionally matured. Do away with the ego trip and come off that high horse when you make a mistake, admit that you have erred and seek forgiveness. Always remember that to err is human and to forgive is divine. We must learn to forgive those who have sinned against us. If you need something to be done for you, say Please; don't have the mindset that people have an obligation to help you out. Some people have what I call the entitlement mentality. The fact that you are in a position of authority or occupy a leadership position does not give anyone the leeway to act disrespectfully towards other people. Same also applies to showing appreciation for gifts received, help offered, or service rendered to us (either paid or unpaid). A popular proverb where I come from says and I quote "Anyone who we help out but does not say "Thank You" is like a thief who has stolen our most precious goods". It does not matter whether it is our parents or family members who have given us the gifts, in every situation and under every circumstance give thanks to those who deserve it. Learn to appreciate the little acts of kindness, when you are grateful for the little then greater things will be committed unto you. Before behaving towards someone in a particular way, put yourself in other people's shoes. If someone else acts towards you in the way you are about to behave or act towards others, will you be happy or upset about it? Good character is precious, it is beauty personified, and it is what defines you.

DO AWAY WITH CARRIERS OF NEGATIVE ENERGY

A lot of people abound in our world today pregnant with negativity; they thrive in seeing the negative in every situation. I call them carriers of negative energy, there is always a "but", and "if" in all their words, they already know a thousand and one reasons why a project will fail. Carriers of negative energy are also serial complainers. They have the victim mentality and are in the habit of having people organise pity-parties for them to whinge about their circumstances.

Be wary of your association with carriers of negative energy; these people can be equated with mosquitoes. Always on the prowl for perpetual victims, there is always someone else to carry the blame for their circumstances. The Bible says in Provs 4:23 "Guard your heart above all else, for it determines the course of your life (NLT). Our words shape our world and we have control over the words that we allow people speak to us. It is not a crime to kick out negative people from your life, neither have you committed any offence when you stop communicating with them.

Dear Friends, I admonish you to develop a motto as a form of defence when you encounter carriers of negative energy. My personal watchword which I use is "All is well". Despite what I might be going through, all is well with me; even amid the raging storm, all is well; when my health fails, all is well; and in every situation, all is well. Any time I make the confession that all is well, the transmitter of the negative message also comes into an agreement with me that "All is well with me"; and the result is that "All is Well" with me.

It is not in all situations that carriers of negative energy speak intentionally or consciously but some sow the seed of the negativity through rumours or word of mouth. There was a time I was changing jobs and an acquaintance of mine told me that my new employers sack people at will. This suggestion was based on unfounded information; I told him I cannot be sacked. The moral of this story, when people give you negative reports, all you need to speak is the report of the Lord. As I did not accept his suggestion as my reality, I was not sacked.

Carriers of negative energy thrive in an atmosphere where fear prevails. I admonish you, friends, instead of fear have faith in God. No matter how long the night might be, it gives way for the dawn of a new day. In your waiting period, trust in the Lord. Even in the wilderness, speak your way to your promised land. Develop a Can-Do attitude and always expect a positive outcome despite the challenges life might throw at you.

THIS TOO SHALL PASS

The wickedness in the world today is of monumental proportions; man's wickedness to man is beyond definition. No matter how evil the days are and how dysfunctional the world has become, please keep hope alive. No matter how long evil seeks to dominate the world, it cannot and will never conquer good. Let this give us hope: there is a time for every event and occurrence on the face of the Earth. No matter the difficulty we might face in our quest for survival, no matter how terrific the wind of evil might blow, never ever give up. There is no situation God cannot turn around.

As a certainty, in our individual lives we will face challenges that will shake and break us, but we can make the best out of every negative situation. No matter how dark the nights might be, the morning gives way to the dawn of a new day. Sorrow and weeping may endure for a night but Joy cometh in the morning. When the reign of terror and oppression dominates the news, when it seems that the evil deeds of people are unending, have faith in God. Instead of allowing fear to dominate our hearts, we need to build up our faith and believe that God can do for us the seemingly difficult things of the world.

I admonish you, friends, cast all your cares upon the Lord. There are times we will feel down and out, the odds as it were might be against us, but in all situations remember to give thanks to the Lord. Our life, times and season belongs to God. If God is for us, who can be against us? Rom 8:31. In your period of low estate, remember that this too shall pass; when the world calls you barren, this too shall pass; in the days of looking at beautiful things with longing eyes and not being able to afford them, this too shall pass. Life is in phases and men are in sizes.

Tough times don't last, no condition is permanent. When there is life there is hope, hope for a change in fortunes, hope for a turnaround in circumstances and hope for a better tomorrow.

BE WARY OF DISTRACTIONS

The mere fact that almost everyone in the world follows a way to get things done does not mean it is the right thing to do. No matter how good people make a corrupt way of life look like, it cannot be termed as good. Our human nature makes us prone to errors, we are not perfect in any way and we are wont to doubt God's promise when it is not happening on time.

My challenge to the person reading this: be wary of the distractions that abound in our world today. The fact that people boycott the process to achieve the results does not mean we should abandon our beliefs in God for short term gains. In the natural, it might seem a foolish idea to wait on the Lord when we can follow the easy route, everybody's way. What is the point of a testimony that we cannot ascribe the glory to God for?

I also understand the fact that distractions can come in various forms, but I admonish you, friends, no matter the scheming and plotting, if God does not grant the increase we are only wasting our time. It could be difficult to take our eyes off the little foxes that tend to corrupt our vine but let us live our lives in the hope that God is able to transform our lives and bless us without short-circuiting the process. God's promise in Romans 9:16 still abides forever. For he says to Moses, "I will have mercy on whom I have mercy, and I will have compassion on whom I have compassion." It does not, therefore, depend on human desire or effort, but on God's mercy. (NIV)

Hand over the issues of your life to God; there is a limit to how far we can navigate the course of our lives based on our own intellect and ideas. The Bible says in 1st Corinthians 3:6 I planted the seed, Apollos watered it, but God has been making it grow. (NIV) There are some people who are called the famous people of yesterday, they were once wealthy but wealth that is not built on the foundation of Christ (Solid Rock) is washed away in the sinking sand. No matter how smart we think we are, we need God to help us make our seed grow.

When it seems as if you are way behind your contemporaries because you chose to wait upon the Lord or you are being mocked by all and sundry because you are not willing to be distracted from your chosen course, do not be dismayed or give up on God; the God that we serve is able to do exceedingly more than we can ever think of or imagine. As you bring your little before the Lord, God is more than able to multiply and bless the works of our hands.

IN HIS PRESENCE

Not having any say in our decision to be born into this world or the family that we belong to should be a pointer to the fact that the same invisible God who orchestrated our life affairs up until this present time is able to do exceedingly greater than we can ever imagine in our life. As humans we live our lives in anxiety; even when we are not a seer we are desperate to have a wonderful tomorrow. What is the essence of all the desires of man? We are here but for a moment; everything is so unreal or at best surreal. All that we ever crave for in this world can be found in the presence of the Lord, so what are the desires of your heart? What things do you hold dear to your heart? You can find all in the presence of the Lord, enduring wealth, salvation, love, joy like a river, divine provision, happiness, deliverance and peace of mind. In the presence of the Lord there is healing, there is provision, just trust in the Lord and believe in the power of his might.

As humans, we perish for lack of knowledge and understanding, we perish because we choose to help ourselves, forgetting the fact that there is a God who formed us and knows us; he is the potter and we are the clay. No matter how big our dreams are, how lofty the ambitions we hold for the future, I have a strong belief in my spirit that there is nothing that we choose to become that we cannot achieve with the help of God alone. I remember a popular saying that the devil does not give out free meals, so if he gives you bread, he will take your butter away or give you sugar without tea. There is a way that seems right to a man, but its end is the way of death (Proverbs 14:12 NKJV).

If your aim in this life is to have enduring wealth, everlasting joy and peace, I admonish you, friends, there is just one right way and path, the narrow road that we are wont to avoid because it is unpopular. The present may not have a semblance of that wonderful future, but my only assurance to you is that when you come to the presence of the Lord your barns will be filled with plenty and overflow.

Today, it is not a very easy task to stand for righteousness because that may not be the popular route. People are wont to have their way because of the fear of tomorrow. There is no point being part of a group taster when you can have all that you want when the main course is being served.

Dear Friends, always remember that all you need to be who God wants you to be is in the presence of the Lord.

YOU CAN WIN YOUR BATTLE!

10 Finally, be strong in the Lord and in his mighty power. 11
Put on the full Armour of God, so that you can take your stand
against the devil's schemes. 12 For our struggle is not against flesh
and blood, but against the rulers, against the authorities, against
the powers of this dark world and against the spiritual forces of
evil in the heavenly realms. 13 Therefore put on the full armour
of God, so that when the day of evil comes, you may be able to
stand your ground, and after you have done everything, to stand.
Ephesians 6:10-14 NIV

The only way by which we can withstand the schemes of the devil is through holiness. The world as we know is controlled by spiritual forces, there is an assembly of the Godly and we have an assembly ruled by the wicked people of this world. So, for us to overcome every scheme of the enemy, we must put on the whole armour of God. Many people suffer from oppression from the devil as they are not fully committed to God, so they are tossed to and fro by the devil. Remember that you cannot serve God and the devil; you can only be a servant to one master at the same time. Hebrew 12:14 "make every effort to live in peace with everyone and to be holy; without holiness no one will see the Lord". (NIV)

A lot of people suffer from demonic oppression and suppression when they are asleep, and they call on the name of Jesus, but the name does not yield to their cries; the story of the seven sons of

Sceva comes to mind. Acts 19:13-15 Some Jews who went around driving out evil spirits tried to invoke the name of the Lord Jesus over those who were demon-possessed. They would say, "In the name of the Jesus whom Paul preaches, I command you to come out." Seven sons of Sceva, a Jewish chief priest, were doing this. One day the evil spirit answered them, "Jesus I know, and Paul I know about, but who are you?" (NIV).

This story of the seven sons of Sceva indicates that we must have a relationship with God to be able to overcome every form of oppression from the camp of the enemy. We must be willing to identify with God to be able to look the devil in the face and take him to the cleaners. We must build our lives on the Word of God and must be ready to give our heart, body and soul to the Lord. The greatest mistake we can ever make in life is to give the devil an opportunity to feast on our inability to follow God whole-heartedly.

We need the grace of God to be able to fight and win our spiritual battles. The forces of evil abound everywhere in this day and age; hence we must carry on the whole armour of God everywhere we go. We must know the Lord for who he is and make him the numero uno in our lives to enjoy a life free from domination of the enemy.

PART 7

MANAGING CHANGE IN THE WORKPLACE

Even if you are on the right track, you will get run over if you just sit there
– Will Rogers

I have had to embrace "Change" at various times in life. During my self-study for my Change Management foundation exams I began to develop greater insights into some of the forces that revolt against Change in the workplace. As humans we find solace in our comfort zone, we always try to resist any Change to the status quo. I remember in my last role working for one of the big four Consultancy firms in London, some of my colleagues were so much in love with London that they always said they were not considering working outside of London due to several reasons. I always shudder at the thought of restricting myself to a certain location either based on friendships, affiliations, family links or love for the city life at the detriment of Career Advancement or the better life as it were.

In every organisation, when ideas that will engender business process improvement, reduce cost and overall productivity are mooted, there are individuals who are wont to resist Change and Change initiatives no matter the benefits it might bring to the organisation. Change initiatives as minute as desk moves or the installation of new software are always met with resistance or complaints, because people love what they are used to. I always ask myself why people resist Change when as individuals we have undergone various degrees of transformation from birth up to our adult life. Change is part of our everyday life, it might be a change in culture, environment, learning a new language, making new friends and seeking out new challenges.

Change is necessary for an organisation to prosper in the 21st century, with the increased competition and advancement in technology in this age, adopting Change as part of the fulcrum of every organisation is vital to avoid being left behind in this fast-paced business environment. Organisations must always communicate the vision in a straightforward way and engage their employees in the Change Process and reduce the uncertainty that the "Change" initiative might create and plan for the Change.

As individuals, we must continually thirst for the new and be dissatisfied with the present. We must embrace change in our career as well; most of the qualifications that were relevant in the 19th century have been thrown in the dustbin of history in the 21st century. Change is vital if we are to remain relevant in our sphere of influence.

DEVELOPING EXCELLENCE AS A WORKPLACE CULTURE

I remember vividly my foray into the financial services sector having worked in the very much conservative and laid back educational sector – it was a new challenge altogether. As these were project environments, there was a lot of pressure left, right and centre and at times unrealistic work-related targets. There were sob stories about how people were getting fired for failure to hit productivity and quality targets. Along the way I discovered that the only solution to be the best in a competitive work environment is to wear the garment of excellence.

Wikipedia defines Excellence as a talent or quality which is unusually good and so surpasses ordinary standards. When the culture of excellence is embedded into the work environment, colleagues are willing to go the extra mile to deliver outstanding service to all organisational stakeholders. An excellent workplace culture means people are willing to use their initiative to get work done and do not wait to be told what to do. Excellent people are uncomfortable with mediocrity, irritated with the status quo; they are always looking to develop faster ways of getting work done while not compromising on quality.

Many people do their job either to earn a living and pay the bills or keep body and soul together, but along this journey I discovered that those who are passionate about what they do, go farther than those who do their job just for the sake of doing it. The Bible verse in Ecclesiastes 9:10 readily comes to my mind, whatever your hand finds to do, do it with all your might, for in the realm of the dead, where you are going, there is neither working nor planning nor knowledge nor wisdom. (NIV) So whether you are the Chief Executive Officer, a Project Manager or a Customer Service Officer, your contribution to the bottom-line must be exceptionally excellent. The only reason I will save up to wear a Ted Baker suit or shirt is because I have discovered there is a tag of excellence ascribed to their products. They are not just in the market to churn out quantity but also pride themselves on designing quality products, which is a subset of excellence, which is a major attribute of their brand.

As individuals we must constantly challenge ourselves to be outstanding, to never be satisfied with your present circumstances. In times past, I have used the illustration of Senior bankers within the Nigerian Banking Industry in the early 1990s who were educated up to Senior Secondary School level but did not deem it fit to improve on their qualifications; they lived in luxury and opulence but did not envisage the wave of downsizing which would soon hit all those who refused to educate themselves up to Bachelors' Degree level and when the tide came, they were all consumed with the wave of downsizing that came along. No matter the wave of downsizing or rightsizing that might consume Organisations, excellent people always stand out. Because excellence does not hide, it does not need to announce itself.

Let's spread the culture of excellence; let's propagate this culture through our Organisations from the top to the bottom. Enough of entitlement mentality, nobody cares how long you have spent in that Organisation or Company. The question should be: are you adding value? What impact are you making? Are you just picking up that pay cheque without putting in the shift? Excellence should be at the front burner, nobody is rewarded for activity rather accomplishments. Let your good works speak for you.

My last word of advice for that excellent man and woman out there who is saying, I do my work in an excellent manner, but things are not working as envisaged, I will end this essay by quoting Gal 6:9 And let us not be weary in well doing: for in due season we shall reap, if we faint not. (KJV). Keep on pushing on, keep on working at being the best version of you. There are still forward-thinking Organisations that value excellence, and there is no stopping you. Politics might shoot mediocrity to the top, but an extraordinary talent will always be one irrespective. Whatever role you find yourself, give it your best shot, as it is an audition for greater things to come.

CHANGE BEGINS WITH YOU

We have heard so many clichés that a successful organisation is a function of its leadership. Today, leaders bear most of the brunt for failings in their organisations. I always watch in sheer amazement whenever companies' results are released to the public and the CEOs face so much scrutiny from the media and organisational stakeholders alike.

The workforce of every organisation has a vital role to play in making the life of the Senior Management very easy. The change we all desire to see in our organisations must begin with us as individuals. Colleagues must not act in ways that are inimical to organisation growth and development. Failings within organisations is a sum of individual failings in the workforce. Effective change must start from the bottom up, so no matter our designation or job title we must always act as a source of positive influence within our department or that small group we belong to.

Everybody cannot be the Chief Executive Officer or the Change Manager; but we all can be a catalyst for change when we all act and think as if we have something to lose when we don't do the right things. The workplace becomes a great environment when the workforce believes in the guiding vision and people are willing to go the extra mile in providing outstanding service. Even though the CEO is the Chief Responsibility Officer, failings caused by the Project Management Office by embarking on white elephant projects or miss-selling of products by the sales and marketing team to those who do not require them are by-products of people not committing to do the right things.

When we all have the right attitude in our work-roles, it becomes a win-win scenario for all organisational stakeholders. Shareholders smile to the bank, Senior Management are lauded for exceptional performance, the entire workforce will also enjoy part of the gains and the agencies that provide contract staff also get more businesses and referrals all because of doing the right things.

I will end this write up by saying: we don't have to be the President of the Country, the Chief Executive Officer of a Blue-Chip company or part of the Senior Management team to make change happen – always remember that the CHANGE begins with YOU.

HOW PREPARED ARE YOU FOR SUCCESS?

Don't ask God to order your steps, if you are not willing to move your feet – Anonymous.

We all want to have a successful career, family life and in all we do be termed as a success. But beyond our goals and dreams to lead successful lives we should not be lax in the place of preparation. We must always be in the know that SUCCESS only comes when opportunity meets PREPARATION. People are wont to ascribe breakthrough to luck, connections and some others might feel it is the law of whatever will be, will be at work. I have come with a message that sowing the seed of preparation is the best way to be ready for success.

An athlete who wants to win a Gold medal at the Olympics must be ready to go through an intense training regimen to achieve their goal; it is not just about confessing it and dreaming about being a success, but we must consciously work towards becoming a success in all that we lay our hands to do. Always remember that faith without works is a waste of time, be ready to sow your "WORKS" to achieve your desired goals. Whenever I see Usain Bolt, I see a man who has gone the extra mile in the place of preparation.

To lead successful lives, we must learn to prioritize our lives each season. Many a time people make the mistake of killing their career before it has even started; we must embrace continuous development. Do not be comfortable with mediocrity or the status quo. Instead of praying for a miracle, we must be the miracle, the solution-provider that people will always be looking out for. There is a time and season for every endeavour under the face of the Earth, there is no gain without pain. How much are we willing to sacrifice to become a success? Most times we know what we need to do to get to the next level, but we refuse to help ourselves in this journey.

A student who burns the midnight candle and is rewarded with an excellent result was not just a fluke, an athlete who incorporates rigorous training regimen to achieve success on the tracks is not fortunate and a Professional who has invested in the place of preparation and is enjoying an accelerated career growth is not blessed because of mother luck. The student, athlete and professional all have one thing in common, PREPARATION. To lead successful lives, we must be ready to cooperate with God and with ourselves. There are so many opportunities the world over, but we miss out because we have slept in the place of preparation.

Always remember that your decisions today will invariably determine the outcome of your lives tomorrow.

THANKSGIVING: THE SECRET TO UNLOCKING THE SUPERNATURAL

On a recent trip to Africa, I began to appreciate the value of being grateful for the trivial things. We have become so used to life and living that we believe it is our fundamental human right to sleep at night and wake up in the morning, so we forget the place of thanksgiving. As humans, we are quick to get lost in the routine of our lives, the quest for survival has taken its toll on us that we forget to count our blessings and name them one by one.

I remember reading the profile of some of the victims of the Malaysian MH-17 plane crash in a major newspaper and turning on the TV to watch the news thereafter; I broke down and wept profusely, I was drenched in my tears as it was hard to fathom how precious lives could easily be cut short based on no fault of theirs. The passengers and crew boarded the plane on that fateful day oblivious of the danger that lurked ahead. Thousands of aeroplanes ply the airspace daily and we have become used to air travel that we rarely bother to give thanks for departing and arriving at our destination safely.

As humans, we have varying degrees of heart desires, but we tend to focus more on what we need than appreciating what we have. Rather than moan and grumble about how bad life is treating us, we should focus on our journey thus far, our testimonies, and the high points. By doing this, we will develop a more positive outlook to life. Our present circumstance which we despise is ultimately another man's heart desire and prayer point.

If you have tried different methods to get ahead in life and what you get in return is disappointments, why not be thankful for the little? Be thankful for life and living; Ecclesiastes 9:4 sums that up "Anyone who is among the living has hope – even a live dog is better off than a dead lion!" (NIV) Be thankful for freedom, be thankful for sanity, be thankful for good health; many are in the hospital bed who would be willing to trade it all for good health. There are so many things that we take for granted in life, making the right decisions, being led by the spirit of God and other things, that is hard for the human mind to decipher.

The past might have been littered with mistakes and failures but quit complaining about the storms that you have experienced; I challenge you to praise your way out of that negative situation. Put an end to the pity parties, quit worrying about what you cannot change, and you will experience a turnaround in all your endeavours.

Be Thankful for something this week.

FEAR: THE DREAM KILLER 1

Many dreams and talents have been buried due to the Fear Factor. Potential is sacrificed daily because we are afraid to take risks. Recently, I was in a discussion with one of my mentors and he shared a story which I would like to also share. There was a man who lived in the city and was attacked in his new home by armed robbers; he was devastated and decided to return to his village as he said he did not want armed robbers to kill him in the City. Upon his return to the village, six months thereafter he was attacked by armed robbers in his village home and was killed. The story really touched me because there are times we take life decisions because of fear; invariably our decision determines our destiny.

Ultimately, our chances of making a success of our lives are not about the world's system or economies. I have heard true life stories of how people's American dreams eventually turned into nightmares. All the hopes and aspirations for a better life were gone with the wind.

Permit me to say, that our fears come in various forms; while some people are afraid to take risks, some others live in the fear of the unknown. Their questions always start with "What if" – what if things go wrong, what if a war breaks out, what if I don't get a job, what if my business fails and the list goes on and on. If we can conquer our fears, then we can go on to achieve greater things. That we are alive is because we have conquered the fear of death.

A Yoruba proverb says, and I quote, "Today's outlook does not in any way determine how tomorrow will look, that is the reason the Herbalist consults the Oracle every 5 days". We must not go to sleep because we feel we are on top of the world. Also, do not let your fears keep you in perpetual slavery. I mentioned that because as humans we have the tendency to be enslaved to our fears, our fear dictates the course of our lives, which is not the proper thing for us to do.

Dear Friends, I admonish you to try new challenges, quit living in fear as this inhibits our progress in life. Irrespective of location, skin colour or lifestyle, we are faced with risks in our day-to-day activities. To harness our full potential, we must freely express our innate desires without any form of limitations. The time for us to conquer new territories, set greater goals and try new adventures is here.

In conclusion, Dear Friends, my wish for you today is that you live a life devoid of fear in every form and I pray that our Lord Jesus Christ grants you the grace to rise above every seed of fear that has been planted in your heart.

FEAR: THE DREAM KILLER 2

Another mentor of mine shared a story which I would like to also share. Death was visiting a town and on his way in, he met a man who asked him how many people he was going to kill within the town. Death told him he would be killing ten people; however, fifty people were killed in the town. On his way out, the man challenged Death saying, 'you told me you were going to kill ten people but fifty people were killed'. Death told the man that he only killed ten people; the other forty people were killed by Fear.

A lot of destinies have been destroyed on the altar of fear; some great ideas never saw the daylight because of the Fear Factor. After my essay on "Fear the Dream Killer", I had my own experience of living in fear for the first time in many years; eventually my faith conquered my fears. Many times, we magnify our fears and allow it to dictate the course of our lives. I live and profess my faith; through this means the spirit of Fear is banished.

A lot of people worry about tomorrow, about the future, but we tend to forget that where we are today is a result of yesterday's decisions. Speak to your fears, speak the word of God, and do not let your fears stop you from fulfilling your God-given destiny. Many kings have been enslaved because of Fear. Always remember that fear is a trap; whatever we choose to fear becomes our master, and Fear is a form of limitation if stimulated which can stop us from fulfilling our potential.

For every seed of Fear substitute it with Faith. At some point in our lives we will face demanding situations and circumstances; however, these situations should not translate to our masters to whom we are perpetually enslaved. The time to start living our dream is here; now is the time to stop living our life in Fear as this limits our lives' outcomes. We can be all that God wants us to be if we believe in him and the power of his word. When negative thoughts come to mind, always nourish your spirit with words that lift and build. Refuse to succumb to Fear; do not let the opinion of others define you. Always remember that everyone is entitled to their opinion; it is in no way our reality.

Dear Friends, I admonish you to speak life to your situation. If God gives you a word, it will definitely come to pass. Do not feed your fears; we need to concentrate on building up our faith in God. At every opportunity we need to water, nourish and grow our faith in God as this is the antidote to our fears. Tomorrow is filled with possibilities if only we can live our dreams and quit living our fears.

NO COMPETITION IN DESTINY

The earlier we realise that life ought to be lived within the context of an individual affair the better it will be for us as human beings. We are not here to compete with one another but to live our life in contentment. The sky is large enough for all birds to fly without any form of hindrance and limitations. The success of friends, family and acquaintances should only challenge us to be the best in whatever we do but not further than that.

Dear Friends, always remember that life is all about time and seasons. There is a time to be born and a time to die, a time to sow and a time to harvest. There is a proverb which I would like to share; it goes thus: "It is when you wake up from bed that is your morning". So, when you understand that fact, then you are happy to be in your own lane. Let me succinctly point out a fact which most people choose to ignore: the world will never run out of houses, of new model cars, of the latest phones and technologies. The moment we own these gadgets, toys and electronics, manufacturers are looking to push out newer models to the market. When new models are launched, then ours becomes obsolete.

Our success is not meant to be a payback check to those friends who despised us in the days of our little beginnings, neither is it to oppress the poor and helpless. Remember that life was never intended to be the races; we all came individually and empty. A lot of people today live false lives; they live their lives to impress other people, they are worried about the opinion of others hence they live above their means. Opinions are like belly buttons, everybody is entitled to one. It is a crime to live your life based on the opinion of others.

The fact that friends within your close circles drive the latest Range Rover cars in town does not in any way mean you should buy one when you cannot afford it. The only competition we must have is with ourselves, to be a better person, to live a productive and fulfilling life and to constantly challenge ourselves to be better than we were yesterday. Also, when people succeed around us, we must celebrate with them. We must throw out the seed of envy and hate as it leads to bitterness. When we celebrate with others, we are also paving the way for our own success.

I admonish you, friends, your only competition is the person you see in the mirror.

NO YARDSTICK, LIFE IS A SOLO RIDE

It is very difficult in these times to use other people as a yardstick for our life goals. The best way to forge ahead with our dreams is to always see Life as an individual affair, a solo ride which can be either smooth or bumpy or a combination of the two scenarios. It would be foolhardy for us to make permanent life decisions based on the failure of a mentor, a role model or a father figure. The fact that a guide has failed does not in any way suggest that we will fail to make our dream come true.

We are all responsible for our life's actions. Be wary of people who want to make right the mistakes of their lives by making your life a replica of the life they never had. Never lose focus that you are the driver of your own car (life). To add to my earlier postulation, never make permanent life decisions based on temporary situations. Life is not a 100 metres dash; the fact that some others never rose to the pinnacle of their career does not suggest that you will be perpetually in the background.

As humans we are unique in our own diverse ways; even identical twins still have unique traits that will distinguish one from the other. My journey is different from your journey. There is no point coveting another man's life as it is the person who wears the shoe that understands where it pinches. As the Chief Responsibility Officer for our lives, we must not evade the headship role and mess around with the destinities that are under our care.

Do things that make you happy, pursue your dreams. Do not quit for the fear of failure; remember winners never quit and quitters never WIN. The world holds no place or recognition for those who almost attained. In truth there is, No winner's medal for 4th place. In my brief time on the face of the Earth, I have seen protocols broken, standing orders shattered, limitations abolished, and I have seen many rags to riches stories to inhibit my future based on the opinion of others.

In conclusion, feel free to explore the world, make new friends, cultivate new relationships, Dream BIG, it costs absolutely nothing; when you fall do not be afraid to rise up again. Forgive yourself for the past and live your life based on your own terms; remember, it's your life, it is your call, it is your responsibility, no yardsticks, and always remember that our life's times and season should not be measured against other people who have embarked on similar journeys as their successes or failures cannot be replicated in our individual lives.

ARE EFFECTIVE ORGANISATIONS THE ANSWER?

The time for organisations to investigate their resource optimization mix is now – what should be done differently to save costs in every department, not just the production department? Are their leakages and what are the steps in place to ensure that resources are optimized judiciously? Organisations that rely solely on diesel for their production should start thinking of alternative and cheaper sources of energy to invest in. In the short term, this could be capital intensive; however, in the long run this could help save costs that would have a positive effect on the bottom-line.

In an era of diminishing consumer spending and increasing cost of production, the HR function within organisations currently have a significant role to play to ensure that they get the best value from the workforce. The era of an over-bloated workforce with overlapping responsibilities is long gone and investment in the right talent to drive an organisation forward should be embraced. Employees should be encouraged to work smart and new processes that can ensure faster alignment towards organisational objectives should be embraced.

The mantra to be adopted should be how to get things done (first time right), using a quicker approach. Everyone from the bottom-up should be ready to be part of the Change process that this new way of working will engender. Also, constant communication from the leadership should be adopted to spread the message among the workforce so everyone is carried along. This will help minimize any form of rebellion and non-conformity to the new way of working.

In times of austerity, when organisations are faced with varying degrees of risk in carrying out their activities, questions should be asked periodically to be sure everyone is focused towards achieving the goals and objectives of the organisation.

In summary, from my own school of thought, I believe organisations should be adaptive and be willing to embrace change. Furthermore, I believe that resource optimization should be a key driver to ensure the right value is received from every layer of the workforce.

STAYING AHEAD OF THE COMPETITION

Competition is the keen cutting edge of business, always shaving away at costs
– Henry Ford

In the 21st century, organisations are investing a lot to stay ahead of the competition. A lot of resources are invested in R & D as organisations begin to think about the next decade and consumers' changing needs and wants. As we all know, some of the goods, products and services that enticed us decades ago are no longer on the shelf because of the refusal of organisations to embrace the notion of changing consumer needs.

In as much as I subscribe to Nancy Pearcey's quote "Competition is always a good thing. It forces us to do our best. A monopoly renders people complacent and satisfied with mediocrity", many businesses have been sent out of the market due to their failure to anticipate the challenges that competition might engender.

For organisations to stay ahead in the marketplace, the quality of their products/service should not be compromised at any stage as this can be leveraged upon by the competition. Furthermore, organisations should be interested in having a robust talent management strategy in place, as the level of success an organisation will enjoy is a function of the calibre of people they are able to attract. A lot of investment should also be done around talent retention as competitors are looking to poach the best hands from rival companies.

Another crucial factor to stay ahead of competition is to always see the business through the eyes of the customer. Anticipating consumer needs and always having a robust strategy to meet the changing needs of the consumer. In as much as organisations have strategies to dominate in the marketplace, they should also have strategies in place to respond to the challenge that competition can bring. While an organisation is looking at new business opportunities and gaining new markets, much should be done in terms of developing strategies to aid customer retention and market share growth.

Also, organisations should do more to entrench brand loyalty among its consumers and end-users. In developing economies, the low-income earners must be active contributors to the top-line and should not be discounted when products, goods and services are being developed for the marketplace.

My advice to organisations who are market leaders is to always be proactive, never underestimate the harm and negative impact that the competition can bring to your business. Do not discount the loss of market share as irrelevant to your bottom-line. It is more difficult to stay at the top than getting to the top of any market segment, so competitor analysis and peer reviews should be done from time to time to deal with any emerging threat in a timely manner.

OWNERSHIP CULTURE: RAISING A NEW GENERATION OF LEADERS

I was fascinated when I read about the culture of one of the top global engineering firms. They believe that the best strategy cannot succeed unless it is supported by a strong culture. And the engine of their sustainable business lies in their Ownership Culture, in which every employee takes personal responsibility for the company's success, always acting as if it were their own company.

The plain truth is that we cannot all be entrepreneurs. While I have heard people talk about the benefits of entrepreneurship as compared to working as an employee, I believe that we don't all have to be entrepreneurs to begin to take the lead in our various departments/work-roles. Organisations must as a necessity begin to indoctrinate the ownership culture within their workforce. In these types of organisations, colleagues are pro-active and take responsibility without being pushed or coerced to get work done. These organisations also foster an environment where employees feel appreciated and know that their ideas and proposals are taken into consideration when decisions are being made.

In organisations where colleagues take the lead without being prompted, growth is inevitable as the entrepreneur in everyone within the organisation is birthed. Employees respond to whatever culture is in place within an organisation. So, when employees are given the chance and opportunity to take responsibility in their work-roles within an enabling environment, it is a WIN-WIN situation for all stakeholders. I also believe that more should be done by the HR function during the induction process so any new entrant to an organisation can tell what an organisation stands for, the work culture and the way of working as this will ensure everyone aligns with the vision, mission and culture within the work-place.

Is it possible to have a new breed of employees, who are not afraid to put a shift in to enhance the growth of their organisations? My answer is a resounding YES. The old-style workplace where people can get off just picking up their pay slips a-la civil service mode can be thrown into the dustbin of history if the right mechanisms are put in place to ensure that leaders are groomed in every sphere of an organisation.

Also, more should be done to ensure that the culture of an organisation should be seen through the leaders/Senior Management. This will help to resonate what an organisation stands for, from the top to the bottom. Leaders must not act contrary to the culture in place within an organisation; they should be role-models in words, through their actions and deeds.

In conclusion, we can give rise to a new generation of leaders within the workplace if we are willing to invest more in the culture within our various organisations.

PERSONAL RESPONSIBILITY: TURNING EVERY RESPONSIBILITY INTO A POCKET OF GREATNESS

Many a time, people are wont to focus on their career while forgetting that the area of concentration should be their unit of responsibility. When you endeavour to make every responsibility a pocket of greatness then you have no fears about stunted career growth or limited opportunities in the labour market as it were.

We live in a time and season when personal responsibility in the workplace is at a deficit, the blame game is rife, and in a bid to protect their careers, some leaders have lost the morality to be truly called leaders. The old cliché where colleagues bruise and batter "pressure" as the fall guy for not getting around to doing the proper things should be discarded forthwith. If we can't deal pressure a fatal blow, then do we still have a right to earn that pay-cheque?

When we take Personal Responsibility for our actions and inactions in the workplace, we are taking the credit for doing the right thing and not afraid to take the blame for our inactions. The fact that you admit to a mistake or a lapse in your work does not in any way indicate that you are less smart than you are; neither does it confer on you an obnoxious title such as "Not good enough". When we take responsibility for our mistakes and lapses, we begin to learn, re-learn and unlearn because until the old dies, we will not be ready to take on the new.

For some leaders, it could be a change of focus from your career to taking care of the people you are leading; it could be as simple as investing in them, building a programme and showing them what's possible, which could inevitably change the lives of your followers.

I make bold to say again, that our focus should be on how we can continuously improve ourselves in the workplace by making every responsibility a showcase of our unique talents; that is why we are not zombies or computers programmed to work and think in a set order; we have the capacity to think outside the box and go the extra-mile to achieve our objectives.

To conclude, the sheer force and unbridled energy colleagues use to protect and grow their careers should be funnelled into turning their KPIs, teams, departments, into a pocket of greatness, and then what we have in return is a model workplace which all stakeholders can be proud of.

I wish you all the very best as we endeavour to commit to take Personal Responsibility in our work-roles.

WORK-LIFE BALANCE

Leaders in the workplace are supposed to show empathy towards their colleagues and teams and not act as if life begins and end at work. Every leader has their style; however, Work-Life balance should be encouraged. When people work they also deserve to rest, go on vacation and spend quality time with their family. It is the place of leaders to raise the bar and make work-life balance and the welfare of all employees a priority. Employees who are capable of balancing their work-life in the long term can contribute more to the growth of the organisations they work for, as a rigid work environment leads to disillusionment and can be counter-productive both in the short and long term.

Many organisations are very much target driven and are more concerned about the bottom line than they are about the welfare of their employees. In other situations, it is the quest to make the extra money that drives people to spend the most valuable time of their life at work, jeopardising the people and relationships that should truly matter to them. Work-life balance should not be a mere slogan or a catchphrase but should be at the heart of every organisation's core values. I worked in a multinational few years ago where it was indeed very difficult for employees to go on holidays and a lot of holidays were accumulated by employees which for some were running into a period of more than 2 months' unused holidays. The truth that we loathe hearing is that no matter your position in that organisation, always remember that no one is indispensable.

Organisations are still in business even after the death of the founder, so an employee should not feel he is indispensable and the work will not go on without him. Well if you think that might be the case, let me awaken you with the reality. It is time to go on that holiday and spend quality time with your family. In the world today, we have many absent parents as everyone is focussed on their career at the expense of their loved ones. It is time for us to prioritise that which should truly matter to us and make work-life balance a vital part of our everyday life.

MESSAGE FOR THE LEADERS: TAKE THE LEAD, REMOVE THE LID AND RAISE THE BAR

This is for the leaders, the real game changers. The men and women who work day and night to effect transformation to the organisations/departments they preside over. While attending the Global Leadership Summit 2015 organized by the **Willow Creek Community Church,** a profound message that I received through one of the keynote speakers, Craig Groeschel, was "If you don't change the way you lead, you will be the lid to that Organisation". Craig's statement was profound for me as I began to have an entirely new perspective on the concept of Leadership and the way the mindset, beliefs and value system of a leader can have a direct correlation to the growth of the organisation and department they lead.

Leaders are expected to always take the initiative, make the difference and offer their teams direction always. The emphasis is not on Leaders being the Alpha and Omega of knowledge or an encyclopaedia of information; however, a leader must be thirsty for continuous improvement. In my career, I have been opportune to work with different leaders from diverse races and each of those leaders have their own unique leadership style. As much as possible, leaders must be open to ideas from their subordinates and teams and not administer the workplace as if it were a one man show where the ideas of others are irrelevant. After all, employees are hired because they have something to offer.

A leader's personality, mindset and belief systems are pivotal in the 21st century as these are the unseen forces that will either propel an organisation to growth or act as the lid that will hinder an organization from achieving its full potential. A risk-averse leader in an Investment Management Company might be unsuitable as he might miss out on vital opportunities due to his fear of taking risks. Leadership entails going the extra-mile, being a step ahead of your teams, taking ownership and personal responsibility for your work and those you lead.

In conclusion, organisational growth is directly proportional to the initiative shown by the leaders to drive growth and inspire change even in challenging times. So far the lid is placed on an organization, which could be the failure to have a proper strategy in place and foresee threats in the marketplace, fear of change, believing in false illusions and being out of touch with economic realities, then it would be a tall order to experience real growth. Real leaders always take the lead, which in turn removes the lid and their organisations experience a new dimension of growth.

REDUCE ACTIVITY!

A lot of people wake up every day and join in the activity that life has become. Life has become a routine to so many people all they do is wake up, go to work, come back home, watch the television set and go to bed depending on the side of the divide you find yourself. For entrepreneurs it is better because the ability to innovate gives ample time for proper thinking, less pressure and the best use of their time.

Activity can be defined as any specific behaviour or the state of being active. The world does not reward activity but excellence. Imagine the people who clean our streets every day – they tend to be more active than the consultants who draw up the blueprint to move such organisations forward. The consultants get more reward for their labour than the people who exert all the energy. For those who thrive on activity, things won't be happening for them – after all they are only buying time and occupying space. Life is more than having an attitude of I don't care about tomorrow, because the society benefits when people learn to accept responsibilities for their actions and inactions. The hands of time cannot be turned back, so there is never a second chance to erase the mistakes of yesterday. We have another opportunity to live out our dreams for the future, seek excellence and remember that knowledge is power. It is what you know in terms of knowledge gained that you can sell to the world. I will elaborate more on this in the next essay.

REDUCE TIME WASTING ACTIVITY

As a sequel to my last essay 'reduce activity', so many people who are professionals, entrepreneurs and Chief Executive Officers of corporations are also involved in mere activity. Anyone who does not have control over his time has lost control over his life. We have people who are perpetual life wasters – they spend long hours on the phone discussing matters that are not relevant; some others are professionals in chatting and can spend the entire day on networking sites. I was discussing with a top manager of a company and he told me he attends to visitors only on Tuesdays because some people are masters in idle talk, they pop into the office without anything concrete to offer just looking for where they can waste their time and invariably succeed in wasting your time.

He who "fails to plan", "plans to fail" – it is very important that we plan our day. We need to account for every minute in our twenty-four hours calendar and not live our life without a plan. Some people are tossed around with no definite plan for their lives; friends plan and run it for them. We all talk about the future, but in truth the future is here; how we spend our days will determine how we spend our lives. Plan your time! Plan your life!

LESSONS

I have been able to learn a few lessons over the past months which I have decided to share.

1. Real leaders admit their mistakes, they don't blame others for their failure or find a basis to attach their failure, and they make use of every opportunity to showcase their capabilities despite every limitation.

2. Real leaders delegate to their subordinates and groom others; no man is an island and one is too small a number to achieve anything meaningful.

3. Service is key; for us to scale up the ladder in our career and business we must learn to serve. Leaders in every sphere of life had served in various capacities before assuming leadership positions, leaders are meant to be servants and not rulers. There are people who have dedicated their lives to the service of others through volunteer work. I remember watching the incident of 9/11 on Cable television and I saw the firefighters and rescue workers trying to save people trapped in the rubble, even at the risk of their own lives while for some others service is a vague term. I met someone recently who was helping me coordinate a project who never believed in service; he believed there is a price tag attached to every assistance you render for others.

Think growth, Think service.

You will succeed.

DON'T STOP LEARNING!

As I sat in class many years ago listening to lectures in a management course, I discovered the day we stop learning is the day we are confirmed intellectually redundant. Life is a teacher; the more we live the more we learn. I believe there is no point when we should call it quits with seeking knowledge. The difference between the rich and the poor is the level of information at their disposal – the "rich" thirst for knowledge and new opportunities to increase their wealth while the "poor" are masters in "passing over opportunities repeatedly".

Every reader is a leader, though not all information we read in books is applicable to our everyday life. The question that bugs my mind is why should I go through a situation someone else has packaged in a book and wants me to learn from? By buying that book, you are invariably saving yourself a whole lot as knowledge is power. With some investment in our knowledge bank account, we could gain a whole lot that cannot be taught in the best business schools in the world. We can improve on every facet of our lives if we learn to invest massively in information. The world is just a click away, with the advent of the internet and search engines like Google which avails us of information when needed.

"We should be informed to avoid being deformed."

TIME: OUR MOST PRECIOUS RESOURCE

Time is the only resource available to the rich and poor, young and old in equal proportion; it is 24 hours that makes up a day for everyone, our president, governors and all the citizenry. The question that bugs my mind is why some people seem to succeed with the management of this resource while others fail. Making the best use of our time is essential to leading successful lives. For how we spend our seconds will determine how we spend our minutes, our minutes will determine our hours, our hours will determine our days and how we spend our days will invariably determine our Life's result. If we could turn back the hands of time, many people will be opportune to correct mistakes made during the journey called life. Time waits for no man; it is important that we make hay while the sun is still shining.

I have a vivid imagination of my past years, my university days, secondary school and growing up. The best it will be for me is fond memories because I can't rewind and relive whatever part that was not pleasing. A Yoruba song says Time owns the world, my friends, don't be lazy.

It is important we learn to value our Time.

ANTICIPATE THE FUTURE, SEE THE POSSIBILITIES!

The future belongs to those who see the possibilities before it becomes obvious
– John Sculley

As the soap opera plaguing the Nigerian Economy continues with no end in sight, this is a time for deep reflection and not losing sight of the big picture. In this generation of the present-day workforce, we are too comfortable with the status quo and we have all forgotten that ideas rule the world.

I can't recount how many times I have heard the swan-song thank God I have a job in the last few months. My question is what if the job was not there? It could be a spur to forever step out of mediocrity and leave indelible marks on the sands of time. Also, it could be a prelude to taking ownership of one's life or it could also end in total disaster. As Ben Carson alluded to in his book 'Take the Risk': No Risk, Pay the cost; Know Risk, reap the rewards.

The time to stop living a life with no picture of the future is here, especially in climes where leaders are wont to not take responsibility for their actions and inactions. You can see the signs, the hand-writing is boldly written on the wall, yet we tend to console ourselves that there is no problem and it is only a sign of the times. However, I will say that irrespective of how fantastic that pay-packet is, do not live a life without a Plan. He, who fails to plan, plans to fail. Every dire economic situation presents an opportunity for the emergence of a new set of millionaires. Every problem presents an opportunity to those who see the possibilities.

We all know that it is risky to take a risk; however, it is far riskier not to take a risk. At all times we should always live in anticipation of the future in mind. If you are on a course that is not working or that you feel might not offer the best outcome, it is better to quickly retrace one's steps before it is too late. A wise man once said, Insanity is doing the same thing repeatedly while expecting a different result. We must always live with an alternative mindset – how can I do things better? What options are available to me? All these are questions that can spur us on to greater heights and ditch the route of mediocrity forever.

The future does not just happen; the future is not a fairy tale as it were. However, when we live consciously oblivious of the future then we can have the future we have always desired.

NO MORE LIMITS!

Many times, we place a ceiling on the level of our ability based on our job title or position and we are confined to act within this sphere. But real growth begins to happen when colleagues are not afraid to take on higher responsibility and remove any form of barriers or limitations that have been placed on them. We must make managing the business of our talent a priority always.

Who says burning the midnight candle ends with higher education? We must always challenge ourselves to be better at what we do. Personal Development should be a continuous process and we should not feel a sense of achievement no matter the post we hold or level we have attained. The goal should always be to be better than our previous best.

The power to experience growth lies within us, that is if we are willing to break free from every form of barrier and limitations that have been placed upon us. The truth is that everyone has inherent gifts and potential waiting to be harnessed. My question is what investments are you making to ensure that your talents are not put to waste? Doing the same thing over and over and expecting different results is a no-brainer. Free yourself from every form of limitations and begin to explore the world without any form of barrier.

A world without limits means no goal is too high to attain and no mountain too high to climb. When we break free from limitations, we believe that all things are possible and the entire world becomes our constituency. A life free of limitations signifies that we are not restricted because of our race, family background, nationality, gender or age. The issues and situations that limited us prior are now history and we can dare to dream.

Can you imagine a life without limitations, where there is no fear of rejection, refusal, or denial? As you consciously try to shake off your limits, you will begin to see growth in every sphere of your life.

START ANYHOW

We all have big dreams, dreams of greatness abound aplenty; however, many only go through the motions in life; the dreaming stage is where it all begins and ends. We are great at wishful thinking – if only I could win the lottery, win a jackpot and the many tall dreams we had in yesteryears – with no means of achieving them. We all want to earn the prize without paying the price; the truth is that there can be no product without a process. I was once in that same boat of having dreams and procrastinating and watching the years roll by. Always remember that time waits for no man.

The good news is that it's not too late to start, it doesn't matter the number of years that have been lost, spent in hiatus; all that matters is that at some point in our lives we come to the realization that our gifts and talents are for a purpose. It will be a big miss if we come to this world and return the way we came, without etching our footprints on the sands of time.

Give life to your vision, drown the negative voices; there will always be obstacles on the way and opposing voices will spring up. Always see the good, don't be discouraged by those who say it can't be done. Do not wait for perfect conditions, or else nothing will be achieved. Start with what you have, quit making excuses about your limitations. You just said not enough time, I am telling you there is more than enough time for everyone.

Some of my colleagues were in awe how I managed to write my book as there is just not enough time to get other things done; however, like I always say, time is Life, use it wisely. It's our responsibility to make sure that our time is spent productively. Time is the only resource every human has in equal measure, so we can't complain of not having enough.

The greatest challenge we face in life is how to start that great idea, business, project, with the fear of failure looming large. The truth remains that it is more honourable to start and fail than quitting from the outset due to perceived challenges and limitations.

In conclusion, start anyhow. Do not be deterred by negative narratives, the stories of those who tried and failed; a hundred and one reasons why the project is bound to fail even before commencement.

Start with your seed, plant it and watch it grow.

WAKE UP IN YOUR OWN MORNING TIME

The truth about life is, it is when we wake up from our sleep that is our morning time. The fact that it is morning in Manchester does not necessarily mean it is morning in New York City, neither does it mean it is morning in Malaysia. We must also apply this concept to our lives – there is no such thing as lost timing. We only awake to our lives' responsibilities at contrasting times. So, the fact that you have friends who woke up early from their slumber does not mean you have failed or does not suggest you are a failure. I believe in the concept of perfect timing; it does not matter when you awake from your slumber, what matters is that you are awake. Thus, waking up by 9am, 2pm or 6pm does not matter as long as we are able to fulfil our lives' objectives in the fullness of time.

Dear Friends, I admonish you to shun competition in Destiny. There is no such thing as competing with friends and family to be the best. It is folly at its best competing with someone who arose from their slumber while you are still in deep slumber. We can live in ignorance for a long time which is not really a problem if we choose to embrace knowledge at some point in our lifetime. Living in ignorance only becomes a problem when he that lives in ignorance does not know that he knows not and is not willing to embrace learning as a solution to gain knowledge.

In furtherance of my teachings, in this world that we live in today, many people live in darkness. Many have been brainwashed to believe that the darkness they live in is the light; however, it is not a crime to be in darkness inasmuch as we see the light at some point in our lifetime. It does not matter how long we have lived in darkness inasmuch as we get to the point of realisation that the light signifies the morning and we awake from our slumber.

In conclusion, the fact that all your friends have been married off does not in any way affect you or your life outcome. Also, the fact that all your friends have built their own houses or the sky rocketing prices of building materials should not in any way be of great concern. In your own morning, I repeat, when you awake from the rigours of the night, things will be easy for you because it will be perfect, without blemish, spot or wrinkles.

ADDENDUM

AS THE NEW YEAR BEGINS

As the New Year begins, have a vision and goals for the year, make the vision plain, write it down and constantly evaluate your progress as we advance further in the year. Imagine driving a car without a destination in mind – make every second count as how we spend our seconds determines our minutes, how we spend our minutes determines our hour, how we spend our hours determines our day, how we spend our days determines our months, how we spend our months determines our year and how we spend our years determines the outcome of our lives. Don't just set goals for the New Year but you must work towards the accomplishment of your goals and plan for the New Year.

Constantly evaluate your relationships, as your relationships are the current that controls your life. Any relationship that will not move you towards your destiny should be discarded. Be careful of your association this year; be wary of friends in the garment of enemies.

It is vital that we put our trust in the Lord. In years past, many people have lived their lives based on their ideologies, human permutations and others have tried to navigate their lives through human wisdom and intellect. Dear Friends, I admonish you to put all your worries and cares onto the Lord. If you have tried to work out the equation of your life based on your own human ability, this is the time to give God a chance and see how he will make your life a beauty to behold. One with God is in the majority.

If you desire a change in the New Year, do things differently. The methods, concepts and plans you used in previous years that failed to yield results should be discarded in totality. In the New Year, try a different approach. Insanity is doing the same thing repeatedly and expecting different results. Evaluate the big decisions of the previous years and see the areas where you need to enforce change.

Finally, I admonish you, dear friends, to do away with every form of addiction in the New Year. There is power in the name of Jesus to break every chain; you can do away with gambling, smoking, masturbation and every form of addiction that is limiting you from reaching your full potential in the New Year. There is no situation God cannot turn around this year; cast all your addictions on the altar and watch God transform you and make your life a testimony.

I trust God that this year will be a wonderful one for us all in the name of Jesus; we will live to celebrate many more years in the land of the living. We will experience God's lifting like never before and my prayer is that we will never have a better last year in Jesus' name.

HAPPY NEW YEAR

At the start of a new year we are opened to new opportunities, a fresh start, forgiving hurts that have been perpetrated against us and purging ourselves of any excesses that can limit us from fulfilling our potential. We need to terminate some friendships, contracts, association, habits and addictions that are holding us back and limiting our growth potential in Life.

The New Year will be profitable for the man who lives in absolute surrender to the father; it is a year when human imagination and thinking will become ineffective. Those who acknowledge that God is more than able to steer the ship of their lives and calm every raging storm in their lives will experience unending joy and happiness.

These are my 20 Nuggets for the New Year:

1. Pray without ceasing
2. Study the Word to show yourself approved.
3. Eat a balanced diet.
4. Eat fruits daily.
5. Drink at least four litres of water daily.
6. Exercise regularly.
7. Take a daily walk.
8. Be eager to get informed to avoid being deformed.
9. Travel within or outside your country of residence.
10. Read books, buy tapes and attend seminars of those who have done what you intend to do.

11. Get a mentor; remember iron sharpens iron.
12. To the unemployed, stop waiting till you get a job – start a business.
13. Be faithful in your relationships.
14. Have a clear-cut vision.
15. Let your goals for the year be the ones that push you to reach new territories.
16. Think outside the box.
17. Challenge the status quo.
18. Do a medical check-up at least once in a year.
19. Live peaceably with everyone.
20. Invest your time, resources and life in the development of others.

Like I always say Time is Life! Use it wisely. Your life is your talent; it is delivered to every person in equal proportion. Every day that we sleep and wake up, this precious resource never comes back, so make your life count. Don't make yourself another addition on the population figure; make glowing impact within your sphere of influence and your community.

In the New Year, shun crowd mentality. Because everyone is doing something does not mean you should do it. The formula that delivered a result for Mr Joshua may not necessarily deliver results for Mr David. Set goals that will challenge conventional thinking, make the vision for the New Year clear and understandable that you will be able to run with it.

I say Happy New Year to the person reading this; I pray that we will fulfil our potential in the New Year. I prophesy divine health into our lives in the New Year.

It's a New Year, New Level, New steps, New Jobs, New business ideas, New qualifications and I pray that grace will be available to you to run the race in the New Year.

TO SUCCEED IN LIFE

To succeed in life, you need two vital ingredients. The first is the God factor and our choices in life.

God is the ultimate; before we were born in our mother's womb he knew us; he knows every season and phase of our lives. There is no happenstance or accident with God; he knows everything that will happen to you in life.

The other vital success factor is our choices. Truly, God has made everything beautiful in his own time, but we also have a role to play if we are to make our life meaningful and beautiful. No witch and wizard can harm you without your permission; remember your passion is your permission.

If you make the right choices, there will be no loopholes for the devil to capitalize on. Everyone has within their grasp the chance to make a choice – make good choices in the morning and afternoon period of your life so the night period will be spent in peace and not tending fields with frail bones.

You cannot change the God-factor because he is omnipotent, he is the alpha and omega, the beginning and end, but the power of choices is within your control, your choices are the seeds of your future.

We have the choice to sow good or evil seeds, we have the choice to invest in our future or not, the choice to procrastinate or work.

Every outcome or result is a function of the choices we make in life; people only heap together the mistakes of their lives and form a monster called destiny.

Phrases like "whatever will be will be" abound in these days, but there is a limit to what will be will be if you make the right choices, there is a limit to living like a victim if you are conscious about your choices.

Make your life count, make the best use of your chances and make good choices. Always remember that we cannot turn back the hands of time. Yesterday is gone, today is another opportunity to do it right and the future is here. Don't put off until tomorrow what you can do today.

The future belongs to those who see the possibilities before it becomes obvious.

TIME IS LIFE: USE IT WISELY

I remember the fireworks that heralded the beginning of the year; it was with great excitement that we all started the year. We all had different acronyms that we coined for the year, now I am writing this essay in the twelfth month of the year.

In this same year, many people who started the year with us are no more today; we are not using this to mock them but it's a way of appreciating God for giving us the grace to be alive today.

It is by the Lord's mercies and grace that we were not consumed by the enemy, we travelled far and wide this year, the Lord preserved our going out and coming in, he kept us at arm's length from danger. We did not receive any evil report over any of our family member and that's a reason to be thankful.

A lot of bachelors and spinsters at the beginning of the year are now married, tenants became landlords, employees became employers, some others became car owners and various testimonies of changed lives in the year.

The major lesson I learnt from the year is that Time is Life, time waits for no one, whether we use it or not the hand of the clock is always in motion. The difference between those who had their new year resolutions become reality and those who did not lies in their use of this precious resource.

Teach us to number our days, oh Lord, that we may apply our hearts to wisdom, teach us not to play with our morning and afternoon season of our lives that we might experience rest at night. Give us the wisdom to understand that we need to sow good seeds in our youth that our harvest may be plenteous in our old age.

I am growing old by the day, new generations come, and the old generations will fade away but those who live useful and successful lives have control over their time: use your time wisely.

And for those whose expectation for the year has not been met, for those who are in tears and are in continuous mourning over their fate during the year , for the person who feels God has not been fair to them in this year and is saying there is nothing to merry over in the year, let me tell you that it is not over until you win; my God is still in the business of turning around dead situations, so you may feel the remaining days are too short to get something worthwhile from the year.

Don't stop trusting and believing, keep on working towards the fulfilment of your dreams and my God will bless you beyond your wildest dreams and imaginations.

Remember it is not how far but how well, it is not the beginning of a story that matters but its end thereof. Make your life count and you will smile at the end.

NEW YEAR! NEW YOU!

After all the hype that usually comes with the start of a new year, the new year resolutions are quickly forgotten when the momentum of starting a New Year has subsided, people are wont to write goals and plans for the year, but this has become a routine for many people.

A New Year is a time to let go of the old; as we advance in our age and years then we should as a priority seek advancement in all aspects of our life. After taking stock of the old and the past years, the New Year is a time to chart out a new beginning, a new course altogether. To experience the leap from where you are to where you are supposed to be, try forgiveness instead of holding on to hurt. In situations where you feel you have wronged others, forgive yourself, instead of wearing the garment of guilt and condemnation.

To experience the newness that comes with the year, you need to be disciplined in letting go of the old, but stopping old habits is never an easy thing to do. Our human nature means we are prone to make mistakes, we can fall and fail; in truth I tell you there is no perfect human being. Experiencing the new takes a lot of self-restraint, diligent work and discipline but it is not an impossible task.

You can make the year all you want it to be, it is your responsibility to make it the best among your years. There is a point you get to in life that you are willing and ready to hand over the wheels of your life to the father, being less reliant on yourself, on human wisdom and ability. The New Year can indeed be the start of a New You. After making the vision plain upon tables, it is also vital to run with it. The New Year is a time to let go of all the garbage of the past, it is a time to throw away all the garbage that has stopped us from moving into the greater places of our desired destiny.

Time indeed waits for no man, so make yours count. I admonish you, dear friends, this year can indeed be the start of your transformation into a new person. Let go of the old with all its garbage, the limitations of the past will come to an end if we make concerted efforts to end our business as usual attitude and we truly make the year a worthwhile one.

I pray that this year will be better than the last year in Jesus' name. (Amen)

GOODBYE TO THE OLD

So, another year has been reduced from our stay on Mother Earth – no human has permanent residency, so we must endeavour to as a necessity move with the times. Don't just count the days, make the days count; there is no point adding years to our age without applying the years to profitable use.

I saw the God who thrives on impossibility manifest himself in my life. I can also brag about the fact that impossible is nothing, it is just an opinion of anyone who feels that giving up too soon is the best option. Yes, you can, you can pursue your dreams irrespective of skin colour or background. When it is your turn to shine, then there is no stopping you.

We can look forward to the New Year with renewed optimism and vigour that the Lord who has done all these remarkable things is able to perfect all that concerns his children in the New Year. There are times we humans can doubt in our heart and limit our capacity to explore the world and ability to make things happen. There are times, situations and circumstances have limited our faith and beliefs system to pursue our dreams, so we join the bandwagon and settle for mediocrity because we have configured our mindset that it is impossible to achieve certain tasks.

In the New Year don't be afraid to dream, don't be afraid to have tall dreams and ambitions; if you can imagine it, then feel free to dream and believe in it – there is no stopping you. If you tried and you failed that sounds more like an attempt, an input, an effort towards getting your heart's desires realized. Don't join the league of quitters even before the race begins.

In the New Year, we must learn to surrender our life totally to God. There are no shortcuts to success, it is not about who you know and what you know, it is about our times and seasons. The Lord Almighty who kept us throughout the past year will make the latter years better than the former; he will bless the work of our hands in the New Year. Always remember that the thought process of man is different from God; man will always calculate where they think you will be at the end of the year based on their limited capacity to comprehend that you serve the God who fetches water with the basket to disgrace the bucket.

I wish you all a wonderful New Year. We will live to celebrate many more years as living souls by the Grace of the one who gave us the life that we live.

YEAR END: IT'S A WRAP

What a glorious and wonderful year it has been. All praise and glory be to the Lord of hosts – that you are alive reading this gem of a book is a testament to the goodness of God. It is indeed a time to count our blessings and name them one by one. Do not let the devil steal your Joy and Praise. Only the living can praise the Lord. Many people started the year with us but are no more today. We are not more righteous or faithful; that we are alive is an evidence of God's unflinching love for us. We travelled by various means of transportation throughout the year and the Lord kept us through it all.

For 365 days, we lay in bed to sleep every night and not by the power in our alarm clocks but through the power of the supernatural God that holds the world in his hand, we awake to testify to the unending mercies of the Lord. I repeat, only the living can praise Jehovah.

The year came with the storms, but we were not drowned. When we walked through the fire our feet did not burn and we were not consumed by the vicissitude of life. The future holds so much promise for us, so we should be buoyant knowing that our greater days are ahead of us. The same way a pregnant woman is expectant for the birth of her baby, our expectations for the New Year will not be cut short in Jesus' name. Always remember that we are work in progress, so if this year did not turn out as expected, your latter years shall exceedingly surpass the former in Jesus' name.

In life, we win some and lose some. The fact that we did not achieve all our goals and aspirations that we penned down at the beginning of the year does not mean we have failed. Life is all about times and seasons. All praise is to the Lord who sustained us through it all. The world has increasingly become a battlefield. Bombs and IEDs detonated for fun, the reign of evil, terror and fear surged through many nations of the Earth.

Therefore, there is enough reason for us to be thankful. Do not take the breath for granted, do not take your access to the good things of life for granted, do not take the fact that you are in good health for granted. Be thankful this day for all the things you have that money can buy and those precious gifts that have been bestowed on us that money cannot buy. We have only one life to live; we must endeavour to live it on purpose.

Dear Friends, I admonish you to put on the garment of praise in honour of the most-high God. He knows the reasons why and he understands everything. Look on the bright side, be thankful for the little, do not despise the days of your little beginning. Our latter years shall be exceedingly great.

ALIVE AND KICKING

As we draw the curtains on an eventful year for some, topsy-turvy for some others, what is not in doubt is that the Lord has been gracious to us all and his mercies abound forevermore. Some days back we were ushered into another year bringing into the front burner how ephemeral the days of man are. Like a candle in the wind, we will, someday, somewhere, somehow embrace the common destiny of every man which is death.

I am sure by now we would have done enough appraisals of the year, what we did right, ways we erred and how we can have a better next year. Don't go into the New Year moaning about the past year, the turbulent winds and all the dreadful things that characterized the year. The fact that you are alive, and kicking says a lot about renewed hope in the face of hopelessness.

The fact that we are victors and not victims should be enough reason to be thankful for this season of our lives. We are not spending the last bit of the year on the hospital bed, we don't need a blood transfusion or infusion, that we are hale and hearty, bubbling with renewed life and energy is testament to the fact that we are in this divide of the universe to fulfil our purpose in life.

For those who find it hard to remember the good things that have happened during the year, don't let the negative occurrences cloud your sense of reasoning. We have a great deal to be thankful for. Alive and Kicking means even though yesterday brought lots of pain with it, the future, our tomorrow, holds a lot of promise.

No matter the situation and circumstances that you might be facing in life, yours is not the worst. Our humanity is fraught with frailties; people face diverse problems yet still pull through. In the face of adversity do not despair; life will get better. No matter the situation and circumstances, never give up on your humanity; never give up on God because he has forever been true.

Your dreams will come true in Jesus' name and you will not have a better last year by his grace. We will live to celebrate many more years in good health and peace of mind.

DO THINGS DIFFERENTLY

As we draw the curtains on what has been an eventful year all over the world, the key message for the New Year is to do things differently. Insanity is doing the same thing repeatedly and expecting different results. This will not be about how long our New Year resolution list is or how desperate we desire a change from the status quo. If you have tried doing things in a set pattern and it didn't work out, then the New Year will be a year for a change. In the New Year we must let go and let God take the glory; if your desire in the New Year is to experience good success, don't forget the place of preparation. In recent times, coaches of sportsmen and women who have experienced success in their sports have talked a lot about how much extra effort they put in on the training ground; this is a pointer to the notion that success comes when opportunity meets preparation. In the New Year success will come to those who are prepared for it.

Many times, we wonder why our financial state has not improved in the past year. The question today is how much are we giving to the poor and the less privileged amongst us? The Bible says in Proverbs 19:17 If you help the poor, you are lending to the LORD – and he will repay you! (NLT) If all you cared about is me, myself and I, then in the New Year you must start to see beyond food for the belly.

People wonder why they have not gotten that dream job or moved up the next level in their businesses, but my question today is what are you doing differently? If your Curriculum Vitae still looks the same way it was five years ago, then you need to start looking out for ways to improve yourself. To remain relevant in the business world, you must constantly seek to innovate and be a step ahead of the competition.

If all you trusted in over the past year to achieve results was your intellect, your connections, your association, then I would encourage you to trust in the Lord in the New Year; let your focus be on the Lord who never fails. God can take us from where we are to where we are supposed to be, he is the God who has the power to change our lives forever. He said in Romans 9:16 "so then it does not depend on the man who wills or the man who runs, but on God who has mercy" (NASB).

If all you ever want in the New Year is advancement, then the key is to carve your own niche, do things differently and you will have tangible results in the New Year.

IT'S HALF TIME: LET'S REVIEW OUR TACTICS

It seems like yesterday when we shouted happy New Year, with lots of plans and goals for the year. Now the referee has blown the whistle for half time and it's time for us to retreat into the dressing room and do a review of our tactics; you may seem down and out like Liverpool was losing to AC Milan 0-3 at half time in the UEFA Champions League final of 2005, but the coach (GOD) says I should tell you the same way Liverpool came back from a three goals deficit to win the game, your recovery is possible if you dare to believe and work at it.

It is pertinent that we review our tactics in this game of life whether we are winning or losing; it's a time to re-evaluate our stand. Insanity is doing the same thing repeatedly and expecting different results. Time is the only constant resource made available to everyone in equal proportion; whether you use it or not, it does not wait for anyone. Use your time judiciously; procrastination they say is the thief of time.

Now the coach needs all the players to perform at their peak – remember it's not over until you win. The first six months of the year might have been filled with disappointments, broken promises, job cuts, scary news, hurricanes, earthquakes, plane crashes, sickness and disease, but I bring good tidings to you, and the next six months will be your best. The race is not always won by the fastest runner, nor the battle won by the strongest man; skill is not always given to men of understanding; your start might have been very slow, but I believe you will finish strong.

Don't be afraid to substitute some players (habits and decisions) that failed to give you your desired goals (breakthrough) in the first six months of the year, change your formation if need be. When you need to defend your territory from opposition attacks please do it as if your life depends on it, don't waste your chances in front of your opponents' goal post, strike with precision as life may not always give us a second chance. Intensify on physical fitness in your training programme; don't lose sight of your ultimate focus which is victory. In your quest to achieve victory, don't chase it at all costs, do not score "hand of God" goals, for the ultimate victory secured without cheating is honourable compared with those who short circuit the process to achieve the results.

Welcome to a new season of your life.

TIMELESS PRINCIPLES

As we all settle into the New Year and we start moving from where we are to where we ought to be, it is a year when we need to plug into our divine heritage and begin to take hold of that which belongs to us financially, economically, politically and spiritually.

It is our right to dream and aspire for the best in our endeavours this year; do not short change yourself. Imagine the possibilities that abound in our life when we have no limitations, when we are free from fear and the things that limit ordinary people. The issues that drive other people crazy, makes them retreat in the battle front and surrender their inheritance for a pittance.

Don't let your past mistakes and disappointments be a reason to give in to failure – success is who you are. The seed of greatness is in you, only you can make your life a model that other people will desire to imitate and emulate. In the quest for greatness, the life without pain, always remember that the prize comes with a price, the product with the process and the gain with the pain. The goldsmith would have to do a lot of pruning before all those priceless ornaments are made, he would have to dip inside hot fire and a lot of other processes before the glittering collection that we all adore is perfected. Hence, if you are faced with difficulty and challenges in life, don't be confounded or overwhelmed by any situation that might confront you. It is the pruning process, which will birth in you a new season, a new level and a new testimony.

Live your life based on God's timing, the race is not always to the swift, nor the battle won by the strongest men, but time and chance happen to them all. Don't live your life oblivious of other people's timing; no matter the success story that you see on the external, it is the man who the shoe pinches who knows exactly how sore the wound is. Be a catalyst for change and a source of blessing to others. To experience true success, endeavour to celebrate and not despise success stories around you. Don't live a life of envy by joining the pull him down syndrome which negates the characteristics of love that should be part of our daily living.

Do not despise the days of little beginning, for your latter end shall be exceedingly great. Every great harvest was because of the seed that was nurtured. Whatsoever talent heaven has deposited in your life, sow your seed and water it in due season and expect an abundance of harvest. Do not bury your talent or despise that which has been entrusted into your care.

Your Life is your seed, make your life count.

NEW YEAR; FRESH START

At the start of a new year, we have another opportunity to start afresh. It's a New Year, hence the slate has been wiped clean for us for a new beginning, gone with the previous year are the habits, addictions and limitations that held us bound. The New Year gives us another chance to ditch the old and effect changes in every area of our life. Here comes a new chance to write the vision down and make it plain upon tables that he may run that reads it.

Take full charge of the spirit realm. Be mindful of your confessions. The most important decisions of our lives are determined in the realm of the spirit. Do not be afraid to exercise your authority in allowing and disallowing in the realm of the spirit. Do not let the opinion of others dictate the direction of your life.

Trust in the Lord with all your heart and do not lean on your own understanding. In all your ways acknowledge the Lord and he shall direct our paths. We must come to an understanding that all our efforts will be in futility except the Lord grants the increase. No matter how much time we invest in planning, it all becomes nought without the divine seal of approval from above. Our total focus must be on the Lord; putting our trust in man leads to deferred hope, broken promises and unfulfilled expectations.

It is very important that we have faith in God. The things that are impossible with man are possible with God; we must come to an understanding that there is power in the name of Jesus. There is a limit we can get to in life through our own scheming, intervention and manipulation; there is no situation too hard for God to resolve. From Day one in the New Year, it is vital that we hand over the wheel of our lives to God. The popular route does not necessarily mean the best route; the fact that everyone is behaving in a certain manner does not give us the licence to live our lives anyhow.

I wish you all an amazing year, your dreams will not die, and we will all fulfil our destinies in Jesus' name. We will not have a better last year in Jesus' name and the mistakes of our past will not mar our future exploits in Jesus' name. (Amen)

BIO

Tolu' Akinyemi is an exceptional talent, out-of-the box creative thinker, a change management agent and a leader par excellence. Tolu' is a business analyst and financial crime consultant as well as a Certified Anti-Money Laundering Specialist (CAMS) with extensive experience working with leading Investment banks and Consultancy Firms. Tolu' is also a personal development and career coach and a prolific writer with more than 10 years' writing experience; he is a mentor to hundreds of young people. He worked as an Associate mentor in St Mary's School, Cheshunt and as an Inclusion Mentor in Barnwell School, Stevenage in the United Kingdom, helping students raise their aspirations, standards of performance and helping them cope with transitions from one educational stage to another.

A man whom many refer to as "Mr Vision", he is a trained Economist from Ekiti State University formerly known as University of Ado-Ekiti (UNAD). He sat his Masters' Degree in Accounting and Financial Management at the University of Hertfordshire, Hatfield, United Kingdom. Tolu' was a student ambassador at the University of Hertfordshire, Hatfield representing the University in major forums and engaging with young people during various assignments.

Tolu' Akinyemi is a home-grown talent; an alumnus of the Daystar Leadership Academy (DLA), he is passionate about people and wealth creation. He believes so much that life is about impacting on others. In his words, “To have a Secured Future we must be willing to pay the Price in order to earn the Prize”.

Tolu’ has headlined and featured in various Open Slam, Poetry Slam, Spoken Word and Open Mic events in the north east of England. He also inspires large audiences through spoken word performances, he has appeared as a keynote speaker in major forums and events in the United Kingdom and facilitates creative writing masterclasses to all types of audiences.

Tolu’ Akinyemi was born in Ado-Ekiti, Nigeria and currently lives in the United Kingdom. Tolu’ is an ardent supporter of Chelsea Football Club, London.

You can connect with Tolu’ on his various Social Media Accounts:

Instagram: @ToluToludo
Facebook: facebook.com/toluaakinyemi
Twitter: @ToluAkinyemi

AUTHOR'S NOTE

Thank you for the time you have taken to read this book. I do hope you enjoyed the essays in it and you are ready to Unravel all your Hidden Gems.

If you loved the book and have a minute to spare, I would really appreciate a brief review on the page or site where you bought the book. Your help in spreading the word is greatly appreciated. Reviews from readers like you make an enormous difference to helping new readers decide to get the book.

Thank you!

Tolu' A. Akinyemi